Compiler Construction

Hanspeter Mössenböck

Compiler Construction

Fundamentals and Applications

Hanspeter Mössenböck
Johannes Kepler University Linz
Linz, Austria

ISBN 978-3-031-84812-4   ISBN 978-3-031-84813-1 (eBook)
https://doi.org/10.1007/978-3-031-84813-1

Translation from the German language edition: "Compilerbau" by Hanspeter Mössenböck, © dpunkt.verlag 2024. Published by dpunkt.verlag GmbH. All Rights Reserved.

© The Editor(s) (if applicable) and The Author(s), under exclusive license to Springer Nature Switzerland AG 2025

This work is subject to copyright. All rights are solely and exclusively licensed by the Publisher, whether the whole or part of the material is concerned, specifically the rights of translation, reprinting, reuse of illustrations, recitation, broadcasting, reproduction on microfilms or in any other physical way, and transmission or information storage and retrieval, electronic adaptation, computer software, or by similar or dissimilar methodology now known or hereafter developed.

The use of general descriptive names, registered names, trademarks, service marks, etc. in this publication does not imply, even in the absence of a specific statement, that such names are exempt from the relevant protective laws and regulations and therefore free for general use.

The publisher, the authors and the editors are safe to assume that the advice and information in this book are believed to be true and accurate at the date of publication. Neither the publisher nor the authors or the editors give a warranty, expressed or implied, with respect to the material contained herein or for any errors or omissions that may have been made. The publisher remains neutral with regard to jurisdictional claims in published maps and institutional affiliations.

This Springer imprint is published by the registered company Springer Nature Switzerland AG
The registered company address is: Gewerbestrasse 11, 6330 Cham, Switzerland

If disposing of this product, please recycle the paper.

Foreword by Niklaus Wirth[1]

You don't speak programming languages—they are formal systems. Programs that translate texts written in programming languages into sequences of computer instructions are called compilers. These are complex programs. In the beginning of compiler development, the languages used were Fortran (1957) and Algol (1960). The design and production of their compilers kept large teams of programmers busy for years. However, using a systematic approach to compiler construction, as presented in this book, has reduced the work needed to a few months for individuals. This has been a tremendous step forward.

Fundamentally new general purpose programming languages are rare these days, as are completely new computer architectures. Compiler construction therefore seems to be a special field reserved for a few specialists in large companies. So why this book?

The reason is simple. Every program, every application, is built according to rules that specify what statements and data declarations should look like. Formalizing these rules increases the clarity and comprehensibility of the application. The key to this is formalization, i.e., specifying a syntax for the input. This enables syntax analysis, which is the basis of compiler construction. Syntax analysis and other techniques described in this book are not only useful for processing programming languages, but can also be applied to many other problems involving the systematic processing of sets of data or texts and an ever increasing range of other structured inputs. These techniques contribute significantly to the correctness and understanding of such applications.

May this book help in this promising development!

Zürich, Switzerland
December 2023

Prof. em. Dr. Niklaus Wirth

---

[1] Prof. Niklaus Wirth died unexpectedly a week after writing this foreword, shortly before his ninetieth birthday.

Preface

Build a compiler? Surely only big companies like Microsoft, Google or Oracle do that. Granted, but almost all computer scientists seem to feel the desire to design their own programming language at some point, even if it is just a domain-specific language or a command language for specific purposes. Of course, they then also want to write a compiler for it! This often fails due to a lack of the required compiler construction knowledge or perhaps because the techniques described in books are too complicated and often mainly deal with advanced topics such as optimization, register allocation or the details of code generation.

Fortunately, the basics of compiler construction are simple—anyone can learn them and add them to their repertoire of skills and techniques. Whilst compilers for programming languages such as Java or C/C++ are indeed only developed by large companies, there are many tasks (even outside of actual compiler construction) that can be solved easily and elegantly using quite elementary techniques. In principle, these techniques can be used whenever there is a structured input that can be described by a grammar. Examples of this are simple command languages, the processing of configuration files, log files, parts lists or data series of measurement data.

This book shows how it's done. It covers the practical basics of compiler construction, from lexical analysis and syntax analysis to semantic processing and code generation. Other topics include the description of translation processes using attributed grammars and the use of a compiler generator to automatically generate the core parts of a compiler. These last two topics in particular are highly relevant in practice although they are not generally included in many books on compilers.

For syntax analysis, this book uses the concept of recursive descent, a simple top-down technique that can also be implemented by hand (i.e. without tools). To round things off, however, bottom-up syntax analysis is also presented at the end of the book, which is more powerful but also more complex than recursive descent.

Techniques can only be fully understood when they are applied to a concrete example, so the development of a small compiler is used as a running case study. The language to be compiled is *MicroJava*, a simple Java-like programming language that is translated to executable bytecode, similar to Java bytecode. The full source code of this compiler can be downloaded and studied from [Download]. Java is used as the implementation language for the compiler, as well as for all the examples in this book.

The target machine of the compiler is a simplified *Java Virtual Machine* (JVM), namely the *MicroJava Virtual Machine* (μJVM), which is simple enough not to be overloaded with unnecessary details, but realistic enough to be used for illustrating and learning the techniques of code generation. The μJVM has a bytecode as its instruction set, which is based on the bytecode of the JVM. An interpreter for this bytecode is provided which makes it possible to execute programs on the computer [Download]. By studying code generation, you also learn about how a computer works, which is another reason to get involved with compiler construction.

At the end of each chapter, there are exercises on the topics covered. Sample solutions can be found under [Download]. You should try to work through the exercises independently, as this will help you to better understand the techniques covered. But even if you can't find the time to solve more than the 70 exercises yourself, at least take a look at the sample solutions, as they provide additional examples for each chapter.

The book is based on a compiler construction course that I have been giving for many years at the Johannes Kepler University Linz and at Oxford Brookes University in England. It can be used as a textbook for an introductory course on compiler construction that can then be followed by a more advanced course on topics such as optimization or register allocation. The PowerPoint slides of the course on which this book is based are available at [Download]. However, the book can also be used for self-study, as it is self-contained and describes all the techniques needed to build compiler-like tools in practice.

I would like to take this opportunity to pay tribute to my former teacher and colleague Prof. Niklaus Wirth (ETH Zürich) who wrote the foreword to this book. He was a master of compiler construction, from whom I have learned and adopted many techniques. I would also like to thank Springer-Verlag for their support of this book project as well as Dr. Brian Kirk who was a tremendous help in translating this book from German. Sincere thanks also to David Lightfoot and Paul Reed for helping to refine the translation.

Linz, Austria   Hanspeter Mössenböck
December 2024

[Download] *https://ssw.jku.at/CompilerBook/*

- Lecture slides
- Source code of the MicroJava compiler
- Sample solutions to the exercises
- Further material

Contents

1 Overview 1
   1.1 A Short History of Compiler Construction 2
   1.2 Dynamic Structure of a Compiler 4
       1.2.1 Single-pass and Multi-pass Compilers 6
       1.2.2 Compiler and Interpreter 8
   1.3 Static Structure of a Compiler 10
   1.4 Grammars 10
       1.4.1 EBNF Notation for Grammars 11
       1.4.2 Example: Grammar of Arithmetic Expressions 12
       1.4.3 Terminal Start Symbols of Nonterminals 13
       1.4.4 Terminal Successors of Nonterminals 14
       1.4.5 Other Terminology of Formal Languages 14
       1.4.6 Recursion 16
       1.4.7 Elimination of Left Recursion 17
       1.4.8 Grammar Classes According to Chomsky 17
   1.5 Syntax Trees 18
       1.5.1 Ambiguity 20
   1.6 MicroJava 21
   1.7 Exercises 22

2 Lexical Analysis 25
   2.1 Regular Grammars and Finite Automata 26
       2.1.1 Limitations of Regular Grammars 28
       2.1.2 Deterministic Finite Automata 28
   2.2 The Scanner as a Deterministic Finite Automaton 29
   2.3 Implementation of a DFA 30
       2.3.1 Implementation of the Scanner 32
       2.3.2 Efficiency Considerations 36
   2.4 Exercises 36

3 Syntax Analysis 39
3.1 Context-free Grammars and Pushdown Automata 39
3.1.1 Pushdown Automata 40
3.1.2 Limitations of Context-free Grammars 42
3.1.3 Context Conditions 42
3.1.4 Comparison of Regular and Context-free Grammars 43
3.2 Recursive Descent Parsing 44
3.2.1 The Parser as a Class 45
3.2.2 Parsing Terminal Symbols 46
3.2.3 Parsing Nonterminal Symbols 47
3.2.4 Parsing Sequences 47
3.2.5 Parsing Alternatives 48
3.2.6 Parsing EBNF Options 49
3.2.7 Parsing EBNF Iterations 49
3.2.8 Dealing with Large Sets of Terminal Start Symbols 50
3.2.9 Avoiding Multiple Checks 51
3.2.10 Computation of Terminal Start Symbols Revisited 53
3.2.11 The Syntax Tree in Recursive Descent Parsing 54
3.3 LL(1) Property 55
3.3.1 Elimination of LL(1) Conflicts 55
3.3.2 Elimination of Left Recursion 56
3.3.3 Hidden LL(1) Conflicts in EBNF Constructs 57
3.3.4 Dangling Else 58
3.3.5 Other Grammar Requirements 59
3.4 Syntax Error Handling 60
3.4.1 Error Handling in Panic Mode 61
3.4.2 Error Handling with General Anchors 61
3.4.3 Error Handling with Specific Anchors 68
3.5 Exercises 72

4 Attributed Grammars 75
4.1 Components of Attributed Grammars 76
4.1.1 Semantic Actions 76
4.1.2 Output Attributes 77
4.1.3 Input Attributes 77
4.2 Examples 78
4.2.1 Processing Variable Declarations 78
4.2.2 Calculating Constant Expressions 79
4.2.3 Sales Statistics 80
4.2.4 Image Description Language 82
4.2.5 Conversion from Infix to Postfix Notation 83
4.3 Exercises 85

5 Symbol Table ... 89
- 5.1 Object Nodes ... 90
  - 5.1.1 Global Variables ... 92
  - 5.1.2 Local Variables ... 93
  - 5.1.3 Inserting Names into the Symbol Table ... 93
  - 5.1.4 Predeclared Names ... 94
- 5.2 Scope Nodes ... 95
  - 5.2.1 Inserting Names into the Current Scope ... 98
  - 5.2.2 Searching Names in Scopes ... 99
- 5.3 Structure Nodes ... 99
- 5.4 Type Checking ... 102
  - 5.4.1 Name Equivalence ... 102
  - 5.4.2 Structural Equivalence ... 102
  - 5.4.3 Variants of Type Compatibility ... 104
- 5.5 Resolving LL(1) Conflicts Using the Symbol Table ... 105
- 5.6 Initializing the Symbol Table ... 106
- 5.7 Exercises ... 108

6 Code Generation ... 111
- 6.1 The MicroJava VM ... 112
  - 6.1.1 Memory Areas ... 114
  - 6.1.2 Instruction Set ... 117
- 6.2 Code Buffer ... 127
- 6.3 Operands of Code Generation ... 128
- 6.4 Loading Values ... 131
  - 6.4.1 Loading Variables ... 132
  - 6.4.2 Loading Constants ... 132
  - 6.4.3 Loading Object Fields ... 133
  - 6.4.4 Loading Array Elements ... 134
- 6.5 Expressions ... 136
- 6.6 Assignments ... 139
  - 6.6.1 Increment and Decrement Statements ... 140
- 6.7 Jumps and Labels ... 141
  - 6.7.1 Forward and Backward Jumps ... 142
  - 6.7.2 Labels ... 143
  - 6.7.3 Conditions ... 145
- 6.8 Control Flow Structures ... 147
  - 6.8.1 While Statement ... 147
  - 6.8.2 If Statement ... 148
  - 6.8.3 Break Statement ... 149
  - 6.8.4 Short-circuit Evaluation of Compound Boolean Expressions ... 150

	6.9	Methods	153
		6.9.1 Calling void Methods	153
		6.9.2 Calling Function Methods	153
		6.9.3 Stack Frames	155
		6.9.4 Method Declarations	156
		6.9.5 Formal Parameters	157
		6.9.6 Actual Parameters	157
		6.9.7 Return Statement	158
	6.10	Object File	159
	6.11	Exercises	160
7	**The Compiler Generator Coco/R**		**163**
	7.1	Scanner Specification	166
		7.1.1 Character Sets	167
		7.1.2 Terminal Symbols	167
		7.1.3 Pragmas	168
		7.1.4 Comments	168
		7.1.5 Characters to Be Ignored	169
		7.1.6 Case Sensitivity	169
		7.1.7 Interface of the Generated Scanner	169
	7.2	Parser Specification	170
		7.2.1 Productions	170
		7.2.2 Semantic Actions	171
		7.2.3 Attributes	171
		7.2.4 Translation into Parser Methods	172
		7.2.5 The Symbol ANY	173
		7.2.6 Generation of the Scanner and the Parser	174
		7.2.7 Interface of the Generated Parser	175
	7.3	Error Handling	175
		7.3.1 Syntax Error Messages	175
		7.3.2 Syntax Error Recovery	176
		7.3.3 Semantic Error Messages	177
		7.3.4 Class Errors	177
	7.4	LL(1) Conflicts	178
		7.4.1 Conflict Resolution by Multi-symbol Lookahead	179
		7.4.2 Conflict Resolution by Semantic Information	180
	7.5	Examples	181
		7.5.1 Reading a Binary Tree	181
		7.5.2 Questionnaire Generator	184
		7.5.3 Abstract Syntax Trees	188
	7.6	Exercises	197

8 Bottom-up Syntax Analysis 201
- 8.1 How a Bottom-up Parser Works............ 201
- 8.2 LR Grammars............ 206
  - 8.2.1 LR(0) Grammars 206
  - 8.2.2 LR(1) Grammars 206
  - 8.2.3 LALR(1) Grammars............ 207
  - 8.2.4 Strengths of Bottom-up Syntax Analysis............ 208
  - 8.2.5 Weaknesses of Bottom-up Syntax Analysis............ 208
- 8.3 LR Table Generation 209
  - 8.3.1 Kernel, Closure, and Successor State............ 210
  - 8.3.2 Table Generation Algorithm 211
  - 8.3.3 LR(1) Conflicts 216
- 8.4 LR Table Compression............ 216
  - 8.4.1 Combining Shift and Reduce Actions 216
  - 8.4.2 Merging Lines 218
  - 8.4.3 Example............ 218
- 8.5 Semantic Processing 219
  - 8.5.1 Semantic Actions 220
  - 8.5.2 Attributes 220
  - 8.5.3 Assessment............ 222
- 8.6 LR Error Handling............ 223
  - 8.6.1 Algorithm for Error Recovery 223
  - 8.6.2 Example............ 224
  - 8.6.3 Guide Symbols for Finding the Escape Route............ 226
  - 8.6.4 Finding the Guide Symbols 227
  - 8.6.5 Assessment............ 229
- 8.7 Exercises 229

A. The MicroJava Language 231

B. The MicroJava Compiler............ 237

References 243

Index............ 245

Overview 1

A compiler is a tool that translates a *source program* (e.g., in Java, Pascal or C) into a *target program*. The language of the target program is usually machine code such as instructions of a processor or Java bytecode. However, the translation target may also be a different source language. In this case, we speak of a *transpiler*.

In addition to compilers, in that strict sense, there are also compiler-like tools which translate any syntactically structured input into another form. Such a tool could, for example, translate a log file into a spreadsheet that displays essentially the same information in a more convenient form for further use.

You might wonder what compiler construction skills are useful for. After all, only big companies like Microsoft, Google or Oracle develop compilers. There are several reasons to study compilers:

- Compilers are among the most frequently used tools in software development. Therefore, we should understand how they are structured and how they work.
- When we deal with compilers, we also learn how a computer works at the machine level. We have to deal with its instruction set, its registers, its addressing modes, as well as its data areas such as the method call stack or the heap. This creates the bridge between hardware and software.
- If you know into which instructions certain language constructs are translated, you can often get a better feel for the efficiency of programs.
- In compiler construction, we must deal with grammars. Just like programming, the ability to describe structured data by grammars, is part of the essential toolkit of any software engineer.

Compiler construction skills can also be useful in general software engineering. Even though few people build compilers in the strict sense, most of them will be faced with the task of developing compiler-like tools at some point in their careers. This ranges from parsing of command-line parameters to processing of parts lists, document description languages (e.g., PDF or postscript) or to static program analysis, which calculates metrics such as a source program's complexity. In all these cases, compiler construction skills come in handy.

This book deals with compiler construction in the strict sense, although the techniques taught can also be used in general software engineering. It describes the complete implementation of a compiler for a simple Java-like programming language (*MicroJava*) that generates executable bytecode (similar to Java bytecode). It is aimed at people with a particular interest in the field. Formal theory is covered only to the extent that is necessary to understand the techniques used. The book deliberately does not cover all the subtleties of compiler construction, but only those techniques that are needed in practice. In particular, it barely covers optimization techniques, which would fill a book of their own and are only relevant to people who write product compilers. Furthermore, it only covers compiler construction techniques for imperative languages. Functional or logical programming languages require different techniques, at least in part, but these are also used less frequently in practical software engineering.

There are many books on advanced compiler construction (e.g., [ALSU06, Appe02, Coop22, FCL09, Much97]). They mainly cover techniques of static and dynamic code analysis, the extensive field of compiler optimization, and the intricacies of code generation and register allocation. These books are most relevant for people who want to develop product compilers for languages such as Java or C++. For beginners, however, they are often rather confusing.

This book concentrates on the essentials. It is based on an established course on the fundamentals of compiler construction and can be used as a textbook for this purpose. However, it is also aimed at practitioners in the field who want to better understand how a compiler works and want to use the techniques to expand their repertoire of skills.

1.1 A Short History of Compiler Construction

The first compilers emerged in the late 1950s. At that time, compiler construction was shrouded in mystery, with a level of hype that can certainly be compared to today's interest in artificial intelligence. At that time few people knew about it, and there were hardly any widely known techniques for compiling programming languages. The development of the first compilers took many person-years. Today, compiler construction is one of the best understood areas of computer science. There are mature techniques now for syntax analysis, optimization, and code generation. As a result, students today can implement a (simple) compiler in a single semester.

This chapter gives a brief (and necessarily incomplete) outline of the history of compiler construction, which is also a history of programming languages and their concepts.

1.1 A Short History of Compiler Construction

The insights and the progress are explained using exemplary languages, which are considered milestones and represent the development of compiler construction techniques in the respective period.

Fortran (1957). One of the first high-level programming languages was Fortran [Back56], which stood for FORmula TRANslation. *John Backus*, who was working for IBM at the time, led a team that set out to replace the assembly language that was common at the time with a higher-level programming language and to implement a compiler that would produce machine code that could match the efficiency of hand-written assembly programs. Many of the basic techniques of compiler construction were developed at that time. In the beginning, for example, it was far from clear how arithmetic expressions (e.g., a + b * c) could be translated into machine instructions in such a way that the precedence of operators reflected the precedence used in standard arithmetic. Also, techniques for the translation of conditional statements and loops into machine instructions had to be worked out, as well as mechanisms for calling procedures or accessing arrays.

1960: Algol. Algol60 [Naur64] was a milestone in the history of programming languages. It was developed by a consortium of experts from Europe and the USA, some of whom came from universities and some from industry. The aim was to be able to express algorithms in a clear, concise and machine-executable form. Important innovations were the block structure with local and global variables, as well as the concept of recursion, which made it possible for procedures to retain their variable values across recursive calls. Algol60 was also remarkable because it was the first programming language whose syntax was formally defined by a grammar. *John Backus* and *Peter Naur* developed the Backus-Naur form (BNF) for this purpose, which is now part of the toolkit of every compiler engineer. BNF is itself a language in its own right and is defined by a grammar.

1970: Pascal. A successor to Algol60 was Pascal [JW75], which was developed by pioneers such as *Niklaus Wirth* and *Tony Hoare*. Although Pascal was designed as a simple teaching language, it introduced important innovations that were also reflected in compiler construction. While older languages only knew predefined data types such as integer or real, Pascal allowed you to define your own data types, which could then be used to declare variables. In addition to arrays, as tables of homogeneous elements, records (also called *structs*) were introduced, which grouped data of different types into a new data type. Although the idea of records had already appeared in Cobol, records as a data type were not introduced until Pascal. Accessing elements of such structured data types required new compiling techniques. In addition, the first Pascal compilers did not generate machine code, but so-called "P-code", which was similar to today's Java bytecode. P-code was much more compact than machine code, which meant that Pascal programs could also run on microcomputers with their very limited memory capacities at the time. This promoted the spread of Pascal but had the disadvantage that P-code could not be executed directly on a machine, but had to be interpreted, which slowed down its running time.

1985: C++. C++ [Stro85] is a successor to the C language, which emerged around the same time as Pascal and was also a successor to Algol60. In C++, the know-how about programming languages and compiler construction was consolidated. Among other things, concepts such as *object orientation*, *exception handling* and *generic* (i.e., parameterizable) *data types* were introduced, which had already existed in other languages, but only became popular with C++. Object orientation required new techniques in compiler construction, such as the representation of inheritance hierarchies and the translation of virtual method calls.

1995: Java. Java [AGH00] was also not a completely new language, but combined concepts from existing languages. However, a new principle was *just-in-time compilation* (JIT compilation), which made Java programs portable. Java programs are translated into bytecode instructions (similar to Pascal's P-code), which can be executed on any computer that has a bytecode interpreter. However, the most frequently executed program parts are translated into machine code of the respective computer at run time (i.e., just in time).

2005: Scala. Scala [Oder08] is a derivative of Java and uses the Java platform (i.e., a bytecode interpreter and a JIT compiler) as its execution environment. Like many current languages, Scala integrates concepts of functional languages with imperative concepts. Functional concepts include *lambda expressions* (functions that are regarded as data and can be passed to other functions as parameters), *lazy evaluation* (evaluation of expressions only when they are needed), and *pattern matching* (recognition of patterns in sequences or tree structures). Of course, these mechanisms also require special compiler construction techniques.

The history of programming languages and compiler construction is far from over. Even today, new language concepts are being invented, which then lead to new compiling techniques. However, they go far beyond the scope of this book, namely to provide an introduction to the fundamental techniques of compiler construction. Anyone interested in the history of programming languages will find background information in the proceedings of the *History of Programming Languages* conference ([HOPL-I, HOPL-II, HOPL-III]).

1.2 Dynamic Structure of a Compiler

As a first overview of how compilers work, let's take a look at their dynamic structure, i.e., the phases in which a compilation takes place (Fig. 1.1).

1.2 Dynamic Structure of a Compiler

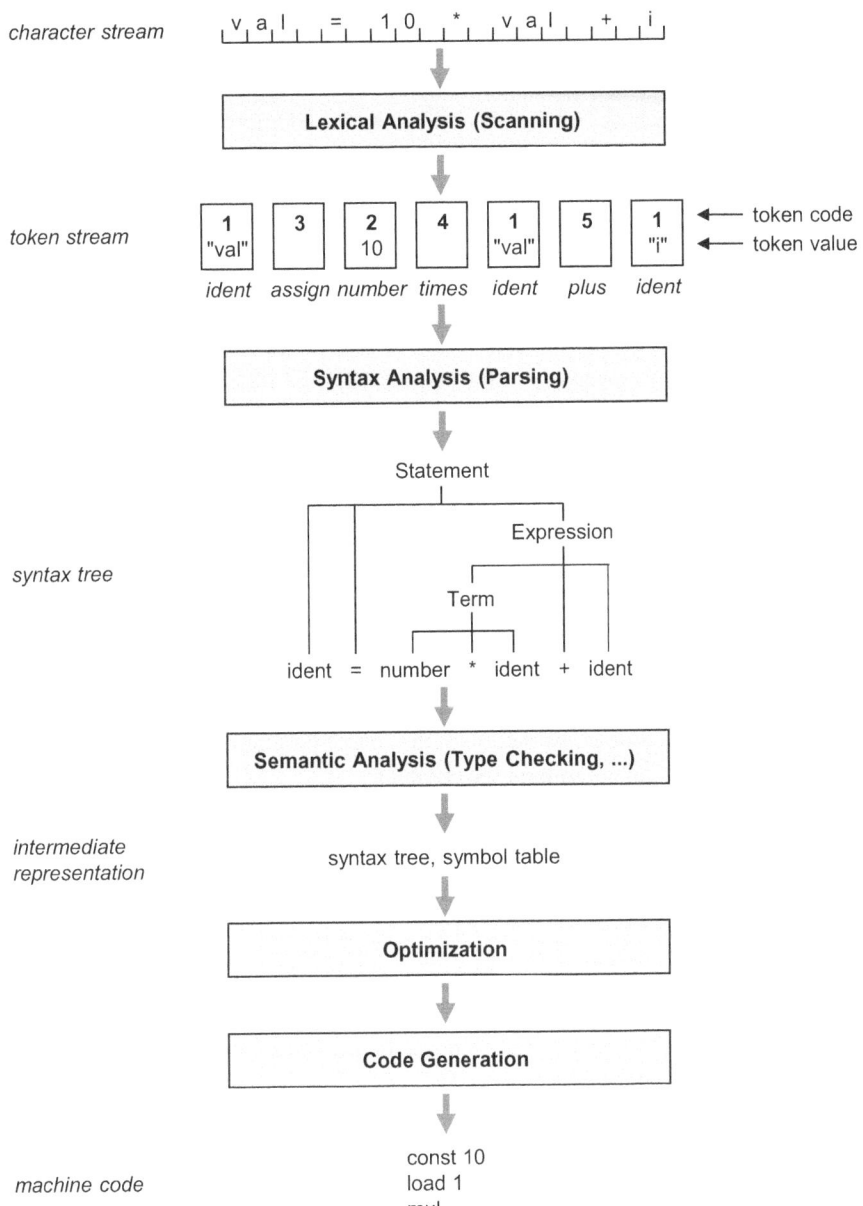

Fig. 1.1 Dynamic structure of a compiler

Lexical analysis. Lexical analysis is the first phase of a compiler. It transforms the character stream of the source program into a token stream. In doing so, it eliminates meaningless characters (e.g., spaces) and combines other characters into symbols (e.g., names, numbers, or operators), which are called *tokens*. Each kind of token is denoted by a unique token code (e.g., 1 for identifiers, 2 for numbers, etc.). For some tokens, there is just a single representation (e.g., the operator "*" is sufficiently identified by its token code). However, other tokens (e.g., identifiers) can have several representations (e.g., there are different identifiers such as "val" or "i"). Therefore, in addition to the token code (e.g., 1 = ident), we also need a token value (e.g., "val"). Each token is an object denoted by a token code and an optional token value. The token stream is an abstraction of the character stream and simplifies the next steps of the compiler. The part of the compiler that performs lexical analysis is called the *scanner*.

Syntax analysis. The next phase of a compiler is syntax analysis (parsing). It analyzes the token stream based on the grammar of the source language and builds a syntax tree that reflects the syntactic structure of the source program. If this succeeds, the program is syntactically correct and so the compiler can proceed to the next phase. If it fails, there is a syntax error that is reported and needs to be corrected by the programmer before the program can be recompiled. The compiler part that performs the syntax analysis is called the *parser*.

Semantic analysis. Syntax analysis only checks the syntactic correctness of a program. Other criteria, such as the requirement that all identifiers must be declared before they are used and that the data types of operands in assignments and expressions must be compatible, are checked in the semantic analysis phase. This phase also builds a *symbol table*, which is a directory of all declared names and their properties. The syntax tree and the symbol table provide a further abstraction of the source program, constituting an intermediate representation of the program in the compiler.

Optimization. Semantic analysis is usually followed by optimization, in which the program is transformed to make it faster or more compact. Optimizations are a vast topic that fills entire books and are essential for product compilers. This book, deliberately does not deal with optimizations. Its focus is on studying the basic techniques of simple compilers or compiler-like tools.

Code generation. The final phase of a compiler is code generation, in which the target code is generated from the intermediate representation of the program.

1.2.1 Single-pass and Multi-pass Compilers

The phases of a compiler can either be interleaved or can run strictly sequentially. In the first case, the compiler is called a single-pass compiler, in the second case, it is called a multi-pass compiler.

1.2 Dynamic Structure of a Compiler

In a *single-pass compiler* (Fig. 1.2) the scanner delivers the next token and the parser checks whether it fits into the grammar at the current position. Then the semantic analysis processes the token, for example, by performing type checks before the code generator generates machine code for it. This cycle then starts all over again until the source program has all been compiled.

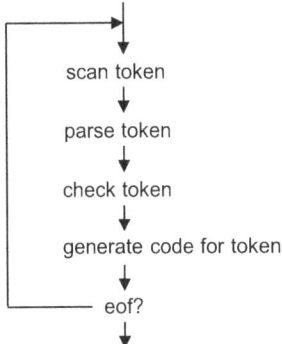

Fig. 1.2 Single-pass compiler

In a *multi-pass compiler* (Fig. 1.3) the individual phases are run one after the other. The scanner reads the source file and generates a token stream, the parser checks its syntactic correctness and generates a syntax tree, the semantic analysis performs further checks and generates a symbol table before the code generator produces the target code from it.

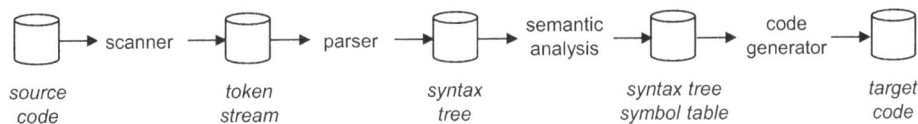

Fig. 1.3 Multi-pass compiler

In the past, multi-pass compilers were often necessary because the computers' memory was small, or the programming language was so complex that it seemed necessary to split a compiler into smaller parts. Both reasons are now irrelevant and so modern compilers are often single-pass. However, for optimizing compilers, a two-pass approach is usually chosen, in which a so-called *frontend* contains the scanner, the parser, the semantic analyzer and a simple code generator which generates an intermediate representation that is then translated into the target code by the *backend* (Fig. 1.4).

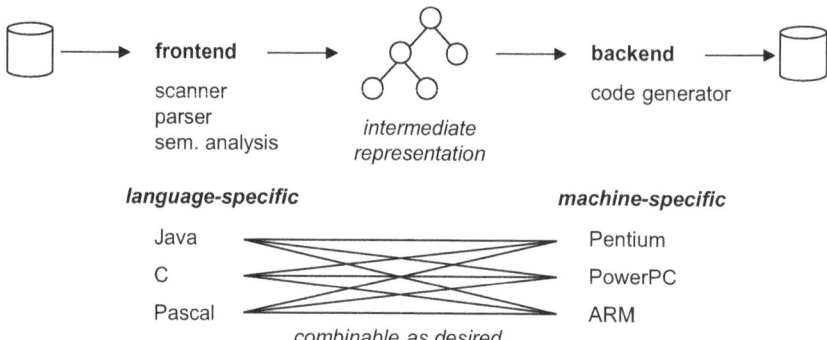

Fig. 1.4 Two-pass compiler with intermediate representation

The frontend is language-specific, because different scanners and parsers need to be implemented for different languages such as Java, C or Pascal. The backend, on the other hand, is machine-specific, because different code generators need to be written for processors such as Pentium, PowerPC or ARM. However, all frontends generate the same intermediate representation and all backends transform the same intermediate representation into the respective target code.

This decomposition offers several advantages. On the one hand, it results in better portability. If we want to implement a compiler for a new language, say C#, all we must do is write a frontend for it. With the various backends, we immediately have C# compilers for all target machines for which there is a backend. In general, any frontend can be combined with any backend to obtain compilers of different source languages for different target machines. The biggest advantage, however, is that optimizations are much easier to perform on the intermediate representation than on the source language. Therefore, almost all optimizing compilers are two-pass compilers.

The disadvantage of two-pass compilers is that they are slower and require more memory than single-pass compilers, because an intermediate representation of the program has to be built in main memory, although with today's fast computers and large memories, this is usually not a problem. Since we don't talk about optimizations in this book, our MicroJava compiler will be a single-pass compiler.

1.2.2 Compiler and Interpreter

A compiler translates a source program directly into machine code, which can then be loaded and executed (Fig. 1.5).

1.2 Dynamic Structure of a Compiler

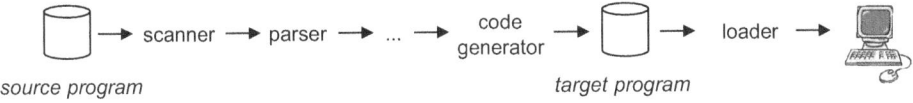

Fig. 1.5 Compiler

An interpreter, on the other hand, executes a program "directly" without first translating it into machine code. However, the program must still be analyzed beforehand, i.e., one needs at least a scanner and a parser that recognizes the structure of the program, but as soon as this structure is known, the program is executed, i.e., interpreted (Fig. 1.6).

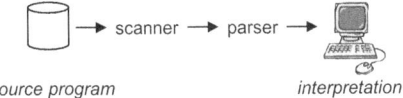

Fig. 1.6 Interpreter

With an interpreter, there is no need for complete compilation. Users have the impression that their program is executed immediately. However, the interpretation is considerably slower than the execution of a compiled program. Statements in a loop, for example, must be reprocessed by the scanner and the parser each time the loop is executed before they can be interpreted. For this reason, many languages (e.g., Java and also MicroJava) use a hybrid approach: a compiler, which does not generate machine code, but rather the code of a "virtual machine" (VM). Java programs, for example, are translated into *bytecode*—a simple instruction format that can then be interpreted by the Java VM (Fig. 1.7).

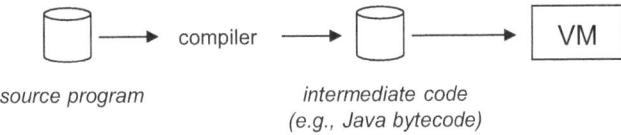

Fig. 1.7 Interpretation of intermediate code

In this way, each statement of the source program only needs to be analyzed and translated once. Furthermore, the interpretation of the bytecode is more efficient than the interpretation of source code. The VM "simulates" a physical machine by executing bytecode instead of machine code. This also has the advantage that the bytecode can be executed on any machine on which there is a corresponding bytecode interpreter. This makes programs portable to any computer which can run the VM.

1.3 Static Structure of a Compiler

The static structure of a compiler describes the relations between its components (i.e., its classes). There are numerous such components in product compilers, but the most important ones that make up any compiler (including the MicroJava compiler) are shown in Fig. 1.8.

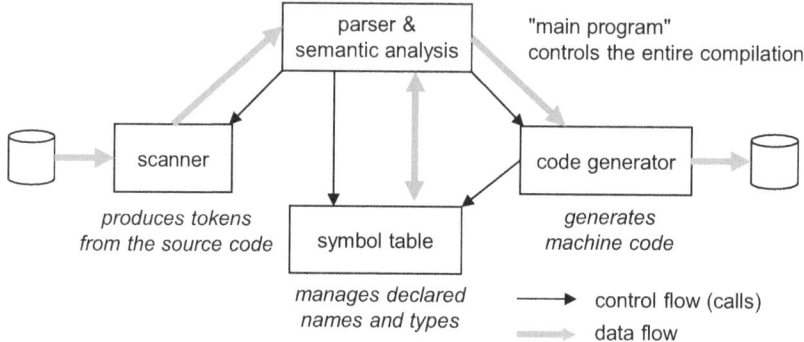

Fig. 1.8 Static structure of a compiler

The parser, which also integrates semantic analysis, assumes the role of the main program and controls the entire translation. Whenever it needs a token, it calls the scanner, which extracts the next token from the source code and delivers it to the parser, which processes it syntactically and semantically. Declared names and their properties are entered into the symbol table by the parser and retrieved from the symbol table when they are used. Finally, the parser calls methods of the code generator to generate instructions of the target code.

The MicroJava compiler is also built using this scheme. We will look at the scanner in Chap. 2, the parser in Chap. 3, the symbol table in Chap. 5, and finally the code generator in Chap. 6.

1.4 Grammars

Like natural languages, programming languages have a syntactic structure that can be described by a grammar. A grammar consists of rules that specify how the individual parts of the language are structured. The following example shows a rule that describes the structure of a while statement:

    WhileStatement = "while" "(" Condition ")" Statement.

A while statement starts with the keyword "while", followed by a condition in parentheses and a statement that represents the body of the loop. In general, grammars consist of the following four parts:

1.4 Grammars

- **Terminal symbols**: A set of symbols (tokens) that cannot be further broken down; they represent the "atoms" of language, so to speak. These include keywords such as "while" or "if", operators such as "+" or "-", special characters such as ";" or "," and finally, symbols such as names or numbers, which are atomic from a grammatical point of view.
- **Nonterminal symbols**: A set of symbols that represent larger parts of the language and therefore need to be broken down into further terminal or nonterminal symbols. This includes, for example, the nonterminal symbol WhileStatement from the example above, but also Condition or Statement.
- **Productions**: A set of grammar rules that describe the decomposition of nonterminal symbols into further terminal and nonterminal symbols. The above example shows the production (and thus the decomposition) of the nonterminal symbol WhileStatement.
- **Start symbol**: The topmost nonterminal symbol from which everything else (i.e., the entire language) can be derived.

Terminal and nonterminal symbols together form the *alphabet* of the language described by grammar, i.e., the set of symbols from which grammar is composed.

1.4.1 EBNF Notation for Grammars

There are various notations for writing grammars. In this book, we use the EBNF (*Extended Backus-Naur Form*) [Wirt77], which is named after the compiler pioneers *John Backus* and *Peter Naur*. It is an extension of pure BNF, to which we will return in Sect. 1.5.

An EBNF production consists of a left-hand and a right-hand side, separated by an equal sign. Each production is terminated by a period:

```
WriteStatement = "write" ident "," Expression ";" .
```

On the left-hand side, there is a nonterminal symbol. The right-hand side consists of a sequence of terminal and nonterminal symbols. Terminal symbols can be names (e.g., ident) or literals (e.g., "write", ",", ";") that denote themselves. Nonterminal symbols are always names. By convention, we write terminal symbols with lowercase letters (e.g., ident) and nonterminal symbols with uppercase letters (e.g., Expression).

In EBNF notation, the right-hand side of a production can also contain meta symbols that separate alternatives, represent optional or iterative parts, or group multiple alternatives using parentheses:

Meta symbol	Purpose	Example	Meaning
|	separates alternatives	a | b | c	a or b or c
(...)	groups alternatives	a (b | c)	ab or ac
[...]	option	[a] b	ab | b
{...}	iteration (0 .. infinitely many times)	{a} b	b | ab | aab | aaab | ...

1.4.2 Example: Grammar of Arithmetic Expressions

As an example, let's consider an EBNF grammar of arithmetic expressions, in which names and numbers (i.e., *operands*) occur in combination with arithmetic *operators* such as "+" or "*":

```
Expr   = ["+" | "−"] Term {("+" | "−") Term} .
Term   = Factor {("*" | "/") Factor} .
Factor = ident | number | "(" Expr ")" .
```

An expression (Expr) begins with an optional *sign* ("+" or "-"), which can be followed by one or more *terms* separated by "+" or "-". A term consists of one or more *factors* separated by "*" or "/". Finally, a factor consists of a name (ident), a number (number) or an expression in parentheses. Note that the round parentheses in Factor are terminal symbols that occur in the input language (that's why they are in quotation marks), whilst the round parentheses in the productions for Expr and Term are meta symbols that merely group alternatives.

Grammars can also be represented graphically by *syntax diagrams* (Fig. 1.9), which connect the symbols of the grammar by lines that can be followed to determine the symbols that can be derived from a nonterminal symbol. While such diagrams are easy to read, they take up a lot of space and are also difficult to process by machine. Therefore, we will use the textual grammar notation in this book.

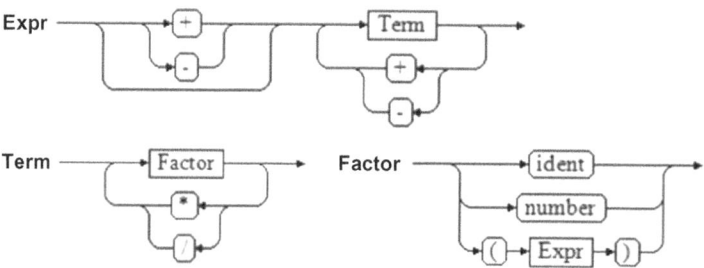

Fig. 1.9 Grammar as syntax diagrams

The nonterminal symbols of the above grammar are Expr, Term, and Factor. With terminal symbols, we distinguish between *simple terminal symbols* ("+", "−", "*", "/", "(", ")"), of which there is only a single representation, and *terminal classes* (ident, number), of which there

1.4 Grammars

can be several representations (for example names can be x, y, or sum and numbers can be 1, 10 or 355). The start symbol of this grammar is Expr.

Grammars can also be used to express *precedence rules* of operators. For example, if the expression

 − a * 3 + b / 4 − c

is analyzed according to the above grammar, the character stream is first converted into terminal symbols, which are then gradually combined into nonterminal symbols (Fig. 1.10).

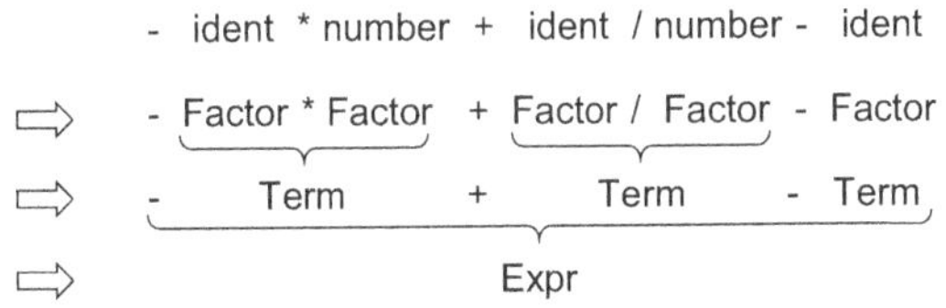

```
        -  ident * number  +  ident / number  -  ident
⇒       -  Factor * Factor +  Factor / Factor -  Factor
⇒       -       Term       +       Term       -  Term
⇒                              Expr
```

Fig. 1.10 Analysis of the expression − a * 3 + b / 4 − c

As you can see, the sign ("−") here refers to the entire term (a * 3) and not just to the variable a. In order to change this, one has to move the optional sign symbol to the production of Factor, so that − ident is combined into a Factor before Factor * Factor is recognized as a Term:

```
Expr   = Term {("+" | "−") Term}.
Term   = Factor {("*" | "/") Factor}.
Factor = ["+" | "−"] (ident | number | "(" Expr ")").
```

So you can influence the precedence rules by changing the grammar. In general, operators at lower grammar levels take precedence over operators at higher grammar levels. Thus, in the grammar above, the unary sign in the production of Factor takes precedence over the binary operators "*" and "/" in the production of Term, and these in turn take precedence over the binary operators "+" and "−" in the production of Expr.

1.4.3 Terminal Start Symbols of Nonterminals

For syntax analysis, it is important to know the *terminal start symbols* of nonterminals, i.e., the terminal symbols with which a nonterminal symbol can begin. For our original grammar

```
Expr   = ["+" | "−"] Term {("+" | "−") Term}.
Term   = Factor {("*" | "/") Factor}.
Factor = ident | number | "(" Expr ")".
```

the production of Factor has three alternatives. The first begins with ident, the second with number, and the third with "(". The terminal start symbols of Factor are therefore:

First(Factor) = **ident, number, "("**

The production of Term begins with Factor, whose terminal start symbols we already know. The following therefore applies:

First(Term) = First(Factor) = **ident, number, "("**

Finally, the production of Expr can begin with a sign ("+" or "-"). But because the sign is optional, it can also begin with a Term whose terminal start symbols are already known:

First(Expr) = "+", "−", First(Term) = **"+", "−", ident, number, "("**

1.4.4 Terminal Successors of Nonterminals

Similar to terminal start symbols, the parser also needs to know the *terminal successors* of nonterminal symbols, i.e., the terminal symbols that can follow a nonterminal symbol in any context. To determine the terminal successors of Expr, we need to look at where Expr occurs on the right-hand side of a production and which terminal symbols can follow there. Expr occurs in the production of Factor, where it is followed by ")". However, since Expr is the topmost nonterminal symbol of our grammar (i.e., the start symbol), it is also followed by a special symbol eof (*end of file*), which marks the end of the input stream (i.e., the expression). So, the terminal successors of Expr are:

Follow(Expr) = **")", eof**

The nonterminal symbol Term occurs in two places in the production of Expr. The first occurrence is followed by an iteration ({...}). If the iteration is entered, "+" or "−" follows. However, iterations can also be executed zero times; in this case, the successors of the iteration follow, here the terminal successors of Expr, which we already know:

Follow(Term) = "+", "−", Follow(Expr) = **"+", "−", ")", eof**

The situation is similar with the nonterminal symbol Factor, which occurs in two places in the production of Term. The first occurrence is followed by an iteration, which can start with "*" or "/". If the iteration is skipped, the terminal successors of Term follow, which we already know:

Follow(Factor) = "*", "/", Follow(Term) = **"*", "/", "+", "−", ")", eof**

1.4.5 Other Terminology of Formal Languages

From a theoretical point of view, programming languages are formal languages. Although we only use as much theory in this book as we need for practical compiler construction, there is some terminology that you need to know.

We have already mentioned that the set of terminal and nonterminal symbols of a grammar forms the *alphabet* of grammar.

1.4 Grammars

The term *string* is used to describe a finite sequence of terminal or nonterminal symbols from an alphabet. Strings are denoted by Greek letters. Examples of strings from the alphabet of our Expr grammar are:

  α = ident + number
  β = − Term + Factor * number

The *empty string*, which does not consist of any symbol, is denoted by ε.

If one replaces a nonterminal symbol in a string α with the right-hand side of its production, one gets a new string β. This is called a *direct derivation* and is written $\alpha \Rightarrow \beta$. In the following example, Factor is replaced by ident:

  − Term + **Factor** * number $\Rightarrow$ − Term + **ident** * number

If the derivation takes place via several intermediate stages,

  $\alpha \Rightarrow \gamma_1 \Rightarrow \gamma_2 \Rightarrow \ldots \Rightarrow \gamma_n \Rightarrow \beta$

this is called an *indirect derivation* and is written as $\alpha \Rightarrow^* \beta$. If the leftmost nonterminal symbol is replaced in a derivation $\alpha \Rightarrow \beta$, this is called a *left-canonical derivation*; if the rightmost nonterminal symbol is replaced, this is called a *right-canonical derivation*.

The reverse of a derivation is called a *reduction*. If a sequence of symbols is found in a string β that corresponds to the right-hand side of a production, and if this sequence is replaced with the corresponding nonterminal symbol, the string β is said to have been reduced to a string α.

Parsers work either *top-down*, by deriving a sentence of the language from the start symbol of a grammar (see Sect. 3.2), or *bottom-up*, by reducing a sentence of the language to the start symbol (see Sect. 8.1).

A string that can be derived directly or indirectly from a nonterminal symbol is called a *phrase* of this nonterminal symbol. For example, the following strings can be derived from Term, which are thus Term phrases:

  Factor
  Factor * Factor
  ident * Factor

A phrase derived from the start symbol is called a *sentential form*. From Expr, for example, the following sentential forms can be derived:

  Term + Term − Term
  Term + Factor * ident − Term
  ...

If a sentential form consists only of terminal symbols, it is called a *sentence* of the grammar. Sentences of our Expr grammar are, for example:

  ident * number + ident
  number * (ident + ident)
  ...

All sentences that can be derived from the start symbol of a grammar form the (*formal*) *language* of this grammar. The MicroJava language is therefore the set of all valid MicroJava programs. There are usually an infinite number of such sentences (i.e., an infinite number of MicroJava programs).

Another concept of formal languages is *deletability*. A string α is called deletable if it can be derived into the empty string ($\alpha \Rightarrow^* \varepsilon$). In the following grammar

```
X = Y Z.
Y = [b].
Z = c | d | .
```

Y is deletable because b is optional and Y can thus be derived into the empty string. The production of Z consists of three alternatives, the last of which is empty; thus Z may also be derived into the empty string and is therefore deletable. Since Y and Z are deletable, X can also be derived into the empty string and is also deletable.

1.4.6 Recursion

The term *recursion* (self-reference) is known from mathematics and also has an important meaning in grammars. A production of a nonterminal symbol X is called recursive if X can be derived into a string which again contains X ($X \Rightarrow^* \omega_1 X \omega_2$). The strings ω_1 and ω_2 can be empty, which results in three possible forms of recursion:

Left recursion	X = b | X a.	$X \Rightarrow Xa \Rightarrow Xaa \Rightarrow Xaaa \Rightarrow ... \Rightarrow baaaaa$
Right recursion	X = b | a X.	$X \Rightarrow aX \Rightarrow aaX \Rightarrow aaaX \Rightarrow ... \Rightarrow aaaaab$
Central recursion	X = b | "(" X ")".	$X \Rightarrow (X) \Rightarrow ((X)) \Rightarrow (((X))) \Rightarrow ... \Rightarrow (((((b)))))$

In the case of left recursion, a nonterminal symbol can be derived into a string that starts again with this nonterminal symbol (ω_1 is empty), in the case of right recursion, it can be derived into a string that ends with this nonterminal symbol (ω_2 is empty). As can be seen from the examples above, this can be used to express repetitions. Central recursion, on the other hand, is used to express nested structures (ω_1 and ω_2 are not empty), where there are exactly as many occurrences of ω_1 as there are of ω_2.

In addition to direct recursion shown in the examples above, there is also indirect recursion. The following simplified Expr grammar

```
Expr   = Term {"+" Term}.
Term   = Factor {"*" Factor}.
Factor = ident | "(" Expr ")".
```

is indirectly central recursive (Expr $\Rightarrow^* \omega_1$ Expr ω_2), because Expr can be derived over several stages into a string which again contains Expr:

Expr $\Rightarrow$ Term $\Rightarrow$ Factor $\Rightarrow$ (Expr)

1.4.7 Elimination of Left Recursion

In top-down parsing, which we will look at in Chap. 3, left recursion is disruptive and must therefore be eliminated. The left-recursive production

    X = b | X a.

consists of two alternatives. The first one starts with b and the second with X, but the terminal start symbols of X are also b. Therefore, if the parser wants to detect an X and finds a b in the input, it cannot decide between the two alternatives because they both start with b.

Fortunately, left recursion can always be transformed into iteration. The nonterminal symbol X can be derived into a sentence as follows:

    X ⇒ Xa ⇒ Xaa ⇒ ... ⇒ baaa... a

It is easy to see that one can transform the left-recursive production of X into an iterative EBNF production that is no longer recursive:

    X = b {a}.

Here is another example: the following left-recursive production

    Expr = Term | Expr "+" Term.

leads to the derivations

    Expr ⇒ Expr + Term ⇒ Expr + Term + Term ⇒ ... ⇒ Term + Term + ... + Term

which in turn reduces to the iterative EBNF production:

    Expr = Term {"+" Term}.

1.4.8 Grammar Classes According to Chomsky

In the 1950s, the American linguist *Noam Chomsky* researched grammars as substitution systems, consisting of rules α = β, by which a string α can be derived into a string β. Depending on the form of α and β, he distinguished four classes of grammars:

Class 0: Unrestricted grammars. Here, α and β can be arbitrary strings of terminal and nonterminal symbols, for example:

    X   = a X b | Y c Y.
    a Y c = d.
    d Y = b b.

For example, X can be derived into a sentence as follows:

    X ⇒ aXb ⇒ aYcYb ⇒ dYb ⇒ bbb

Unrestricted grammars are the most powerful class because they can generate languages according to complex rules. However, there is no general algorithm to analyze such languages. Such languages are said to be recognizable by *Turing machines*.

Class 1: Context-sensitive grammars. Here, $|\alpha| \leq |\beta|$ must hold. The left-hand side can be a string of any length, for example:

    a X = a b c.

but it must not contain more symbols than the right-hand side. As can be seen, the context of a nonterminal symbol is taken into account here: X can only be derived to b c if it is preceded by an a. Context-sensitive grammars can be used to generate languages that are recognizable by *linear-bounded automata* (a variant of Turing machines).

Class 2: Context-free grammars. In these grammars, α consists of a single nonterminal symbol, while β can be any string, for example:

    X = a b c.

In principle, it is also required that β must not be empty, but it can be shown that productions where β is empty can be transformed into productions where β is not empty. Context-free grammars generate languages that can be recognized with *pushdown automata* (see Chaps. 3 and 8).

Class 3: Regular grammars. Again, α consists of just a single nonterminal symbol, but β can only be a terminal symbol, or a terminal symbol followed by a nonterminal symbol, for example:

    X = b.
    X = b Y.

Regular grammars generate languages that can be recognized by *finite automata* (see Chap. 2).

For compilers, only context-free and regular grammars are relevant as there are efficient algorithms for processing them. Context-free grammars are used in syntax analysis, whilst regular grammars are used in lexical analysis.

1.5 Syntax Trees

The parser analyzes a sentence of a language according to its grammar and checks its syntactic correctness. This involves building a syntax tree that describes the decomposition of the sentence into individual parts.

To build a syntax tree, it is easier to work with pure BNF (*Backus-Naur form*), which, unlike EBNF, does not have brackets for grouping alternatives ((...)), for representing

1.5 Syntax Trees

optionality ([...]) and for representing iterations ({...}). Optionality must be expressed by several alternatives and iteration by left recursion. Our Expr grammar looks like this in pure BNF:

```
Expr   = Sign Term | Expr AddOp Term.
Term   = Factor | Term MulOp Factor.
Factor = ident | number | "(" Expr ")".
Sign   = "+" | "–" | .
AddOp  = "+" | "–".
MulOp  = "*" | "/".
```

For example, for the input 10 + 3 * x, the syntax tree shown in Fig. 1.11 is constructed:

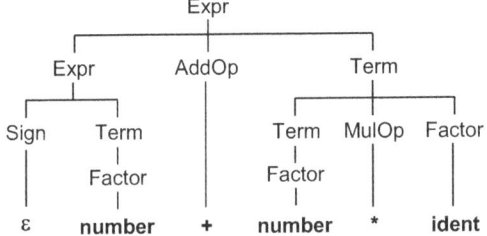

Fig. 1.11 Concrete syntax tree for the sentence 10 + 3 * x

This reflects all derivations from the start symbol to the sentence (Expr ⇒ Expr AddOp Term, Term ⇒ Term MulOp Factor, etc.). Such a syntax tree is therefore called the *concrete syntax tree* (*parse tree*).

In addition to the concrete syntax tree, there is also the *abstract syntax tree*, which reflects the logical structure of a sentence and is much more compact than the concrete syntax tree. Its leaves represent the operands and its inner nodes represent the operators (Fig. 1.12).

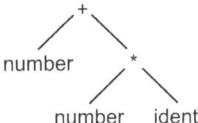

Fig. 1.12 Abstract syntax tree for the sentence 10 + 3 * x

The abstract syntax tree is often used in optimizing compilers for the internal representation of a program on which optimizations can then be performed.

1.5.1 Ambiguity

A grammar is ambiguous if multiple (concrete) syntax trees can be built for a specific sentence. For example, from the following grammar (T stands for Term and F for Factor)

```
T = F | T "/" T.
F = id.
```

the sentence id / id / id can be derived:

$T \Rightarrow T/T \Rightarrow T/T/T \Rightarrow F/F/F \Rightarrow id/id/id$

As can be seen from Fig. 1.13, two different syntax trees can be built for this sentence.

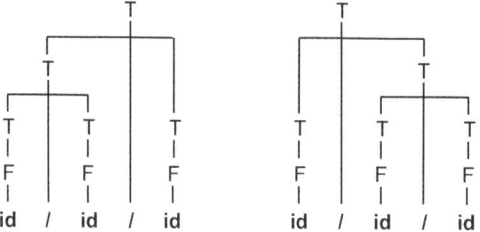

Fig. 1.13 Different syntax trees for the sentence id / id / id

Ambiguous grammars are unsuitable for syntax analysis because they allow different interpretations of the sentence. For example, the left syntax tree in Fig. 1.13 states that the first two occurrences of id are divided first, while the second syntax tree states that the last two occurrences of id are divided first.

Fortunately, in this example, it is not the language that is ambiguous, but only the grammar. If the grammar is transformed to

```
T = F | T"/" F.
F = id.
```

the same sentences can be generated, but the divisions are always carried out from left to right. The ambiguity has therefore been removed.

However, there are languages that are inherently ambiguous, and you don't have to look far to find one. Most of the languages in the C family (C, C++, C#, and Java) contain an inherent ambiguity called the *dangling else*. The if statement can take two forms in these languages:

```
Statement = "if" Condition Statement
          | "if" Condition Statement "else" Statement
          | ... .
```

If you look at the following nested if statement

```
if (a < b) if (b < c) x = c; else x = b;
```

the keyword else can either belong to the first if or to the second. This means that two different syntax trees can be built (see Fig. 1.14), which represents an ambiguity. In this case, the language itself is ambiguous and not just the grammar. It is not possible to transform the grammar in such a way that the ambiguity disappears.

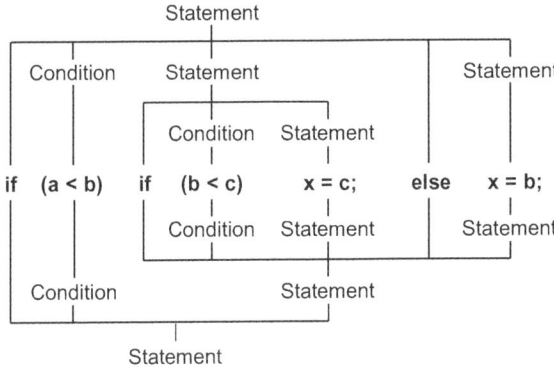

Fig. 1.14 Ambiguity in the "dangling else"

This ambiguity is solved by associating the else with the immediately preceding if. If the parser analyzes the two alternatives of the if statement and finds an else in the input stream, it proceeds with the second alternative instead of terminating the first one. So, the lower syntax tree from Fig. 1.14 applies, but this is just a convention that does not actually eliminate the ambiguity.

1.6 MicroJava

This book demonstrates the principles of compiler construction using the programming language *MicroJava*. The following section gives a brief overview of this language. A more detailed description of its syntax and semantics can be found in Appendix A.

MicroJava is a subset of Java and is simple enough to develop a complete compiler for it in a one-semester course, but also realistic enough to study the most important principles of compiler construction.

A MicroJava program consists of a single file that starts with the keyword program and can contain global data and methods. The main method, where the program execution starts, is called main(). There are the following elements in MicroJava:

- *Value types*: int and char; char values are stored in a single (ASCII) byte.
- *Reference types*: These are one-dimensional arrays, as well as classes with fields but without methods or inheritance. Variables of these types contain references.
- *Constants*: int constants (e.g., 3) and char constants (e.g., 'x'), but no string constants.
- *Variables*: These can be local to a method or global to the entire program.

- *Methods*: These are global to the program; there are no class-local methods.
- *Comments*: End-of-line comments that go from "//" to the end of the line.

The following example shows a MicroJava program with all the essential elements:

```
program P
  final int size = 10;      // constant declaration
  class Table {             // class declaration (without methods)
    int[] pos;              // array declaration (one-dimensional)
    int[] neg;
  }
  Table val;                // declaration of a global variable

  {
    void main()
      int x, i;             // declaration of local variables
      //---------- initialize val ------------
      val = new Table;
      val.pos = new int[size];
      val.neg = new int[size];
      i = 0;
      while (i < size) {
        val.pos[i] = 0; val.neg[i] = 0;
        i++;
      }
      //---------- read values ---------
      read(x);
      while (x != 0) {
        if (0 <= x && x < size) {
          val.pos[x]++;
        } else if (-size < x && x < 0) {
          val.neg[-x]++;
        }
        read(x);
      }
    } // main
  } // P
```

MicroJava programs are translated into MicroJava bytecode that can be executed by the MicroJava VM (see Chap. 6).

1.7 Exercises

There are sample solutions for all exercises in this book, which can be downloaded from [Download].

1. *Grammar of e-mail addresses*. Write a grammar for e-mail addresses. These consist of an address part and a domain part, separated by "@". Both the address part and the domain part should consist of a list of names (ident) separated by periods. While the

address part may consist of just a single name, the domain part must have at least two names, for example:

   john.doe@some.company.com

2. *Grammar of simplified Boolean expressions.* Write a grammar for Boolean expressions that has identifiers (ident) as well as the constants true and false as operands and &&, || and ! as operators (where ! takes precedence over &&, and && takes precedence over ||). It should also be possible to enclose subexpressions in parentheses. Use the grammar of arithmetic expressions from Sect. 1.4 as a template. Example:

   (big || small) && ready || big && ! ready

3. *Grammar of Roman numbers.* Write a grammar of the Roman numbers from 1 to 20 (i.e., I, II, III, IV, V, VI, VII, VIII, IX, X, XI, XII, XIII, XIV, XV, XVI, XVII, XVII, XVII, XVIII, XIX, XX). Terminal symbols are I, V, and X.

4. *Terminal start and successor symbols (1).* List the terminal start and successor symbols of all nonterminal symbols in the following grammar (note: names beginning with lowercase letters are terminal symbols):

   ```
   Course  = Intro Section {Section} Final.
   Intro   = lecture [questions].
   Section = {lecture | questions} (project | test).
   Final   = [panic] test.
   ```

5. *Terminal start and successor symbols (2).* List the terminal start and successor symbols of all nonterminal symbols in the following grammar:

   ```
   Message = Header [Data] Status.
   Header  = "get" | "put" [number | "final"].
   Data    = number {number}.
   Status  = "ok" | Number.
   ```

6. *Elimination of left recursion (1).* Transform the following left-recursive grammar into an equivalent non-recursive grammar using EBNF iteration:

   ```
   A = A B | a b.
   B = B d | c.
   ```

7. *Elimination of left recursion (2).* Transform the following left-recursive grammar into an equivalent non-recursive grammar using EBNF iteration:

   ```
   List = List number | .
   ```

8. *Syntax trees (1).* Consider the following BNF grammar for simplified arithmetic expressions:

   ```
   Expr   = Term
   Expr   = Expr AddOp Term.
   Term   = Factor
   Term   = Term MulOp Factor.
   Factor = number
   ```

```
Factor  = "-" Factor
Factor  = "(" Expr ")".
AddOp   = "+"
AddOp   = "-".
MulOp   = "*"
MulOp   = "/".
```

(a) Draw the concrete and the abstract syntax tree for the expression 3 + 5.

(b) Draw the concrete and the abstract syntax tree for (7 - 2) * 5 + 1.

9. *Syntax trees (2)*. Consider the following strongly simplified grammar of statements:

```
Statement =
    ident "=" ident "-" ident
  | "{" Statement {";" Statement} "}"
  | "if" "(" ident ">" ident ")" Statement
  | "while" "(" ident ">" ident ")" Statement.
```

Draw the abstract syntax tree for the following program

```
if (a > b) {
   while (a > b) a = a - b;
   b = b - a
}
```

where "if", "while", "=", ">", "-" and ";" are operators and identifiers are operands. The operator ";" concatenates two statements.

10. *Ambiguity*. The grammar

```
List = ident | List "," List.
```

is ambiguous because different syntax trees can be built for certain sentences.

(a) Draw all possible syntax trees for the sentence ident, ident, ident.

(b) Transform the grammar in such a way that it produces the same language but is unambiguous.

Lexical Analysis

2

The first phase of the compilation process is lexical analysis (*scanning*). It converts the character stream of the source program into a sequence of terminal symbols, i.e., a token stream (Fig. 2.1).

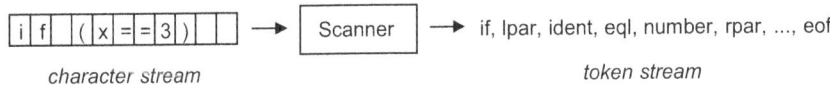

Fig. 2.1 Conversion of the source program into a token stream

In this example, the characters "i" and "f" become the token if, the character "(" becomes the token lpar (*left parenthesis*), "x" becomes ident, "=" and "=" become eql, and ")" becomes rpar. Note that the token stream is always terminated by a special eof token that marks the end of the input.

As we saw in Chap. 1, each token is described by a *token code* that specifies the kind of token (e.g., identifier, number, operator). Tokens, of which there are several forms (e.g., identifiers), also have a *token value* in addition to their token code. In the case of an identifier the token value is the text of the identifier.

Another task of lexical analysis is to filter out insignificant characters (blanks, tabs, line endings, and comments) from the input stream, as they are irrelevant for syntax analysis. After that, the token stream contains only the relevant symbols, which can then be processed much more easily by the parser than the original source code.

Lexical and Syntactic Structures

The structure of terminal symbols can be described by a grammar, for example:

    ident   = letter {letter | digit}.
    number = digit {digit}.

```
if     = "i" "f".
eql    = "=" "=".
...
```

Why are these lexical structures not viewed as part of the language's syntax? For example, why is ident considered to be a terminal symbol rather than a nonterminal symbol that can be broken down into letters and digits?

There are several reasons for this. If syntax analysis were done at character level, it would be much harder to distinguish between identifiers and keywords. For example, the following production

```
Statement = ident "=" Expr ";"
          | "if" "(" Expr ")" Statement
          | ... .
```

would then have to be written as

```
Statement = "i" ( "f" ( "(" Expr ")" Statement
                       | (letter | digit) {letter | digit} "=" Expr ";"
                       )
                | not_f {letter | digit} "=" Expr ";"
                )
          | not_i {letter | digit} "=" Expr ";"
          | ... .
```

which would be much harder to understand. Also, blanks and other irrelevant characters would have to be considered in all sorts of places in the grammar, for example:

```
Statement = "i" "f" {Blank} "(" {Blank} Expr {Blank} ")" {Blank} Statement {Blank} ... .
Blank     = " " | "\n" | "\t" | Comment.
```

That would bloat the grammar and make it much harder to read. A third reason is that for terminal symbols regular grammars are sufficient, which can be analyzed more efficiently than context-free grammars that are used for syntax analysis.

For these reasons, lexical structures are recognized by the scanner, which provides them as a stream of tokens. The syntactic structures can then be described by a simple grammar that treats the lexical structures as terminal symbols.

2.1   Regular Grammars and Finite Automata

In Chap. 1, we defined regular grammars by saying that the left-hand side of their productions must consist of a single nonterminal symbol, and the right-hand side must consist of a terminal symbol, or a terminal symbol followed by a nonterminal symbol:

```
X = a.
X = b Y.
```

2.1 Regular Grammars and Finite Automata

This can be used to write a regular grammar for identifiers, for example:

```
ident = letter
      | letter Rest.
Rest  = letter
      | digit
      | letter Rest
      | digit Rest.
```

All these productions have the required form. The identifier xy3 can be derived as:

ident ⇒ letter Rest ⇒ letter letter Rest ⇒ letter letter digit

For our purposes, however, we use a simpler definition of regular grammars: a grammar is *regular* if it can be expressed by a *single* EBNF rule *without recursion*. For example, the grammar for identifiers can be expressed by the following non-recursive EBNF production:

```
ident = letter {letter | digit}.
```

It is therefore regular. What about the following grammar, is it regular?

```
E = T {"+" T}.
T = F {"*" F}.
F = ident.
```

It consists of several productions, but F can be substituted in the production of T:

```
T = ident {"*" ident}.
```

and then T in the production of E:

```
E = ident {"*" ident} {"+" ident {"*" ident}}.
```

By transforming it, we have obtained a grammar that just consists of a single non-recursive EBNF rule. Thus, the grammar is shown to be regular. Let's look at a third example. Is the following grammar regular?

```
E = F {"*" F}.
F = ident | "(" E ")".
```

We could try using the same trick, substituting F in the production of E:

```
E = (ident | "(" E ")") {"*" (ident | " (" E ")")}.
```

This results in a single EBNF rule, but it is recursive (more precisely, central-recursive). It is simply not possible to eliminate the recursion by further inlining E into this production. This highlights the main limitation of regular grammars: they cannot deal with central recursion.

2.1.1 Limitations of Regular Grammars

Regular grammars cannot deal with central recursion. In other words, they cannot express nested structures. However, nested structures are quite common in programming languages, for example:

nested expressions: **Expr** ⇒* "(" **Expr** ")"
nested statements: **Statement** ⇒ "do" **Statement** "while" "("**Expr**")"
inner classes: **Class** ⇒ "class" "{" ... **Class** ... "}"

Thus, the syntax analysis of programming languages requires the next higher class of grammars, namely context-free grammars. For lexical structures, however, regular grammars are sufficient, for example:

names   ident   = letter {letter | digit}.
numbers   number = digit {digit}.
character constants charCon = "\'" noQuote "\'".
keywords   keyword = letter {letter}
operators   geq   = ">" "=".

The only exception is for nested comments:

/* ... /* ... */ ... */

They cannot be described by a regular grammar and therefore would require special treatment in the scanner. For this reason, many languages such as Java do not allow nested comments.

2.1.2 Deterministic Finite Automata

A *deterministic finite automaton* (DFA) is a mechanism for recognizing regular languages. It consists of states with transitions defined between them (Fig. 2.2).

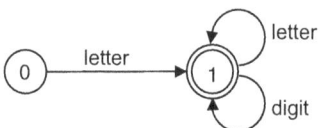

Fig. 2.2 Deterministic finite automaton for recognizing an identifier

States are represented by numbered circles, final states by double circles. By convention, the start state always has the number 0. State transitions are represented by labeled arrows. If the automaton in Fig. 2.2 is in state 0 and the next input character is a letter, it consumes this character and transitions to state 1. If further letters or digits are encountered in state 1, they are also consumed and the DFA stays in state 1. If a character other than a letter or digit is seen in state 1, the automaton terminates. If the automaton terminates in a final state (like in state 1), it has recognized a sentence of the language (in this case, an identifier). If, on the other hand, a character other than letter were to appear in state 0, this would be an error.

The state transitions can also be represented as a table (Fig. 2.3), which has as many rows as there are states and as many columns as there are input symbols. The table represents the *state transition function* δ: From state 0, letter takes us to state 1 and digit to an error state. The automaton is called "finite" because δ can be described by a finitely large table.

δ	letter	digit
s0	s1	error
s1	s1	s1

Fig. 2.3 State transition function δ represented as a table

Thus, a DFA consists of the following five parts:

- Q: a set of states
- S: a set of input symbols
- $\delta: Q \times S \to Q$: a state transition function
- s_0:   a start state
- F: a set of final states

The language recognized by a DFA is the set of all symbol sequences that lead from the start state to one of the final states. A DFA has recognized a sentence

- if it is in a final state, *and*
- if the input is finished *or* a state transition with the next input symbol is no longer possible.

How do we get from a regular grammar to a DFA? We do not give an algorithm for this, but it is easy to see that the DFA from Fig. 2.2 is derived from the production.

    ident = letter {letter | digit}.

First a letter must be recognized, which can then be followed by any number of letters or digits (including none). That is exactly the behavior of our DFA.

2.2 The Scanner as a Deterministic Finite Automaton

The scanner can be considered as a large DFA that is invoked by the parser to recognize terminal symbols. Each time it is invoked, it starts in state 0, skips irrelevant characters, and then branches off to a sub-automaton that recognizes one of the terminal symbols and returns it to the parser (Fig. 2.4).

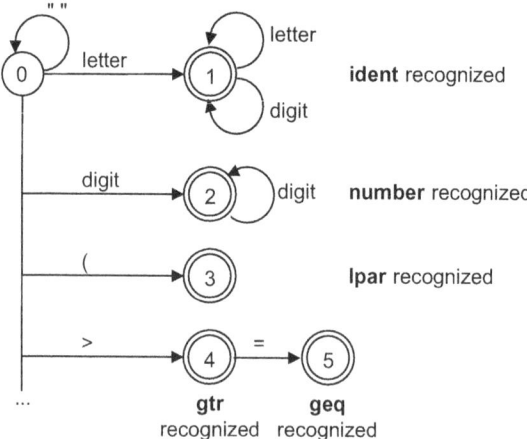

Fig. 2.4 Scanner as a deterministic finite automaton (DFA)

For the input character stream

max >= 30

the scanner starts in state 0, moves to state 1 with the character "m" and stays in state 1 with "a" and "x". Since the next character is a blank and there is no transition with it in state 1, the DFA terminates here. In this final state, it has recognized the token ident with the value "max" and returns it to the parser.

On the next call, the scanner starts again in state 0. Since there is still a blank left from the last call, it skips it, staying in state 0. With ">" it then goes to state 4, and because another transition is possible with "=", it goes to state 5. The next character is again a blank, for which there is no transition defined in state 5. The DFA therefore terminates and returns the token geq (*greater or equal*) to the parser.

On the third call, the scanner again skips the left-over blank in state 0 and then goes to state 2 with "3", where it stays with "0", both being digits. If the following character is again a blank, the DFA terminates here (in state 2 there is no transition with a blank) and returns a number token with the value 30 to the parser.

2.3 Implementation of a DFA

A DFA can either be implemented as a table-driven algorithm, which contains the state transition function as a table that drives the analysis, or the states and transitions can be implemented directly in code.

Let's now consider both alternatives. First we will look at the table-driven variant using the regular grammar

X = a {b} c.

2.3 Implementation of a DFA

This grammar results in the DFA shown in Fig. 2.5 together with the equivalent state transition function represented as a table.

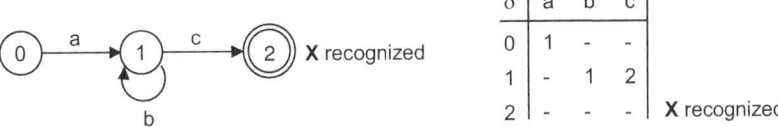

Fig. 2.5 DFA and its state transition table

The table can be implemented as a two-dimensional array, with error entries encoded as -1. This results in the following algorithm (in Java-like pseudocode, simplified):

```
int[][] delta = { {1, -1, -1}, {-1, 1, 2}, {-1, -1, -1} };  // state transition table
int state = 0, lastState;       // the DFA starts in state 0
do {
   char ch = read();            // read next character
   lastState = state;
   state = delta[state][ch];    // look up successor state
} while (state != -1);
assert(lastState is a final state);
return recognizedToken[lastState];
```

In the loop, the next input character and the current state are used to look up and transition to the next state until no further transition is possible (state == -1). The DFA should then be in a final state, otherwise there is an error. Finally, the token recognized in this final state (lastState) is determined using a further table recognizedToken and is returned to the parser.

Note that this algorithm is "universal" in the sense that it can be used for all regular grammars. It just needs to be initialized with the appropriate state transition table to recognize tokens of the corresponding grammar. However, the algorithm is not particularly efficient, which is why we will now look at an algorithm in which the states and the state transitions are encoded directly.

Using the DFA from Fig. 2.5 as an example, states are now implemented as case labels of a switch statement, which is addressed using the current state.

```
int state = 0;
loop:
for (;;) {
   char ch = read();
   switch (state) {
      case 0:  if (ch == 'a') { state = 1; break; }    // go to state 1
               else break loop;
      case 1:  if (ch == 'b') { state = 1; break; }    // go to state 1
               else if (ch == 'c') { state = 2; break; } // go to state 2
               else break loop;
      case 2: return X;
   }
}
return errorToken;
```

No table accesses are needed here. Instead, we branch to the current state using a switch statement in each iteration of the loop. In case of an error, the loop is exited with break loop.

Even better, however, is to abstract away from the states and their transitions altogether and implement the DFA as follows:

```
char ch = read();
if (ch == 'a') {
  ch = read();
  while (ch == 'b') ch = read();
  if (ch == 'c') { ch = read(); return X; }
  else return errorToken;
} else return errorToken;
```

Here, the DFA is only implicit, but the code is extremely efficient. Hence this style will be used for the MicroJava scanner in the next section.

2.3.1 Implementation of the Scanner

We will now consider the implementation of a scanner for MicroJava. The scanner is a class with two public methods that are static because there is just a single scanner in the compiler.

```
public class Scanner {
    public static void init (Reader r) {...}
    public static Token next() {...}
}
```

The method init() initializes the scanner and passes it a Reader object that represents the input stream (i.e., the source program). A call to init() might look like this:

```
InputStream s = new FileInputStream(sourceFileName);
Reader r = new InputStreamReader(s);
Scanner.init(r);
```

The method next() is called repeatedly by the parser and returns the next token on each call. A token is an object of the following class:

```
public class Token {
    public int    kind;    // token code
    public int    line;    // token line (for error messages)
    public int    col;     // token column (for error messages)
    public String val;     // token value
    public int    numVal;  // numeric token value (for number and charCon)
}
```

Each token has a *token code* (kind) that specifies the kind of token. Some tokens also have a *token value* that is stored in the numVal field for numbers and character constants and in the val field for identifiers. For error messages, each token also contains the line and column number at which it occurs in the source code.

2.3 Implementation of a DFA

Each kind of token is denoted by a unique token code. The token codes for MicroJava are as follows:

```
static final int
// error token
none = 0,
// token classes    operators and special characters                    keywords
ident   = 1,        plus  = 4,  /* + */       assign    = 17, /* = */    break_   = 29,
number  = 2,        minus = 5,  /* - */       pplus     = 18, /* ++ */   class_   = 30,
charCon = 3,        times = 6,  /* * */       mminus    = 19, /* -- */   else_    = 31,
                    slash = 7,  /* / */       semicolon = 20, /* ; */    final_   = 32,
                    rem   = 8,  /* % */       comma     = 21, /* , */    if_      = 33,
                    eql   = 9,  /* == */      period    = 22, /* . */    new_     = 34,
                    neq   = 10, /* != */      lpar      = 23, /* ( */    print_   = 35,
                    lss   = 11, /* < */       rpar      = 24, /* ) */    program_ = 36,
                    leq   = 12, /* <= */      lbrack    = 25, /* [ */    read_    = 37,
                    gtr   = 13, /* > */       rbrack    = 26, /* ] */    return_  = 38,
                    geq   = 14, /* >= */      lbrace    = 27, /* { */    void_    = 39,
                    and   = 15; /* && */      rbrace    = 28, /* } */    while_   = 40,
                    or    = 16, /* || */
// end of file token
eof = 41;
```

The current status of the scanner is stored in global variables:

```
static Reader in;                   // input character stream
static char ch;                     // next unprocessed character
static int line, col;               // line and column number of ch
static final char eofCh = (char) -1;  // character indicating end of file
```

At each point in time, ch holds the next unprocessed character, and line and col contain its position in the source code, with line and column numbers starting at 1.

The init() method initializes the global variables of the scanner and reads the first character of the source code by calling the nextCh() helper method:

```
public static void init (Reader r) {
    in = r;
    line = 1, col = 0;
    nextCh(); // reads the first character into ch and increments col to 1
}
```

The nextCh() method reads the next character of the source code, stores it in the global variable ch, and updates the line and column numbers:

```
private static void nextCh() {
    try {
        ch = (char) in.read(); col++;
        if (ch == '\n') { line++; col = 0; }
    } catch (IOException e) { ch = eofCh; }
}
```

The core of the scanner is the method next(), which is called by the parser each time it needs the next token. It implements a DFA in the style as demonstrated at the end of the last section. The following code shows an excerpt of it:

```
public static Token next() {
    while (ch <= ' ') nextCh(); // skip blanks, tabs, end of line characters
    Token t = new Token(); t.line = line; t.col = col;
    switch (ch) {
        // identifiers and keywords
        case 'a': case 'b': ... case 'z': case 'A': case 'B': ... case 'Z':
            readName(t); break;

        // numbers
        case '0': case '1': ... case '9':
            readNumber(t); break;

        // character constants
        case '\'':
            readCharCon(t); break;

        // single-character tokens
        case ';': nextCh(); t.kind = semicolon; break;
        case '.': nextCh(); t.kind = period; break;
        case eofCh: t.kind = eof; break; // no further nextCh()
        ...
        // multi-character tokens
        case '=': nextCh();
            if (ch == '=') { nextCh(); t.kind = eql; } else t.kind = assign; break;
        case '&': nextCh();
            if (ch == '&') { nextCh(); t.kind = and; } else t.kind = none; break;
        ...
        // comments or slash operator
        case '/': nextCh();
            if (ch == '/') {
                do nextCh(); while (ch != '\n' && ch != eofCh); // skip comment
                t = next(); // call scanner recursively
            } else t.kind = slash; break;

        // invalid characters
        default: nextCh(); t.kind = none; break;
    }
    return t;
} // ch holds the next as yet unprocessed character
```

The method first skips irrelevant characters (blanks, tabs, line endings) that are all less than or equal to ' '. After that, ch holds the first character of the next token. Therefore, a new token object t is created and its line and column numbers are set to the line and column numbers of ch.

Now the method branches depending on the first character of the token. If it is a letter, readName() is called, which processes the remaining characters of a name or keyword; if it is a digit, readNumber() is called, which processes the remaining characters of a number, and so on.

2.3 Implementation of a DFA

For tokens that consist of a single character, the corresponding token code is immediately set (e.g., semicolon for ';'). For tokens that consist of multiple characters, it is necessary to read on. For example, a single '=' represents the assign token, but two consecutive '=' represent the eql token. It is important that after each character that is read, nextCh() is called, which reads the next character into ch and ensures that the scanner makes progress.

The above implementation also shows the processing of comments. A single '/' means the token slash, but two consecutive '/' represent the beginning of a comment. Comments are skipped to the end of the line. But which token should then be returned? After all, comments are meaningless to the parser and do not result in a token. Therefore, the next token after the comment must be returned, which is done by calling next() recursively. If several comments follow one another, next() is called recursively until a token is found (in the worst case eof), which is then returned to the parser.

If ch is not a valid start of a token, the error token none is returned. Note that at the end of next() the global variable ch contains the next unprocessed character with which the method continues at its next call.

The method next() invokes some helper methods that recognize names, numbers, or character constants. They have the following tasks:

private static void readName (Token t)
When readName() is called, ch holds the first letter of a name and t is already initialized with the correct line and column number. The method now reads further letters or digits and stores them in t.val. Eventually, ch holds the first character after the name. Since identifiers and keywords have the same structure, it is necessary to check whether the recognized name is a keyword. To do this, the name is searched in a table of all MicroJava keywords. If it is found, t.kind is set to the token code of the found keyword, otherwise to ident.

private static void readNumber (Token t)
When readNumber() is called, ch holds the first digit of the number. The method now reads further digits and stores them in t.val. The digit sequence is then converted into a number and stored in t.numVal. If the number is too large for the type int, an error must be reported, but the token code t.kind is still set to number so that the parser can continue working with the recognized number. Once that number is completely recognized, ch holds the first character after the number.

private static void readCharCon (Token t)
When readCharCon() is called, ch holds an apostrophe ('\''). The method now reads further characters up to the closing apostrophe or to the end of the line and stores them in t.val. Those characters are then analyzed. In the case of a valid character constant (e.g., 'x', '\r'. '\n' or \t), t.kind is set to charCon and t.numVal is set to the corresponding character value. In the case of an invalid character constant (e.g., an empty character constant, 'xy', '' or 'x) an error must be reported, but t.kind is still set to charCon so that the parser can continue working with the character constant. On completion, ch now holds the first character after the character constant.

2.3.2 Efficiency Considerations

Although lexical analysis is the simplest phase of a compiler, it is also one of the most time-consuming phases (aside from optimizations). After all, a large number of characters have to be read, and nextCh() has to be called for each of them. Therefore, special attention must be paid to efficiency during lexical analysis.

This is also the reason why the next character read is not treated as a return value of nextCh(), but is stored in a global variable ch.

For very large source programs, it is worth using buffered reading to improve performance, i.e., using a BufferedReader:

```
InputStream s = new FileInputStream(sourceFileName);
Reader r = new BufferedReader(new InputStreamReader(s));
Scanner.init(r);
```

However, with small source programs (as is the case in MicroJava), the difference in speed would be hardly noticeable.

2.4 Exercises

1. *Regular grammars (1).* Write a regular grammar for non-nested bracket comments (/* ... */). You can denote all characters that are neither '/' nor '*' with char.

2. *Regular grammars (2).* Is the following grammar for clock times regular? If not, can it be transformed into a regular grammar?

   ```
   Time    = Hours ':' Minutes.
   Hours   = digit digit.
   Minutes = digit digit.
   ```

3. *Regular grammars (3).* Is the following grammar for lists regular? If not, can it be transformed into a regular grammar?

   ```
   List    = '(' Element {',' Element} ')'.
   Element = ident | List.
   ```

4. *Conversion of a regular grammar into a DFA.* Draw the DFA for the following regular production describing floating-point numbers:

   ```
   Float = digit {digit} '.' {digit} ['E' ['+' | '-'] digit {digit}].
   ```

5. *Conversion of a DFA into a regular grammar.* Specify the regular grammar for the DFA in Fig. 2.6 that recognizes a hexadecimal number (e.g., 1A5X) starting with a decimal digit:

2.4 Exercises

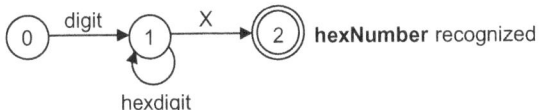

Fig. 2.6 DFA for recognizing hexadecimal numbers

6. *Introduction of a new token.* What would you have to do to introduce a power operator ** (e.g., x**y = x^y) as a new token in MicroJava?

7. *Processing nested bracket comments.* Modify the implementation of the method next() so that, in addition to end-of-line comments, (nested) bracket comments (/* ... /* ... */ ... */) are recognized and filtered out of the token stream.

8. *Scanning names.* Implement the readName() method according to its specification in the previous section. This method is called by next() to recognize a name or a keyword. The token kind should be stored in t.kind and the text of the name in t.val.

9. *Scanning numbers.* Implement the readNumber() method according to its specification in the previous section. This method is called by next() to recognize a number. The token kind number should be stored in t.kind and the value of the number in t.numVal. If the number is too large for the type int, an error message should be printed.

10. *Scanning character constants.* Implement the readCharCon() method according to its specification in the previous section. This method is called by next() to recognize a character constant (e.g., 'x'). The token type charCon should be stored in t.kind and the numeric value of the character constant in t.numVal. If the character constant is invalid (e.g., '', 'abc'), an error message should be printed.

11. *Implementation of the scanner.* Implement the entire MicroJava scanner as described in this chapter, observing MicroJava's lexical structure as described in Appendix A. Stick to the scanner's interface (Sect. 2.3) and implement the helper methods nextCh(), readName(), readNumber(), and readCharCon() in addition to the methods init() and next().

Then download the file TestScanner.zip from [Download] and use it to test your scanner. All valid terminal symbols should be recognized and an error should be reported for invalid terminal symbols.

Syntax Analysis

3

After lexical analysis, the source program is available as a token stream containing only the relevant tokens; all blanks, tabs, line endings and comments have been eliminated.

The task of the syntax analyzer (the *parser*) is now to analyze the token stream according to the given grammar and to build (at least implicitly) a syntax tree. If this is successful, the program is syntactically correct and can be processed further. If it fails, there is a syntax error that must be reported; syntax analysis should then be continued so that further errors can be detected.

As with lexical analysis, we will start with a short theory section in which we will look at context-free grammars and their recognition mechanism, namely pushdown automata.

3.1 Context-free Grammars and Pushdown Automata

In Chap. 2 we saw that regular grammars cannot deal with central recursion. However, since central recursion is common in programming languages, we need the next higher grammar class to describe such languages, namely *context-free grammars* (CFG). A grammar is context-free if all productions are of the form:

$x = \alpha.$

On the left-hand side there is a single nonterminal symbol and the right-hand side α consists of a sequence of terminal and nonterminal symbols; grammars in EBNF can also contain meta symbols such as |, (...), [...] and {...}. A simple example of a context-free grammar is the following indirectly central-recursive grammar of arithmetic expressions:

```
Expr = Term {("+" | "−") Term}.
Term = Factor {("*" | "/") Factor}.
Factor = ident | number | "(" Expr ")".
```

Context-free languages are recognized by *pushdown automata*, which we will now take a closer look at.

3.1.1 Pushdown Automata

Like a deterministic finite automaton (DFA), a *pushdown automaton* (PDA) consists of states and state transitions. However, in contrast to a DFA

- a PDA allows state transitions not only with terminal symbols, but also with nonterminal symbols;
- a PDA remembers the state transitions using a stack and can thus go back after recognizing a nonterminal symbol and continue from there with the recognized nonterminal symbol.

Let's take a very simple central-recursive grammar as an example:

E = x | "(" E ")".

The PDA for recognizing the language of this grammar looks like this, in a first version (Fig. 3.1):

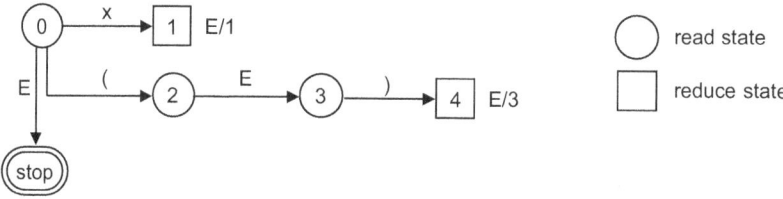

Fig. 3.1 Preliminary PDA for E = x | "(" E ")"

We can see that there are two types of states. In *read states* (represented by circles), the next input symbol is read, like in the DFA, and the automaton transitions to a successor state (e.g., from 0 with x to 1). In *reduce states* (represented by squares), a nonterminal symbol has been recognized. Therefore, the most recently parsed symbols are reduced to this nonterminal symbol, whereby the PDA goes back part of its way and then continues with the recognized nonterminal symbol. The reduce states in Fig. 3.1 are labeled with an action. In state 4, this action is "E/3", which means that the PDA has recognized the nonterminal symbol E and must go back 3 edges (to state 0). From there, it continues with E and enters the stop state. This also explains the meaning of transitions with nonterminal symbols.

There is also a transition with E from state 2 to state 3. However, before this transition can take place, the nonterminal symbol E must first be recognized. You can think of this as if the E automaton is invoked recursively in state 2. After the recognition of E, the recursively invoked automaton returns to state 2 and the transition with E takes place (Fig. 3.2).

3.1 Context-free Grammars and Pushdown Automata

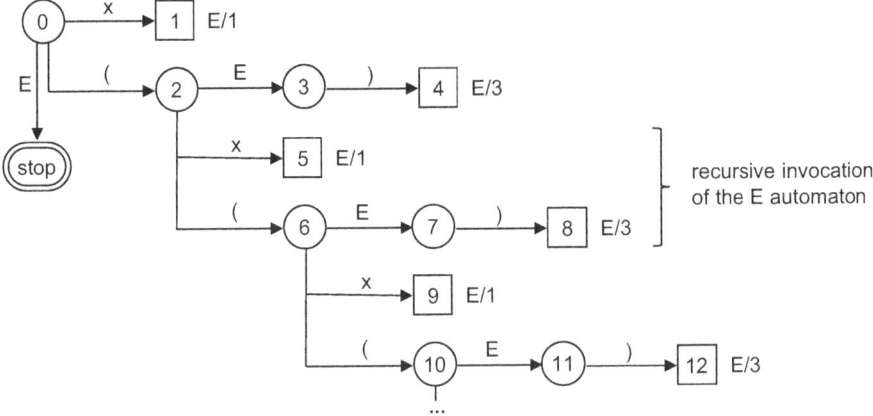

Fig. 3.2 Recursive invocation of the E automaton in state 2

However, the problem remains: In state 6, another transition with E takes place, so that the E automaton has to be invoked again, and so on. This would lead to endless recursion.

But if we look more closely, we see that states 1 and 5 are identical, and so are states 2 and 6. Thus, we can go from 2 with x to 1 and from 2 with "(" back to 2. This results in the following final PDA (Fig. 3.3):

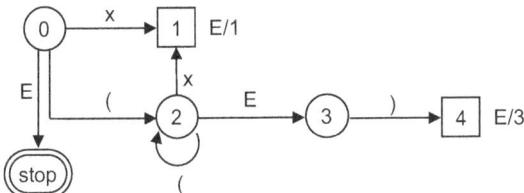

Fig. 3.3 PDA for E = x | "(" E ")"

When recognizing the sentence ((x)), the PDA goes through the following states:

stack	action
0	shift with (to state 2
0 2	shift with (to state 2
0 2 2	shift with x to state 1
0 2 2 1	reduce x to E and go back one edge
0 2 2	shift with E to state 3
0 2 2 3	shift with) to state 4
0 2 2 3 4	reduce (E) to E and go back 3 edges
0 2	shift with E to state 3
0 2 3	shift with) to state 4
0 2 3 4	reduce (E) to E and go back 3 edges
0	shift with E to the stop state
0 **stop**	sentence recognized

As you can see, the PDA remembers the path it has taken (i.e., the states it has passed through) in a stack and can therefore go back along this path after a reduction and continue from there with the recognized nonterminal symbol. The PDA is therefore more powerful than the DFA, because it remembers its "history" and can go back after a reduction. Thus, unlike a DFA, it can handle central recursion.

3.1.2 Limitations of Context-free Grammars

As we have seen, regular grammars cannot handle central recursion. Are there similar limitations for context-free grammars? Yes, there are: context-free grammars cannot express context conditions.

A context-free grammar only describes the *syntax* of a language, but not its (static) *semantics*. The semantics is expressed in terms of context conditions, which must also be checked by the compiler. Examples of such context conditions are:

- *Every name must be declared before it is used.*
  A name is usually declared many lines before it is used, so the declaration belongs to the context of the use. Thus, the statement

    x = 3;

  can be correct or incorrect, depending on whether x was declared or not. This cannot be expressed with context-free grammars.

- *In expressions, the types of the operands must be compatible.*
  The types of the operands are specified when the operands are declared and thus belong to the context of the expression.

How can this problem be solved? One option would be to switch to the next higher grammar class, i.e., to context-sensitive grammars. However, these are too complicated for compiler construction and cannot be analyzed efficiently.

Therefore, we solve the problem by postponing the check of the context conditions to semantic analysis. The program

    char x;
    ...
    x = 3;

is therefore recognized by the parser as syntactically correct. The incompatibility in the assignment is only detected and reported during semantic analysis.

3.1.3 Context Conditions

To describe the semantics of programming languages, there are formal notations (e.g., [Schm86, GTWW77]), but they are usually complex to write and difficult to read. We therefore use a semi-formal notation, in which the context conditions to be checked are listed in natural language for each production of the grammar.

Here are some examples. The full list of context conditions for MicroJava can be found in Appendix A.

Statement = Designator "=" Expr ";".
- Designator must denote a variable, an array element, or an object field.
- The type of Expr must be *assignment compatible* with the type of Designator.

Factor = "new" ident "[" Expr "]".
- ident must denote a type.
- The type of Expr must be int.

Designator$_0$ = Designator$_1$ "[" Expr "]".
- The type of Designator$_1$ must be an array.
- The type of Expr must be int.

As you can see, the context conditions refer to the symbols in the productions (e.g., ident, Expr or Designator). If a symbol occurs more than once (as in the third production), we distinguish the occurrences by subscripts (e.g., Designator$_1$).

We will see later that semantic analysis is not a separate phase of the compiler, but is integrated into the parser. The semantic analysis of a production is carried out in step with its syntax analysis. In this process, the corresponding context conditions are checked and any errors are reported.

3.1.4 Comparison of Regular and Context-free Grammars

To summarize, let us again compare regular and context-free grammars and look at their usage, their characteristics and their limitations (Fig. 3.4).

Regular grammars are used in lexical analysis; context-free grammars are used in syntax analysis. The recognition mechanism of regular languages is the deterministic finite automaton (DFA); the recognition mechanism of context-free languages is the pushdown automaton (PDA). The PDA is more powerful than the DFA because it remembers the "history" of the analysis in a stack and so can also process nested structures (with central recursion).

The productions of regular grammars may only contain a terminal symbol or a terminal symbol followed by a nonterminal symbol on the right-hand side (according to another definition, they may only consist of a single non-recursive EBNF rule), while the productions of context-free grammars may contain any EBNF constructs on the right-hand side.

Regular grammars cannot deal with nested structures and thus cannot handle central recursion. With context-free grammars, central recursion is not a problem; however, they cannot express context conditions and thus cannot describe the requirements for the semantic correctness of a program.

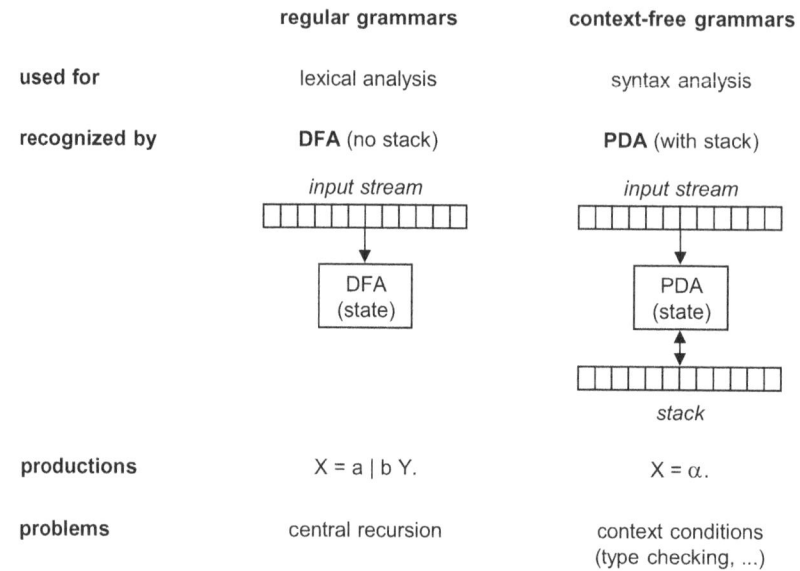

Fig. 3.4 Regular versus context-free grammars

3.2 Recursive Descent Parsing

We now come to the actual syntax analysis, i.e., the implementation of a parser for a given grammar. There are several syntax analysis techniques. Here we describe the simplest one, which is also the only one that can be implemented "by hand" without using tools such as a parser generator. An alternative technique is described in Chap. 8.

The technique described here is called *recursive descent*. It is a top-down technique in which the syntax tree for a given input is built from top to bottom. As an example, let's take the following grammar

X = a X c | b b.

and the input a b b c. The analysis begins with the start symbol of the grammar (in this case X) at the top and the input sentence a b b c at the bottom. In between, a syntax tree must be built that maps the start symbol to the input sentence (Fig. 3.5).

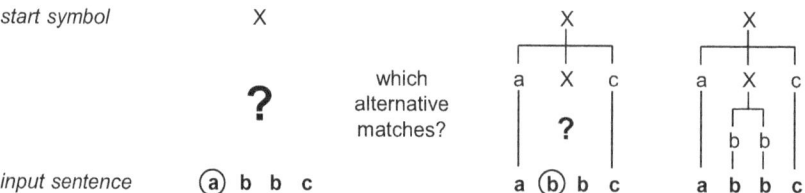

Fig. 3.5 How top-down parsing works

3.2 Recursive Descent Parsing

The first input symbol is a. Which of the two alternatives of X matches it? The first alternative is a X c, the second b b. Therefore, only the first alternative can fit, since only it begins with an a. So we put it as the next layer under the start symbol X and can match the first and last symbol of the input sentence with a X c.

This leaves the nonterminal symbol X in the tree and the still unmatched remainder of the input (b b). The first symbol of this remainder is b, which only matches the second alternative of X. So we use this alternative (b b) as the next layer of the syntax tree and can thus cover the rest of the input. The syntax tree is now complete and the input has been recognized as syntactically correct.

In general, the parser always selects the appropriate alternative of a nonterminal symbol based on the next input symbol (the *lookahead symbol*) and the *terminal start symbols* of these alternatives.

3.2.1 The Parser as a Class

Like the scanner, the parser is a class with global fields and methods. At any point in time, it looks ahead one token and uses it to control the analysis. This token is called the *lookahead token*. Its token code is stored in a global field sym:

```
private static int sym;   // token code of the lookahead token
```

The parser also remembers the two recent tokens t and la:

```
private static Token t;   // most recently recognized token
private static Token la;  // lookahead token (not yet recognized)
```

Token is the type of the tokens supplied by the scanner for the individual terminal symbols (see Chap. 2). Figure 3.6 shows the relationship between t, la and sym.

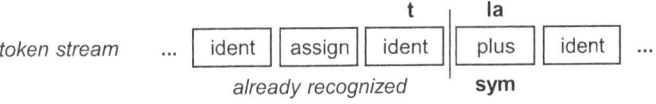

Fig. 3.6 Current tokens in the token stream

The vertical line indicates the current parser position. t is the last recognized token, la is the lookahead token that has not yet been recognized, and sym is its token code. Each time a token is recognized by the parser, the parser position is advanced by one token using the helper method scan():

```
private static void scan() {
    t = la;
    la = Scanner.next();
    sym = la.kind;
}
```

At the beginning of the syntax analysis, scan() is called so that the first token of the input stream is in la and its token code is in sym; t is still undefined.

We will now look at how to systematically (almost mechanically) derive and implement a parser from a given EBNF grammar. For each element of the grammar (i.e., for terminal symbols, nonterminal symbols, alternatives, options, and iterations) we will provide a pattern that shows how to convert this element into a piece of parser code.

3.2.2 Parsing Terminal Symbols

If a terminal symbol a occurs on the right-hand side of a production, the corresponding parser action is check(a).

check() is a helper method that takes the token code of the token to be recognized as a parameter and checks whether it matches the lookahead symbol sym. If this is the case, the next token is requested from the scanner, otherwise an error is reported.

```
private static void check (int expected) {
    if (sym == expected) scan(); // token recognized => move ahead
    else error(name[expected] + "expected");
}
```

As an error message, we simply report which token was expected but not found. To do this, we use a global array name initialized with the names of the individual tokens in the order of their token codes:

```
private static String[] name = {"?", "identifier", "number", ..., "+", "-", ...};
```

The error() method prints the error message along with the corresponding line and column number, the values of which are taken from the lookahead token la:

```
private static void error (String msg) {
    System.out.println("line " + la.line + ", col " + la.col + ": " + msg);
    System.exit(1); // for a better solution see later
}
```

After the error has been reported, the compilation is aborted here with System.exit(1). Of course, this is not a good solution, because we want to detect as many errors as possible in a single run. We will look at how to do this in Sect. 3.4.

The token codes that we use as parameters of check() are declared as named constants as in the scanner (see Chap. 2):

```
static final int none = 0, ident = 1, number = 2, ...;
```

3.2.3 Parsing Nonterminal Symbols

If there is a nonterminal symbol X on the right-hand side of a production, the corresponding parser action is to call a method X() that parses this nonterminal symbol:

```
private static void X() {
    ... actions to parse X ...
}
```

So, for every nonterminal symbol there is a parser method with the same name as this nonterminal symbol.

The start symbol of the MicroJava grammar is MicroJava and so the parser has a method of that name, which parses the entire MicroJava program by calling other parser methods and recognizing terminal symbols with check(). The main method of the Parser class is therefore:

```
public static void parse() {
    scan();        // fill la and sym
    MicroJava();   // parse the whole MicroJava program
    check(eof);    // make sure that there is nothing left after the program
}
```

3.2.4 Parsing Sequences

We can now put these two patterns together and look at how sequences of terminal and nonterminal symbols are parsed. For the grammar

```
X = a Y c.
Y = b b.
```

we have to write parser methods for X and Y. The parser method for X looks like this:

```
private static void X() {
    // sym holds the first token of X
    check(a);
    Y();
    check(c);
    // sym holds the first token after X
}
```

The patterns for parsing terminal and nonterminal symbols can be applied mechanically to parse the sequence a Y c. Figure 3.7 shows a simulation of how the parser methods for X and Y work.

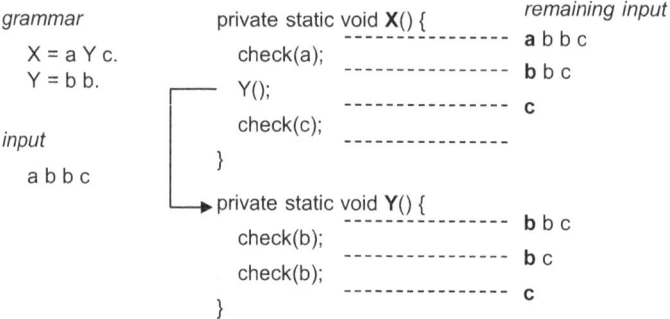

Fig. 3.7 Simulation of the parser methods for X and Y

Each call of check() consumes the next token of the input stream until it is empty.

3.2.5 Parsing Alternatives

If there are alternatives α | β | γ on the right-hand side of a production (where α, β and γ denote arbitrary EBNF expressions), the parser action looks as follows (in pseudocode):

```
if (sym ∈ First(α)) { ... parse α ... }
else if (sym ∈ First(β)) { ... parse β ... }
else if (sym ∈ First(γ)) { ... parse γ ... }
else error("..."); // find a meaningful error message
```

The alternatives are checked in turn to see whether the lookahead symbol sym matches one of them (where, for example, First(α) denotes the terminal start symbols of α). If this is the case, the corresponding alternative is parsed. If none of the alternatives match, an error is reported, for which a meaningful error message must be chosen. Let's look at an example. For the following grammar

```
X = a Y | Y b.
Y = c | d.
```

let's first determine the terminal start symbols of their alternatives:

```
First(c) = {c}
First(d) = {d}
First(aY) = {a}
First(Yb) = First(Y) = {c, d}
```

We can now implement the parser methods for X and Y as follows:

```
private static void X() {
    if (sym == a) {                       // if sym matches the first alternative
        check(a);
        Y();
    } else id (sym == c || sym == d) {    // if sym matches the second alternative
```

3.2 Recursive Descent Parsing

```
        Y();
        check(b);
    } else error("invalid start of X");
}

private static void Y() {
    if (sym == c) {          // if sym matches the first alternative
        check(c);
    } else if (sym == d) {   // if sym matches the second alternative
        check(d);
    } else error("invalid start of Y");
}
```

The error messages here are that the lookahead symbol is not a valid start of X or Y.

3.2.6 Parsing EBNF Options

If there is an optional EBNF expression [α] on the right-hand side of a production, the corresponding parser action is:

```
if (sym ∈ First(α)) { ... parse α ... } // no error branch!
```

For the production

```
X = [a b] c.
```

the parser method for X looks like this:

```
private static void X() {
    if (sym == a) {          // if sym matches the start of the option, i.e., a
        check(a);
        check(b);
    }
    check(c);
}
```

If the input is a b c, the option is entered, which parses a and b. Then, c is parsed. If, on the other hand, the input is only c, the option is skipped and only c is parsed. The optional part [a b] may therefore be missing.

3.2.7 Parsing EBNF Iterations

If there is an iteration {α} on the right-hand side of a production (where α can again be an arbitrary EBNF expression), this is translated into parser code as follows:

```
while (sym ∈ First(α)) { ... parse α ... }
```

As an example, let's consider the following grammar:

```
X = a {Y b} c.
Y = d | e.
```

The terminal start symbols of the iteration {Y b} are the terminal start symbols of Y, i.e., d and e. Thus, the parser method for X is:

```
private static void X() {
  check(a);
  while (sym == d || sym == e) {   // while sym matches First(Y)
    Y();
    check(b);
  }
  check(c);
}
```

If the set of terminal start symbols of an iteration is large, it may be more efficient to execute the loop until a terminal *successor* to the iteration occurs. However, the loop should then also be terminated with eof to be on the safe side:

```
private static void X() {
  check(a);
  while (sym != c && sym != eof) {
    Y();
    check(b);
  }
  check(c);
}
```

If possible, however, the first form of the loop pattern should be used, otherwise the loop would only be exited with eof if the terminal successor (here c) is missing from the input.

3.2.8 Dealing with Large Sets of Terminal Start Symbols

When parsing alternatives, options, and iterations, the lookahead symbol sym must be compared with the terminal start symbols of these constructs. The number of terminal start symbols can be very large. So what is the best way to deal with it?

As a rule of thumb: If the set of terminal start symbols has more than four elements, the class BitSet should be used. For example, if the start symbols of the nonterminal symbols X and Y are:

```
First(X) = {a, b, c, d, e}
First(Y) = {f, g, h, i, j}
```

one can declare these sets in the parser as follows:

```
import java.util.BitSet;
...
```

3.2 Recursive Descent Parsing

```
private static BitSet firstX = new BitSet();
private static BitSet firstY = new BitSet();
```

and initialize them accordingly at the beginning of the parser:

```
firstX.set(a); firstX.set(b); firstX.set(c); firstX.set(d); firstX.set(e);
firstY.set(f); firstY.set(g); firstY.set(h); firstY.set(i); firstY.set(j);
```

Parsing the production

Z = X | Y.

can then be implemented as:

```
private static void Z() {
    if (firstX.get(sym)) X();        // if sym ∈ First(X)
    else if (firstY.get(sym)) Y();   // if sym ∈ First(Y)
    else error("invalid start of Z");
}
```

If a set of terminal start symbols has fewer than five elements, it is more efficient to check those elements directly. For the set

First(X) = {a, b, c}

it is more efficient to check them one by one:

```
if (sym == a || sym == b || sym == c) ...
```

3.2.9 Avoiding Multiple Checks

So far, we have specified patterns that can be systematically used to translate an EBNF grammar into parser code. Although the resulting parser is correct, it may contain inefficiencies because some checks may be performed multiple times. This can be optimized. For the production

X = a | b.

the non-optimized parser method would be:

```
private static void X() {
    if (sym == a) check(a);
    else if (sym == b) check(b);
    else error("invalid start of X");
}
```

The call to check(a) checks whether sym == a and in this case calls scan() to get the next token. However, sym == a has already been checked in method X(), which makes this second check redundant. In general, each check(x) can simply be replaced with scan() if sym == x has already been checked before. This results in the following optimized solution:

```
private static void X() {
   if (sym == a) scan();
   else if (sym == b) scan();
   else error("invalid start of X");
}
```

In this way, many double checks can be avoided, as with the following grammar:

```
X = {a | Y d}.
Y = b | c.
```

The non-optimized parser method for X is:

```
private static void X() {
   while (sym == a || sym == b || sym == c) {
      if (sym == a) check(a);
      else if (sym == b || sym == c) { Y(); check(d); }
      else error("a, b or c expected");
   }
}
```

Again, check(a) can be replaced with scan(). But we can do even more: since the loop is only entered if sym is a, b, or c, the check in the first else branch is redundant. If sym is not a, then it must be b or c. The check can therefore be eliminated and the error branch can also be dropped. The optimized solution is:

```
private static void X() {
   while (sym == a || sym == b || sym == c) {
      if (sym == a) scan();
      else /* unconditionally */ { Y(); check(d); }  // no error branch
   }
}
```

But even that is not optimal. Here, sym == a is checked twice, which can be avoided by the following implementation:

```
private static void X() {
   for (;;) { // endless loop
      if (sym == a) scan();
      else if (sym == b || sym == c) { Y(); check(d); }
      else break;
   }
}
```

In this solution, each check is performed only once. This pattern can be used whenever there is an iteration of alternatives, e.g., {α | β | γ}. The iteration is then implemented using an endless loop in which the alternatives are checked one by one. If none matches, the loop is exited.

3.2.10 Computation of Terminal Start Symbols Revisited

In Sect. 1.4, we looked at how to compute the terminal start symbols of nonterminal symbols. In the parser methods of the previous sections, we also computed the terminal start symbols of alternatives, options, and iterations. In principle, this is simple, but there are certain subtleties that need to be taken into account.

If we want to compute the terminal start symbols of an EBNF expression $\alpha_0 \alpha_1$ and if α_0 is deletable, we have to take not only the terminal start symbols of α_0 into account, but also the terminal successors of α_0, i.e., the terminal start symbols of α_1. In the following grammar

```
X = Y a.
Y = {b} c    // can start with b and c
  | [d]      // can start with d and a(!)
  | e.       // can start with e
```

the first alternative of Y begins with the deletable element {b}. The alternative must therefore be chosen if b or c is seen in the input. The second alternative is completely deletable. It must be chosen if we see d or a successor of [d] (here a as the successor of Y). So the parser method of Y is:

```
private static void Y() {
    if (sym == b || sym == c) {
        while (sym == b) scan();
        check(c);
    } else if (sym == d || sym == a) {
        if (sym == d) scan();
    } else if (sym == e) {
        scan();
    } else error("invalid start of Y");
}
```

If the second alternative of Y were not also entered with a, an error would be reported when we see an a at the beginning of Y. However, since this alternative is entered with a, the option [d] is skipped and a is recognized as the successor of Y in the parser method of X.

Here is another example: in the following grammar

```
U = V e    // can start with d (i.e., First(V)) and e, since V is deletable
  | f.     // can start with f
V = {d}.
```

the nonterminal symbol V is deletable. Since the first alternative of U begins with V, it must be entered if we see a terminal start symbol of V (here d) or a terminal successor of V (here e). So the parser methods of U and V are:

```
private static void U() {
    if (sym == d || sym == e) {
        V(); check(e);
    } else if (sym == f) {
```

```
    scan();
  } else error("invalid start of U");
}
private static void V() {
  while (sym == d) scan();
}
```

When the first alternative of U is entered with e, V() is first called. However, V() returns without executing the loop, and then e is recognized in U.

Thus, when computing the terminal start symbols of an EBNF expression, deletability must also be taken into account.

3.2.11 The Syntax Tree in Recursive Descent Parsing

At the beginning of this chapter, we claimed that the parser builds a syntax tree over the token stream. But where is this syntax tree? The parser actions described above do not build one.

The answer is: with recursive descent parsing, the syntax tree is only built implicitly, i.e., it is represented in the parser methods that are currently active, or in other words, in the productions that are currently being worked on. As an example, let's consider the following grammar:

X = a Y d.
Y = b c.

When calling the parser method of X, we are working on a subtree with the root X and its children a, Y, and d (see Fig. 3.8a).

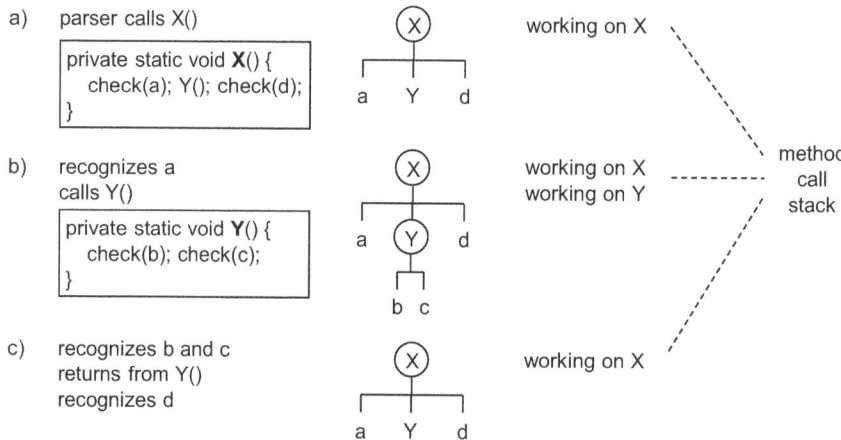

Fig. 3.8 Implicit construction of a syntax tree in recursive descent parsing

3.3 LL(1) Property

The parser method X() recognizes an a and then calls Y(), implicitly adding another layer with the children b and c to the syntax tree (Fig. 3.8b).

Y() recognizes b and c and then returns to X, by which the implicit subtree with the root Y is removed again (Fig. 3.8c).

Thus, the syntax tree is not built explicitly during recursive descent parsing, but exists only implicitly, namely in the form of all productions that the parser is currently working on.

Also, the stack of the PDA exists only implicitly in recursive descent parsing, namely in the form of the call stack of all currently active parser methods. If X() calls Y(), the call stack grows; if Y() returns, it shrinks again. You can think of it as if the PDA—after recognizing Y—goes back to the beginning of Y and then continues with Y in the parser method of X.

3.3 LL(1) Property

For a grammar to be suitable for recursive descent parsing, it must satisfy the LL(1) property. LL(1) means that the sentences of the grammar must be recognizable from **left** to right with **left**-canonical derivations and **1** lookahead symbol. However, this definition is not particularly helpful. Therefore, we use the following definition:

- A grammar is LL(1) if all its productions are LL(1).
- A production is LL(1) if for all alternatives $\alpha_1 \mid \alpha_2 \mid ... \mid \alpha_n$ in it the following holds:
  $\forall\, i \neq j$: $First(\alpha_i) \cap First(\alpha_j) = \{\}$.

It must hold that the terminal start symbols of all alternatives in a production are pairwise disjoint. In other words, all the alternatives in it must start with different terminal symbols, so that the parser can clearly choose one of them based on the lookahead symbol. If this is not the case, there is an LL(1) conflict.

Unfortunately, many grammars that are found in language descriptions or on the internet do not meet this requirement. However, they can usually be transformed so that they become LL(1) and are thus suitable for recursive descent.

3.3.1 Elimination of LL(1) Conflicts

LL(1) conflicts can usually be eliminated by *factorization*, i.e., by extracting the common beginnings of alternatives. Let's take a look at the production of the if statement in Java:

```
IfStatement  =  "if" "(" Expr ")" Statement
             |  "if" "(" Expr ")" Statement "else" Statement.
```

The two alternatives of this production both start with if, which is why the production is not LL(1). It is also not LL(k) for an arbitrary k, because Expr and Statement can be arbitrarily long, and therefore, in the worst case, one has to look ahead indefinitely to find out whether an else follows or not.

However, if one extracts the common beginnings of the alternatives and lets the alternatives start only afterwards, one obtains

```
IfStatement = "if" "(" Expr ")" Statement  (
                                            | "else" Statement
                                           ).
```

or in EBNF notation

```
IfStatement = "if" "(" Expr ")" Statement ["else" Statement].
```

The alternatives have disappeared and with them the LL(1) conflict. However, we will see later that there is still a further LL(1) conflict, which we will deal with further down in the section on the *dangling else*.

To better see LL(1) conflicts and to be able to eliminate them by factorization, it is sometimes helpful to replace a nonterminal symbol with the right-hand side of its production. Let's consider the following grammar:

```
Statement  =  Designator "=" Expr ";"
           |  ident "(" [ActualParameters] ")" ";".
Designator =  ident {"." ident}.
```

Here, a Statement can be an assignment or a method call with optional parameters. Both alternatives start with ident, but this is easier to see if one *inlines* Designator in Statement:

```
Statement  =  ident {"." ident} "=" Expr ";"
           |  ident "(" [ActualParameters] ")" ";".
```

Now it is obvious that both alternatives start with ident. By extracting ident, one can eliminate the LL(1) conflict:

```
Statement = ident (  {"." ident} "=" Expr ";"
                  |  "(" [ActualParameters] ")" ";"
                  ).
```

The production still contains alternatives, but the first one starts with "." or "=" and the second one starts with "(". Thus, the terminal start symbols of the alternatives are disjoint, so that the LL(1) conflict has been eliminated. The parser can decide which alternative to choose based on the lookahead symbol.

3.3.2 Elimination of Left Recursion

Left recursion is always an LL(1) conflict and must therefore be eliminated before a grammar is suitable for recursive descent parsing. However, we have already seen in Chap. 1 that this is always possible. Let's take a look at the following left-recursive grammar:

```
IdentList = ident | IdentList "," ident.
```

3.3 LL(1) Property

It generates the following sentences:

```
ident
ident "," ident
ident "," ident "," ident
...
```

It is easy to see that the same sentences can also be generated by the following EBNF grammar:

```
IdentList = ident {"," ident}.
```

In this way, left recursion can always be replaced by EBNF iteration.

3.3.3 Hidden LL(1) Conflicts in EBNF Constructs

The LL(1) property requires that the parser must always be able to select the appropriate alternative based on the lookahead symbol. In addition to explicit alternatives, which we have seen in the examples above, there are also implicit alternatives that are hidden behind EBNF options or EBNF iterations.

If the parser is faced with an option [α] β, it can either enter the option and recognize α or skip it and continue with β. This represents implicit alternatives α β | β. Therefore, the terminal start symbols of α and β must be disjoint.

The same applies to iterations. If the parser is faced with an iteration {α} β, it can either enter the iteration and recognize α, or skip it and continue with β (remember that iterations mean zero or more repetitions). Therefore, the terminal start symbols of α and β must also be disjoint here.

Thus, whenever an option or iteration appears in a grammar, the following must be checked:

$$[α] β \quad \text{First}(α) \cap \text{First}(β) \text{ must be } \{\}$$
$$\{α\} β \quad \text{First}(α) \cap \text{First}(β) \text{ must be } \{\}$$

If an option or iteration is at the end of a production, its terminal start symbols must be disjoint from the successors of that production:

$$X = α [β]. \quad \text{First}(β) \cap \text{Follow}(X) \text{ must be } \{\}$$
$$X = α \{β\}. \quad \text{First}(β) \cap \text{Follow}(X) \text{ must be } \{\}$$

This also applies to the special case where a production has an empty alternative:

$$X = α \,|\,. \quad \text{First}(α) \cap \text{Follow}(X) \text{ must be } \{\}$$

Fortunately, such hidden LL(1) conflicts can usually be eliminated by transforming the grammar. For example, in the production

```
Name = [ident "."] ident.
```

a hidden LL(1) conflict occurs because the option starts with ident and is also followed by ident. So if the parser is in front of the option and the lookahead symbol is ident, it cannot decide whether to enter the option or skip it. To eliminate the LL(1) conflict, we have to transform the production. Let's think about which phrases can be generated:

    ident "." ident
    ident

The production can therefore be written as follows:

    Name = ident ["." ident].

The LL(1) conflict is gone, but we still have to check whether the terminal start symbols of the option (i.e., ".") and the terminal successors of Name are disjoint. To do this, we would have to compute the successors of Name, which is not shown here.

Here is another example that is not so trivial:

    Program = Declarations ";" Statements.
    Declarations = Decl {";" Decl}.

When an iteration occurs, we must check if its terminal start symbols (i.e., ";") and its successors (here the successors of Declarations) are disjoint, which is not the case here, because Declarations is followed by a ";". One can see this LL(1) conflict better by inlining Declarations in Program:

    Program = **Decl {";" Decl}** ";" Statements.

If the parser is in front of the iteration and the lookahead symbol is ";", it cannot decide whether to enter the iteration or skip it. However, the production of Program can be transformed into

    Program = Decl ";" {Decl ";"} Statements.

The LL(1) conflict has disappeared, but we still have to check whether First(Decl) ∩ First(Statements) = {}, for which we would have to look at the productions of Decl and Statements, which is not shown here.

Checking the LL(1) property of a grammar is time-consuming, but can be supported by tools (see Chap. 7). In the MicroJava grammar (Appendix A), all LL(1) conflicts have already been eliminated. However, if a grammar is taken from an external source, the LL(1) property must be checked and any LL(1) conflicts must be eliminated before the grammar can be used for recursive descent parsing.

3.3.4 Dangling Else

In Chap. 1, we saw that with nested if statements such as

    if (a < b) if (b < c) x = c; else x = b;

an ambiguity arises, which is called the *dangling else*: the else can be considered to belong either to the outer or the inner if. By convention, this ambiguity is resolved by always assigning the else to the immediately preceding if.

3.3 LL(1) Property

However, the dangling else also represents an LL(1) conflict. Let's look at the grammar

```
Statement  =  "if" "(" Expr ")" Statement ["else" Statement]
           |  ... .
```

The grammar contains an option at the end of the production. Therefore, the terminal start symbols of the option (i.e., else) and the terminal successors of Statement must be disjoint. As we can see, however, a Statement can be followed by an else, which constitutes an LL(1) conflict. If the parser is in front of the option and the lookahead symbol is else, it cannot decide whether it should enter the option and thus assign the else to the inner if, or whether it should skip the option and thus assign the else to the outer if.

Unfortunately, this LL(1) conflict cannot be eliminated by transforming the grammar—it is inherent. So how can the problem be solved?

Consider what the parser does if an LL(1) conflict is not eliminated. If the lookahead symbol matches more than one alternative, the parser will always choose the first matching alternative. In the grammar

```
X  =  a b c
   |  a d.
```

both alternatives start with a. If the lookahead symbol is a, the parser will always choose the first alternative; the second one will never be entered. This is certainly not the desired behavior, so this LL(1) conflict must be eliminated by transforming the grammar, which is easy:

```
X = a (b c | d).
```

But what about the dangling else? If the parser is in front of the option in the grammar

```
Statement  =  "if" "(" Expr ")" Statement ["else" Statement]
           |  ... .
```

and if it has to decide whether to enter or skip the option when it sees the lookahead symbol else, it chooses the first variant: It enters the option and thus assigns the else to the inner if. This is exactly the desired behaviour, so we do not need to eliminate the LL(1) conflict in this case. The parser implicitly does the right thing here.

Thus, an LL(1) conflict is just a warning that the parser will choose the first of several suitable alternatives. If this is the desired behaviour, as in the case of the dangling else, the LL(1) conflict can be ignored, otherwise it must be eliminated.

3.3.5 Other Grammar Requirements

In addition to the LL(1) property, a grammar must also meet other properties in order to be suitable for syntax analysis. These apply not only to recursive descent parsing, but to all syntax analysis techniques.

- **Completeness**. For each nonterminal symbol, there must be a production. For example, the grammar

    X = a Y Z.
    Y = b b.

    is incomplete because there is no production for Z.

- **Terminalizability**. Each nonterminal symbol must be directly or indirectly derivable into a sequence of terminal symbols. For example, the grammar

    X = a Y | c.
    Y = b Y.

    is not terminalizable because Y cannot be derived into a sequence of terminal symbols, but leads to an endless recursion.

- **Non-circularity**. A nonterminal symbol must not be derivable into itself, i.e., there must not be a derivation of the form $X \Rightarrow \alpha_1 \Rightarrow \alpha_2 \Rightarrow ... \Rightarrow X$. For example, the grammar

    X = a | Y.
    Y = b | X.

    is circular, because there is a derivation $X \Rightarrow Y \Rightarrow X$.

3.4 Syntax Error Handling

If the parser detects a syntax error, it must report it. Afterwards, however, it should continue parsing in order to discover further syntax errors. In general, good syntax error handling should meet the following requirements:

- The parser should find as many errors as possible in a single run.
- The parser must not crash even with severe errors.
- Error handling should not slow down error-free parsing.
- Error handling should not unduly increase ("bloat") the parser code.

These requirements are sometimes contradictory. The better the error handling should be, the more effort has to be put into the parser, which in turn bloats the parser code and usually also slows down the analysis of error-free programs. Therefore, there are various error handling techniques for recursive descent parsing that meet these requirements to varying degrees:

- Error handling in *panic mode*
- Error handling with *general anchors*
- Error handling with *specific anchors*

3.4 Syntax Error Handling

Let's take a look at these techniques in order. Error handling in panic mode is the simplest technique, but it can only detect a single error per compilation. The other techniques can detect multiple errors, but are more complex and therefore meet the last two requirements less well.

3.4.1 Error Handling in Panic Mode

This is the technique we used so far. If the parser detects an error, it reports it by calling the error() method and then aborts parsing.

```
private static void error (String msg) {
    System.out.println("line " + la.line + ", col " + la.col + ": " + msg);
    System.exit(1); // abort parsing
}
```

This technique has the advantage that it is cheap and does not bloat the parser code, as it does not contain any error handling other than the error() method. If the source program is error-free, parsing is not slowed down in any way. However, only the first error is detected. After correcting the error, the program must be recompiled to detect any further errors.

For languages in which programs are short (e.g., for command languages), this technique is perfectly adequate. However, for languages such as Java or MicroJava, in which programs can be longer, this technique is not satisfactory. For such languages, one of the other techniques should be used.

3.4.2 Error Handling with General Anchors

With this technique, an *error recovery* takes place after a syntax error is detected, i.e., the parser and the faulty program must be synchronized in such a way that parsing can continue and any further errors can be detected. For this purpose, a set of *anchors* is collected, with which the parser can "get hold" again after a syntax error and can thus synchronize itself with the source program. Let's look at an example. Suppose we have the following grammar

```
X = a Y e f.
Y = b c d.
```

and the input is

```
a b x y e f eof
```

As can be seen from Fig. 3.9, X is called and a is recognized. Then Y is called and b is recognized before the parser detects that the next symbol x does not match the expected symbol c. The error is reported. The parser then collects all terminal symbols that can follow the error location in the grammar. These form the set of *anchors* with which parsing can continue at some point in the grammar.

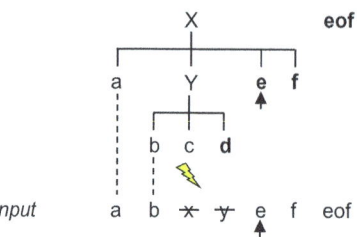

Fig. 3.9 Collecting anchors

Let's now take a closer look at the recovery process. It consists of the following three steps:

1. From the grammar, a set of anchors is calculated, which can be used to resume the analysis after the error location. The error was detected because the expected symbol c did not match the input symbol x. The anchors are all terminal successors of the symbols on which the parser is currently working. The parser works on c, whose successor is d. It is also working on Y, whose successors are e and f, and on X with the successor eof. So the anchors are {d, e, f, eof}.

2. All symbols in the input that are not anchors will now be skipped, i.e., the symbols x and y are skipped before e occurs, which is in the set of anchors. The input stream has thus been synchronized: the next symbol e can be used to continue parsing at some point in the grammar.

3. In the last step, the parser is steered to the point in the grammar where the anchor e is expected. To do this, the parser simply continues until it reaches that point (see arrow in Fig. 3.9). The input and the grammar are now synchronized, and parsing can continue from there.

To calculate the anchors, each parser method is given the successors of the corresponding nonterminal symbol as a parameter, for example:

```
private static void X (BitSet sux) {
    ...
}
```

Depending on the context in which this nonterminal symbol occurs, the successor set sux can be different, as can be seen in Fig. 3.10.

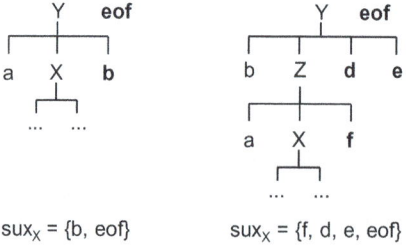

Fig. 3.10 Successors of a nonterminal symbol X in different contexts

3.4 Syntax Error Handling

Therefore, the context-specific successors of a nonterminal symbol must be passed to its parser method as a parameter. Note that the symbol eof is always in the successor set, because it is a successor of the start symbol. This ensures that synchronization happens with eof at the latest.

For error handling with general anchors, the patterns for parsing terminal and nonterminal symbols, alternatives, options, and iterations need to be adapted; that is our next topic.

Parsing Terminal Symbols

When a terminal symbol **a** appears on the right-hand side of a production, followed by other elements α_i (which can be symbols, alternatives, options, or iterations)

$X = \ldots$ **a** $\alpha_1\ \alpha_2\ \ldots\ \alpha_n$.

the parser action looks as follows (in pseudocode):

check(**a**, First(α_1) ∪ First(α_2) ∪ ... ∪ First(α_n) ∪ sux$_x$);

In other words, the check() method is given the successors of the terminal symbol a as a second parameter:

```
private static void check (int expected, BitSet sux) {
    if (sym == expected) scan();
    else error(name[expected] + " expected", sux); // pass sux to the error method
}
```

The first part of the successor set (First(α_1) ∪ First(α_2) ∪ ... ∪ First(α_n)) can be calculated statically from the grammar. However, the successors of the nonterminal symbol (sux$_x$) must be added at run time. The parser method for the production

$X = a\ b\ c$.

therefore reads (in pseudocode):

```
private static void X (BitSet sux) {
    check(a, {b, c} ∪ sux);
    check(b, {c} ∪ sux);
    check(c, sux);
}
```

The sets are managed as BitSets, which are declared and initialized at the beginning of the parser. For example, the set {b, c} is created as follows:

```
BitSet fs1 = new BitSet();
...
fs1.add(b); fs1.add(c);
```

The first call to check() in the parser method X() is then in Java:

```
check(a, ((BitSet)fs1.clone().or(sux));
```

Note that a copy of fs1 must be created (so as not to destroy fs1) before sux can be added to it. Of course, this is tedious to write, bloats the parser code and also slows down parsing.

Parsing Nonterminal Symbols

The parsing of nonterminal symbols is similar to that of terminal symbols. If a nonterminal symbol Y appears on the right-hand side of a production (followed by other elements α_i)

$X = \ldots Y\ \alpha_1\ \alpha_2 \ldots \alpha_n.$

the parser method of Y is called with the successors of Y as a parameter:

$Y(First(\alpha_1) \cup First(\alpha_2) \cup \ldots \cup First(\alpha_n) \cup sux_X);$

Again, the first part ($First(\alpha_1) \cup First(\alpha_2) \cup \ldots \cup First(\alpha_n)$) can be calculated statically from the grammar, while sux_X must be added at run time. The production

X = a Y c. // assume First(Y) = {b}

is parsed as follows (in pseudocode):

```
private static void X (BitSet sux) {
    check(a, {b, c} ∪ sux);
    Y({c} ∪ sux);
    check(c, sux);
}
```

The start symbol MicroJava is parsed by calling MicroJava({eof}).

Skipping Erroneous Symbols

If a syntax error occurs, the error() method is called, which is passed an error message and a set of anchors as parameters:

```
private static void error (String msg, BitSet sux) {
    System.out.println("line " + la.line + ", col " + la.col + ": " + msg);
    errors++;
    while (!sux.get(sym)) scan(); // while (sym ∉ sux) scan();
    // sym ∈ sux
}
```

The error() method uses scan() to skip tokens from the input stream until a valid anchor from the set sux occurs. Since multiple errors can now be detected, they must be counted using the variable errors that is declared at the beginning of the parser as follows:

```
public static int errors = 0; // error counter
```

This variable can be queried at the end of parsing to see how many syntax errors were detected.

After synchronizing the input stream in the error() method, the lookahead symbol sym now contains an anchor with which parsing can be continued.

3.4 Syntax Error Handling

Synchronization with the Grammar

After erroneous symbols have been skipped, the parser must finally be steered to the point in the grammar where it can continue with the detected anchor. To do this, the parser simply continues (and possibly produces follow-up error messages) until it gets to the point in the grammar where the detected anchor is expected. Let's look at an example: for the production

```
X = a b c.
```

the parser method is (in pseudocode):

```
private static void X (BitSet sux) {
    check(a, {b, c} ∪ sux);
    check(b, {c} ∪ sux);
    check(c, sux);
}
```

Suppose the input is not a b c, but is x y c. The parser tries to recognize an a by calling check(a, {b, c} ∪ sux), but the next input symbol is x and not a, so an error is reported. The anchor set is {b, c} ∪ sux. The error() method skips all symbols that are not in this set. So x and y are skipped, but c is an anchor, so skipping stops here (sym == c).

The parser now simply continues and comes to check(b, {c} ∪ sux). The recognition of b also fails because sym contains the symbol c. Therefore, another error is reported. The anchor set is now {c} ∪ sux. This time, however, nothing is skipped, because the lookahead symbol c is in this set.

If the parser now continues and comes to check(c, sux), c is recognized, and the synchronization is thus complete. The parser can resume parsing and can try to detect more errors.

Suppressing Follow-up Error Messages

As we have seen, once a syntax error has been detected, the parser simply continues until it gets to the point in the grammar where the detected anchor is expected. This can produce follow-up error messages, which are of course undesirable because they are not real errors, but a consequence of the original error.

Follow-up error messages can be suppressed by a simple heuristic: Errors are only reported if at least three symbols have been correctly recognized since the last error. To do this, we introduce a global variable errDist for the current distance to the last error:

```
private static int errDist = 3;
```

Initially, we pretend that the last error was already three symbols ago. Whenever a symbol has been correctly recognized and consumed (i.e., scan() is called), the error distance is incremented:

```
private static void scan() {
    ...
    errDist++; // another token correctly parsed
}
```

In the error() method, we only report an error if errDist >= 3. After skipping erroneous symbols, we reset errDist to 0, and counting starts again:

```
private static void error (String msg, BitSet sux) {
  if (errDist >= 3) {
    System.out.println("line " + la.line + ", col " + la.col + ": " + msg);
    errors++;
  }
  while (!sux.get(sym)) scan();
  errDist = 0; // restart counting
}
```

This simple heuristic suppresses follow-up error messages. However, if there are less than three correctly recognized symbols between two syntax errors, the second error goes unreported (but will be detected in a recompilation). In most cases, however, syntax errors are not so close to each other, so that the heuristic works well in practice.

Parsing Alternatives

The pattern for parsing alternatives also needs to be adapted for error handling with general anchors. In order to parse alternatives such as

$X = \alpha \mid \beta \mid \gamma.$

we have so far used the following pattern (in pseudocode):

```
private static void X() {
  if (sym ∈ First(α)) ... parse α ...
  else if (sym ∈ First(β)) ... parse β ...
  else if (sym ∈ First(γ)) ... parse γ ...
  else error("invalid X");
}
```

If sym does not match any of the alternatives, an error will be reported in the last else and erroneous symbols will be skipped, but we will then no longer be able to enter one of the alternatives. Therefore, it is better to check whether sym matches one of the alternatives before parsing them. If not, we can already report the error there, skip any erroneous symbols, and can then still enter one of the alternatives. So the new pattern is (in pseudocode):

```
private static void X (BitSet sux) {
  if (sym ∉ First(α) ∪ First(β) ∪ First(γ))
    error("invalid X", First(α) ∪ First(β) ∪ First(γ) ∪ sux);
  // sym matches one of the alternatives or sux
  if (sym ∈ First(α)) ... parse α ...
  else if (sym ∈ First(β)) ... parse β ...
  else if (sym ∈ First(γ)) ... parse γ ...
  // no error branch
}
```

The error() method skips erroneous symbols until one from the specified set occurs. This is then either a valid start of one of the alternatives or a valid successor of X. The set First(α)

∪ First(β) ∪ First(γ) can again be calculated statically from the grammar, while sux has to be added at run time. As you can see, we no longer need an error branch, because any error has already been reported before.

Parsing EBNF Options

Similarly, for EBNF options, we have to check before the option whether the lookahead symbol matches the option or its successors and otherwise report an error. For the production

$X = [α] β.$

the new pattern is (in pseudocode):

```
private static void X (BitSet sux) {
    if (sym ∉ First(α) ∪ First(β)) error("invalid X", First(α) ∪ First(β) ∪ sux);
    if (sym ∈ First(α)) ... parse α ...
    ... parse β ...
}
```

Parsing EBNF Iterations

For EBNF iterations, we use a completely new pattern, i.e., a loop that will be entered in any case. In the loop, we check whether the lookahead symbol matches the iteration or its successors. If not, we report an error, but remain in the loop so that we can continue with the next iteration after skipping any erroneous symbols. For the production

$X = \{α\} β.$

the pattern is (in pseudocode):

```
private static void X (BitSet sux) {
    for (;;) { // enter loop even if sym ∉ First(α)
        if (sym ∈ First(α)) ... parse α ...            // correct case 1: process α
        else if (sym ∈ First(β) ∪ sux) break;          // correct case 2: leave loop and process β
        else error("invalid X", First(α) ∪ First(β) ∪ sux); // error case: synchronize and stay in loop
    }
    ... parse β ...
}
```

The error() method reports the error and then skips symbols until a terminal start of α occurs (with which the next iteration can begin), or a terminal start of β (with which the iteration is exited), or a symbol from sux (with which the iteration is also exited; in this case follow-up errors would be reported when parsing β, but these would be suppressed).

Example

Finally, let's look at an example where the patterns for all EBNF constructs (alternatives, options, and iterations) are used. For the grammar

$X = a\ Y\ |\ b\ \{c\ d\}.$
$Y = [b]\ d.$

the parser methods with error handling look like this (for readability, pseudocode is again used for the calculation of the anchor sets):

```
private static void X (BitSet sux) {
    If (sym != a && sym != b) error("invalid X", {a, b} ∪ sux);
    if (sym == a) {
        scan(); Y(sux);
    } else if (sym == b) {
        scan();
        for (;;) {
            if (sym == c) {
                scan();
                check(d, {c} ∪ sux); // c is also a successor of d
            } else if (sym ∈ sux) {
                break;
            } else {
                error("c expected", {c} ∪ sux);
            }
        }
    }
}

private static void Y (BitSet sux) {
    if (sym != b & sym != d) error("invalid Y", {b, d} ∪ sux);
    if (sym == b) scan();
    check(d, sux);
}
```

Summary

Error handling with general anchors results in a good and quick error recovery. It can be applied systematically by using patterns for parsing terminal symbols, nonterminal symbols, alternatives, options, and iterations.

The disadvantage, however, is that it is somewhat complicated, bloats the parser code and slows down the parsing of (even error-free) programs, since anchor sets have to be calculated and passed to the parser methods at run time.

3.4.3 Error Handling with Specific Anchors

With this error handling technique, the recovery after syntax errors happens only at particularly "safe" synchronization points, i.e., at locations where keywords are expected that do not occur elsewhere in the grammar. Such locations are, for example:

- the start of a *statement* where keywords such as if or while are expected, or
- the start of a *declaration* where keywords such as public or void are expected.

3.4 Syntax Error Handling

When we see an if, we know that we are at the beginning of a statement because that keyword does not occur anywhere else in grammar. When we see a void, we know that a declaration begins.

For each of these locations, we calculate a set of anchors, i.e., the set of all symbols that are expected there. However, at the beginning of a statement or a declaration, the symbol ident can also occur, which is not a safe anchor, because ident can also occur in many other places in the grammar. Therefore, we remove ident from the set of anchors.

At each of these synchronization points, we insert the following code into the parser (in pseudocode):

```
if (sym ∉ expectedSymbols) {
   error(...); // called without a parameter for successors; no synchronization in error
   while (sym ∉ anchors ∪ {eof}) scan(); // synchronization
   errDist = 0;
}
```

If sym is not one of the symbols that are expected at the synchronization point, we report an error. We then skip symbols from the source program until an anchor appears that is expected there. This can then be used to resume parsing. When skipping symbols, we also stop on finding eof to avoid an infinite loop.

The advantage of this technique is that neither the parser methods nor the error() method need a parameter denoting their successors. The anchors at the synchronization points can be statically calculated from the grammar and do not need to be computed at run time, which keeps the parser code compact and contributes to the efficiency of the parser. After a syntax error occurred, the parser simply continues until it gets to the next synchronization point, where the recovery takes place.

As an example, let's look at the synchronization point at the beginning of a statement. The symbols expected there (ident, if, while, ...) are stored in a global variable firstStat:

```
private static BitSet firstStat = new BitSet();
...
firstStat.set(ident); firstStat.set(if_); firstStat.set(while_);
...
```

Furthermore, we create a "safe" anchors set syncStat, which is identical to firstStat, but does not contain ident, because that would be an unsafe anchor; instead, we add eof as an anchor:

```
private static BitSet syncStat;
...
syncStat = (BitSet) firstStat.clone();
syncStat.clear(ident); syncStat.add(eof);
```

The parser method for Statement then looks like this:

```
private static void Statement() {
   if (! firstStat.get(sym)) { // synchronization
      error("invalid start of statement");
      while (! syncStat.get(sym)) scan();
      errDist = 0;
   }
```

```
// parse statement
if (sym == if_) {
    scan();
    check(lpar); Condition(); check(rpar);
    Statement();
    if (sym == else_) { scan(); Statement(); }
} else if (sym == while_) {
    ...
}
```

As you can see, error handling and synchronization only take place at the beginning of Statement. The rest of the parser code remains unaffected. No anchors have to be calculated there, nor is there any need to pass them as parameters to the parser methods or to check(). The parser code is thus not bloated and remains efficient.

Also, the error() method does not need a set of anchors as a parameter and does not skip erroneous symbols, because this happens at the synchronization points (e.g., at the beginning of Statement). The error distance heuristic is used as described above to suppress follow-up error messages.

```
private static void error (String msg) {
    if (errDist >= 3) {
        System.out.println("line " + la.line + ", col " + la.col + ": " + msg);
        errors++;
    }
    errDist = 0;
}
```

Let's look at how error handling with specific anchors works when analyzing the following flawed MicroJava statement:

```
if a > b , max = a;
```

The parser enters Statement() (see above) with the lookahead symbol being if. Since the keyword if is a valid start of a statement, no error is reported and if is consumed by scan(). When check(lpar) is called, an error is detected because the next symbol is an ident. The error message is "(expected". The parser now simply continues and calls Condition(), which correctly parses a > b. The subsequent call to check(rpar) again reports an error (") expected"). After that, the parser continues, calls Statement() and comes to the synchronization point. The next symbol comma is not a valid start of a statement, which is why error() is called again. However, since the last error was less than three symbols ago, the error message is suppressed (follow-up error). The parser now skips symbols until an anchor from syncStat appears, which is the case with the semicolon. A semicolon is a valid start of a statement (an empty statement) and can thus be used to continue parsing. The recovery was successful, and the missing parentheses around a > b were reported as errors. The code piece ", max = a" was skipped, and parsing will continue with the semicolon.

As you can see, error handling with specific anchors synchronizes only in a few places, and code pieces may be skipped before recovery succeeds. However, this technique is

3.4 Syntax Error Handling

much simpler than error handling with general anchors and leads to more compact and efficient parser code.

Synchronization at the Beginning of an Iteration

The technique described above can still be improved. If a synchronization point is at the beginning of an iteration, a suboptimal recovery may occur. As an example, let's look at the production of Block:

```
Block = "{" {Statement} "}".
```

The parser method for Block looks like this (in pseudocode):

```
private static void Block() {
  check(lbrace);
  while (sym ∈ First(Statement)) {
    Statement();
  }
  check(rbrace);
}
```

However, if lbrace is not followed by a valid start of a statement, the loop will not be entered and the synchronization point in Statement() will not be reached. This hampers recovery. One way to fix this is to rewrite the parser method as follows:

```
private static void Block() {
  check(lbrace);
  while (sym ∉ {rbrace, eof}) {
    Statement();
  }
  check(rbrace);
}
```

Instead of checking whether sym is a terminal start of Statement, we check whether it is a terminal successor of a statement sequence (or eof, to avoid an infinite loop). As a result, the loop will also be entered if sym is not a terminal start of Statement, and the synchronization point in Statement() will be reached. In the event of an error, the parser will skip symbols there until it finds the next start of a statement, and the analysis can continue. However, we also have to include rbrace in syncStat so that skipping will stop with this symbol as well. Thus, a certain amount of "tuning" is necessary here.

Summary

Error handling with specific anchors requires just a few small modifications of the parser code. Synchronization happens only at locations where particularly "safe" symbols are expected that do not occur anywhere else in grammar. The rest of the parser remains unchanged. This keeps the parser code compact and efficient.

However, this technique is not quite as systematic as error handling with general anchors. It requires a certain amount of experience and sometimes a bit of "tuning" to compute the right set of anchors. The parser of the MicroJava compiler uses error handling with specific anchors.

3.5 Exercises

1. *Pushdown automaton.* Draw the pushdown automaton for the grammar

    E = x | E "+" x.

    As in the example for Fig. 3.3, specify how the input x + x is parsed and which states are on the stack at each analysis step.

2. *Recursive descent (1).* Write a parser method for the production

    Assignment = ident "=" Expr ";".

    Here and in the following exercises, use the token codes declared in Sect. 2.3. You do not need to implement any error handling.

3. *Recursive descent (2).* Write parser methods for the following productions:

    VarDecl = ("static" | "final") Type ident {"," ident} ";".
    Type   = ident.

4. *Recursive descent (3).* Write parser methods for the following productions:

    MethodCall = ident "(" [Parameters] ")" ";".
    Parameters = Param {"," Param}.
    Param   = ["out" | "ref"] ident.

5. *Recursive descent (4).* Write parser methods for the following productions:

    Signature = ["public" | "private"] ("void" | Type) ident "(" [Param {"," Param}] ")" ";".
    Type   = ident ["[""]"].
    Param   = Type ident.

6. *Recursive descent (5).* Write parser methods for the following productions:

    EnumType = Visibility "enum" ident "{" [IdentList] "}".
    Visibility = ["public" | "private"].
    IdentList = ident {"," ident}.

7. *LL(1) property (1).* Given the following grammar:

    Decl   = Type Variable ";"
            | Decl Type Variable ";".
    Type   = "int"
            | "string"
            | Type "*".
    Variable = ident
            | ident "[" "]".

    (a) Find all LL(1) conflicts.
    (b) Transform the grammar so that it is LL(1).

3.5 Exercises

8. *LL(1) property (2)*. Given the following grammar:

    ```
    DeclStatList = DeclStat | DeclStatList DeclStat.
    DeclStat     = Declaration | Statement.
    Declaration  = Type ident ";".
    Type         = "int" | ident.
    Statement    = ident "=" Expr ";".
    ```

    (a) Find all LL(1) conflicts.
    (b) Transform the grammar so that it is LL(1).

9. *LL(1) property (3)*. Given the following grammar (back, contents, cover, index, intro, page and preface are terminal symbols):

    ```
    Book    = cover Heading Body back.
    Heading = [preface] contents.
    Body    = {Chapter} Chapter [index].
    Chapter = intro | Chapter page.
    ```

    (a) Find all LL(1) conflicts.
    (b) Transform the grammar so that it is LL(1).

10. *Syntax error handling with general anchors*. Write parser methods for the following grammar and implement error handling with general anchors (Sect. 3.4.2). You can write the operations on sets in pseudocode.

    ```
    A = { b C | d }.
    C = [ c ] e.
    ```

    A is the start symbol of this grammar whose successor is eof.

11. *Syntax error handling with specific anchors*. Write parser methods for the following grammar and implement error handling with specific anchors (Sect. 3.4.3).

    ```
    Program     = "program" ident {Declaration} "{" {Statement} "}".
    Declaration = ("public" | "private") Type ident ";".
    Type        = ident ["[""]"].
    ```

    Since public and private are keywords that only occur at the start of a declaration, the start of the declaration is a good synchronization point. You do not need to implement the parser method for Statement.

12. *Implementation of the parser*. Implement the complete parser of MicroJava according to the grammar in Appendix A. Implement error handling with specific anchors and choose the start of declarations (in Program) as well as the start of Statement as synchronization points.

    Then download the file TestParser.zip from [Download] and use it to test your parser. All syntax errors in the sample program BuggyParserInput.mj (in TestParser.zip) should be reported.

Attributed Grammars 4

The parser only checks the syntactic correctness of a source program; it does not perform any translation. This is now done in the next phase of the compilation process called *semantic analysis*. The following tasks have to be performed:

- **Checking context conditions**. The compiler must check conditions that cannot be described by context-free grammars, such as the requirement that every name must be declared before it is used, or that the types of operands in expressions must be compatible. As a result, further (semantic) errors may be detected.
- **Symbol table management**. A directory of all declared names must be created, along with their properties such as their types or addresses. This core data structure of the compiler is called the *symbol table* (see Chap. 5). It also keeps track of data types, such as arrays or classes, as well as the scopes of names.
- **Code generation**. If no syntactic or semantic errors have been detected, the target code can finally be generated. To do this, methods are called that generate instructions for the target machine, manage jump labels, and ensure that memory is allocated for the local variables of each method called in the source program.

In a single-pass compiler (such as the MicroJava compiler), these actions are integrated directly into the parser. We will discuss this in more detail in Chaps. 5 and 6. To specify these actions, however, we first introduce a notation that can be used to describe translation processes in a simple and compact way, namely *attributed grammars*.

Attributed grammars (ATGs) were introduced by *Donald Knuth* [Knut68]. In their original form, they assume that a syntax tree is built from the source program, which is then traversed once or several times, decorating the tree nodes with attributes such as types or addresses. Code is then generated from this attributed syntax tree.

In this book, however, we use a simpler form of attributed grammars, in which semantic actions are executed immediately during syntax analysis. This form of attributed grammars is therefore also called *syntax-directed translation*. It is particularly suitable for single-pass compilers.

4.1 Components of Attributed Grammars

Let's first look at the components of attributed grammars and then show examples of how to use them (also outside of compiler construction proper). In later chapters, especially in code generation, we will use attributed grammars extensively to describe the translation of MicroJava programs.

4.1.1 Semantic Actions

Semantic actions are pieces of code (e.g., in Java) that are inserted into a grammar at the point where they are to be executed during parsing. Let's look at an example:

Number = digit {digit}.

A number consists of a sequence of digits. In principle, numbers are part of the lexical structure of a language, but we use them here as if they were part of the syntax of the language in order to create a simple example.

Assume that the "translation" of numbers consists of counting the number of digits they contain. This leads to the following grammar:

Number =
    digit   (. int n = 1; .)
    { digit (. n++; .)
    }   (. System.out.println(n); .) .

As you can see, semantic actions are inserted into the grammar as pieces of code between the brackets (. and .) and are executed by the parser at the position where they appear. After the first digit has been recognized, a counter n is set to 1. For each subsequent digit, n is incremented. At the end of the digit sequence, n is finally printed.

To aid readability, attributed grammars are written in tabular form: the syntax is on the left and the semantic actions that are to be executed according to the recognized symbols are on the right. Our "translation" of numbers yields the following example result for n:

    123   => 3
    4711 => 4

4.1.2 Output Attributes

Syntax symbols can provide values (*output attributes*) that can then be used in semantic actions. Such values act like output parameters of the recognized symbols. For example, the recognition of a digit can provide the value of that digit as an output attribute val:

    digit <↑val>

Attributes are enclosed in angle brackets (< and >). Their direction of flow is indicated by an arrow. So digit returns an output attribute val.

We can now make our translation a little more interesting, and instead of just counting the digits of a number, we can calculate and print the value of the number:

    Number   (. int val, n; .)
    = digit <↑val>
      { digit <↑n>   (. val = 10 * val + n; .)
      }   (. System.out.println(val); .) .

The first digit provides a value val. Each subsequent digit provides a value n, which is added to val shifted by a power of ten. Finally, the value of the number is printed.

4.1.3 Input Attributes

Nonterminal symbols can also have *input attributes*, i.e., parameters that are passed to them by the production in which they occur. This allows us to parameterize nonterminal symbols. In our example, an input attribute base can be used to specify the base (e.g., 10 or 16) to which the value of a number is to be calculated:

    Number <↓base, ↑val> (. int base, val, n; .)
    = digit <↑val>
      { digit <↑n>   (. val = base * val + n; .)
      } .

Number has an input attribute base and an output attribute val. The first digit provides the initial value of val. Each subsequent digit provides a value n, which is added to the number with base * val + n. The result is not printed here, but returned by Number as an output attribute val. The result of our translation is therefore:

    base = 10, digit sequence = 123   => val = 123
    base = 16, digit sequence = 123   => val = 291 (= 1*16^2 + 2*16^1 + 3*16^0)

To summarize, an attributed grammar is a compact notation for describing translation processes. It consists of the following three parts:

- **Productions** in EBNF. For example:

    IdentList = ident {"," ident}.

- **Attributes** as parameters of syntax symbols, for example:

    ident <↑name>   // output attribute (providing a translation result)
    IdentList <↓type>   // input attribute (providing context)

- **Semantic actions** as arbitrary statement sequences (e.g., in Java):

    (. *arbitrary statement sequence* .)

4.2 Examples

Attributed grammars are an extremely useful and compact notation. We will use them extensively in later chapters of this book to describe the translation of MicroJava programs. However, they are also useful outside compiler construction proper, which is why we look at some examples here that demonstrate such use.

4.2.1 Processing Variable Declarations

Let's start with an example from the MicroJava compiler that shows how variable declarations are processed. Variable declarations such as

    int a, b, c;

start with a type followed by a list of names. The declaration should cause the declared names and their type to be inserted into the symbol table (Tab). The attributed grammar for this looks as follows:

```
VarDecl                    (. Struct type; .)
= Type <↑type>
  IdentList <↓type>
  ";" .

IdentList <↓type>          (. Struct type; String name; .)
= ident <↑name>            (. Tab.insert(name, type); .)
  { "," ident <↑name>      (. Tab.insert(name, type); .)
  } .
```

Type provides a type description in the form of an output attribute of type Struct that is passed to IdentList. In IdentList, each declared name and its type are entered into the symbol table using Tab.insert().

But how is an attributed grammar mapped to compiler code? To do this, we simply integrate the attributes and semantic actions into the parser code. Attributes become parameters of parser methods, and semantic actions are inserted into the parser methods as pieces of code. This then looks as follows (attributes and semantic actions are shown in gray here):

4.2 Examples

```
private static void VarDecl() {
  Struct type;
  type = Type();
  IdentList(type);
  check(semicolon);
}
private static void IdentList (Struct type) {
  String name;
  check(ident); name = t.val;
  Tab.insert(name, type);
  while (sym == comma) {
    scan();
    check(ident); name = t.val;
    Tab.insert(name, type);
  }
}
```

Input attributes become parameters, and output attributes become return values of parser methods. The output attributes of terminal symbols are taken from the last recognized token t, for example:

```
check(ident); name = t.val;
```

As you can see, attributed grammars are more compact and easier to read than parser methods. The syntax is more clearly separated from the semantics. The representation of EBNF alternatives, options, and iterations is more compact than in parser code. Therefore, in the following chapters of this book, we will always describe translation processes by using attributed grammars.

4.2.2 Calculating Constant Expressions

In this example, we want to parse and evaluate constant expressions such as

$3 * (2 + 4)$

This can be described by an attributed grammar as follows:

```
Expr <↑val>           (. int val, val1; .)
= Term <↑val>
  { "+" Term <↑val1>  (. val = val + val1; .)
  | "-" Term <↑val1>  (. val = val - val1; .)
  } .

Term <↑val>           (. int val, val1; .)
= Factor <↑val>
  { "*" Factor <↑val1> (. val = val * val1; .)
  | "/" Factor <↑val1> (. val = val / val1; .)
  } .
```

Factor <↑val>   (. int val; .)
= number <↑val>
| "(" Expr <↑val> ")" .

Each Expr, Term, and Factor returns a value as an output attribute, which is then combined with other values according to the respective operator. Figure 4.1 shows an (imaginary) syntax tree of the constant expression, in which the nonterminal symbols are annotated with the values of their output attributes.

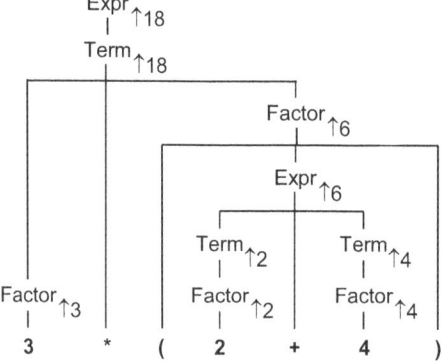

Fig. 4.1 Syntax tree of a constant expression (with output attributes)

Let's again take a look at how attributed productions are implemented as parser methods. As an example, we choose the production of Expr:

```
private static int Expr() {
    int val, val1;
    val = Term();
    for (;;) {
        if (sym == plus) {
            scan; val1 = Term(); val = val + val1;
        } else if (sym == minus) {
            scan(); val = Term(); val = val - val1;
        } else break;
    }
    return val;
}
```

Note that the output attribute of Expr is returned as a function value. Expr must therefore be implemented as a function method.

4.2.3 Sales Statistics

The next example does not come from the area of compiler construction in a strict sense, but rather describes the processing of sales figures into a sales statistic. Nevertheless, attributed grammars can be used here as well.

4.2 Examples

Let's assume we have a file in which articles (denoted by article numbers) and their sales quantities are stored. Each article line is terminated by a semicolon:

```
3451   2 5 3 7 ;
3452   4 5 1 ;
3453   1 1 ;
...
```

We want to sum up and print the sales quantities per article, i.e.:

```
3451   17
3452   10
3453    2
```

The input file has a syntactic structure, namely:

```
File   = {Article}.
Article = Code {Amount} ";".
Code   = number.
Amount = number.
```

Whenever an input is syntactically structured, we can process it using compiler construction techniques. To do this, we first write an attributed grammar:

```
File                        (. int code, amount; .)
= { Article <↑code, ↑amount>  (. System.out.println(code + " " + amount); .)
  }.

Article <↑code, ↑amount>    (. int code, x, amount = 0; .)
= number <↑code>
  { number <↑x>             (. amount += x; .)
  }
  ";".
```

We can now translate this grammar into parser methods. Article has two output attributes. However, since a parser method can only return a single function value, we need to combine the two attributes into an object of a helper class ArticleInfo:

```
class ArticleInfo {
    int code, amount;
}
```

Now we can implement the parser methods (attributes and semantic actions are shown in gray again):

```
private static void File() {
    while (sym == number) {
        ArticleInfo a = Article();
        System.out.println(a.code + " " + a.amount);
    }
    check(eof);
}
```

```
private static ArticleInfo Article() {
  ArticleInfo a = new ArticleInfo();
  check(number); a.code = t.numVal;  // value of number is taken from t.numVal
  while (sym == number) {
    scan(); int x = t.numVal;
    a.amount += x;
  }
  check(semicolon);
  return a;
}
```

All that is missing now is a mini scanner that returns the terminal symbols number, semicolon, and eof. However, this is trivial to implement.

Although the example is simple, compiler construction techniques have helped us to implement it in a systematic and compact way. One of the goals of this book is to make readers aware of such situations. Whenever a syntactically structured input needs to be processed, the techniques of compiler construction can be put to good use.

4.2.4 Image Description Language

Again, this example does not come from compiler construction proper, but deals with the processing of an image description language. An image described in this language can consist of several figures (rectangles, circles, polygons, etc.) that are encoded in a specific format. Let's focus on (closed) polygons here. For example, a polygon is encoded as follows:

   POLY (10, 30) (50, 50) (40, 30) (50, 10) END

It consists of several points, each defined by an x and y coordinate. Polygons of this type are to be read from a file and drawn on the screen (see Fig. 4.2).

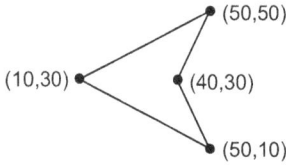

Fig. 4.2 Representation of a polygon on the screen

For drawing, we use the so-called "turtle graphics", in which a pen (like a turtle) runs across the drawing area and draws a line. We use the following two operations:

   Turtle.start(p);   sets the pen to the point p
   Turtle.move(q);   moves the pen to the point q, drawing a line

As experienced compiler engineers, we start by writing a context-free grammar for the description of polygons, which looks like this:

4.2 Examples

```
Polygon = "POLY" Point {Point} "END".
Point   = "(" number "," number ")".
```

We can now turn this into an attributed grammar, where Point should return an output attribute of the type

```
class Pt { int x, y; }
```

The attributed grammar looks like this:

```
Polygon             (. Pt p, q; .)
= "POLY"
  Point <↑p>        (. Turtle.start(p); .)
  { Point <↑q>      (. Turtle.move(q); .)
  }
  "END"             (. Turtle.move(p); .) .

Point <↑p>          (. Pt p = new Pt(); .)
= "(" number <↑p.x>
  "," number <↑p.y>
  ")" .
```

The first point defines the starting point of the polygon. Each additional point causes the pen to move to that position. Finally, we move the pen back to the starting point, which closes the polygon. A point is defined by two numbers that we assign directly to the coordinates p.x and p.y.

All we need to do now is translate this attributed grammar into parser methods and write similar productions for the other types of figures (rectangles, circles, etc.), then the processing of our image description language is complete. As we can see, the techniques of compiler construction could also be put to good use here.

4.2.5 Conversion from Infix to Postfix Notation

The final example is again closer to compiler construction. We want to convert an arithmetic expression in infix notation into an equivalent expression in postfix notation. In infix notation, the operators are placed between the operands, in postfix notation they are placed after the operands, thus:

infix notation	postfix notation
3 + 4 * 2	3 4 2 * +
(3 + 4) * 2	3 4 + 2 *

In the first postfix expression, for example, the operands 4 and 2 are multiplied before the result is added to the operand 3.

This task may seem complicated, but it is very easy to solve with some compiler construction knowledge. The trick is to output each operand immediately and delay the output of the operators until both of their operands have been output. This allows us to write down the attributed grammar immediately:

Expr
= Term
   { "+" Term   (. print("+ "); .)
   | "-" Term   (. print("- "); .)
   }.

Term
= Factor
   { "*" Factor   (. print("* "); .)
   | "/" Factor   (. print("/ "); .)
   }.

Factor
= number <↑val> (. print(val + " "); .)
| "(" Expr ")".

If a factor is a number, its value is printed immediately. If a term consists of Factor * Factor, the two factors have already been printed in the Factor production, so that the operator "*" must be printed after them in the Term production. The situation is similar for terms: If we have Term + Term, the two terms have already been printed in the Term production, so the operator "+" is printed after them in the Expr production. If a factor is an expression in parentheses, it is printed by calling Expr, which in turn calls Term and Factor to print the components of the expression.

To illustrate how this attributed grammar works, we look in Fig. 4.3 at the (imaginary) syntax tree of the expression

(3 + 4) * 2

and annotate it with the outputs of the elements of the postfix expression.

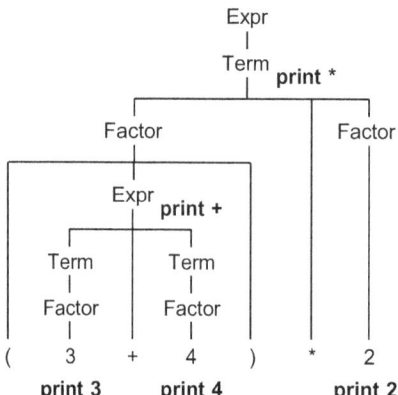

Fig. 4.3 Conversion of the infix expression (3 + 4) * 2 to a postfix expression

Expr calls Term and this Factor. Factor recognizes the opening parenthesis and then calls Expr. Expr calls Term and Factor again. Factor recognizes the number 3 and prints it. Then Factor and Term return. Expr recognizes the "+" operator, but does not print it yet. Rather, it calls Term and Factor again. Factor recognizes the number 4 and prints it. Then Factor and Term return. The two terms have now been printed, so the delayed operator "+" is emitted in Expr. And so the processing continues. This results in the postfix expression 3 4 + 2 *.

4.3 Exercises

1. *Understanding attributed grammars.* Given the following attributed grammar:

    ```
    N <↑n>      (. int n, x; .)
    = D <↑n>
      { D <↑x> (. n = 2 * n + x; .)
      }.
    D <↑x>      (. int x; .)
    = "0"       (. x = 0; .)
    | "1"       (. x = 1; .).
    ```

    (a) What does this grammar do, i.e., what does N return as an output attribute?
    (b) Translate the two productions into parser methods that also contain the attributes and semantic actions. The terminal symbols "0" and "1" can be denoted by the token names zero and one in the parser.

2. *Roman numbers.* Consider the following context-free grammar for a simplified form of the Roman numbers between 1 and 19 ("I" means 1, "V" means 5, and "X" means 10):

    ```
    RomanNumber = OneOrMore | FiveOrMore | TenOrMore.
    OneOrMore   = "I" ["I" ["I" ["I"]]].
    FiveOrMore  = "V" [OneOrMore].
    TenOrMore   = "X" [OneOrMore | FiveOrMore].
    ```

    Turn this grammar into an attributed grammar so that RomanNumber returns the integer value of the Roman number as an output attribute.

3. *Calculating with clock times.* The following context-free grammar describes expressions that can be used to add and subtract clock times:

    ```
    TimeExpr = Time { "+" Time | "-" Time }.
    Time     = Hours ":" Minutes.
    Hours    = digit [digit].
    Minutes  = digit digit.
    ```

    Turn it into an attributed grammar that returns the number of minutes of a time expression as the output attribute of TimeExpr, for example:

    ```
    3:24 + 1:00         => 264
    21:15 + 0:30 - 12:00 => 585
    ```

The grammar should also check the following context conditions:

- The hours must be in the range 0..23.
- The minutes must be in the range 0..59.

You can assume that digit returns an output attribute val.

4. *Address assignment in variable declarations.* Consider the following context-free grammar for variable declarations:

   ```
   VarDeclList = VarDecl {VarDecl}.
   VarDecl    = Type ident {"," ident} ";".
   Type       = "boolean" | "char" | "int".
   ```

   Turn it into an attributed grammar that prints the address of each declared variable and, finally, the total amount of memory required for all variables. Variables of type boolean require 1 byte, of type char 2 bytes, and of type int 4 bytes. For the declarations

   ```
   boolean x, y;
   int b;
   char c;
   ```

   the output should look as follows:

   ```
   x: 0
   y: 1
   b: 2
   c: 6
   Total = 8 bytes
   ```

5. *Courses and participants.* Given is a text file that describes courses and their participants. Each course has a name and a list of participants according to the following grammar:

   ```
   Courses     = {Course}.
   Course      = "course" CourseName ":" Participants.
   Participants = {Participant}.
   CourseName  = string.
   Participant = string.
   ```

   Turn it into an attributed grammar, which builds a global hash table that contains for each participant the list of attended courses. Use the following global data structure:

   ```
   HashMap<String, ArrayList<String>> participants;
   ```

   At the end, print this list. Take the value of the terminal symbol string from t.val.

6. *Evaluation of prefix expressions.* Arithmetic expressions can be written in prefix notation, where the operator *precedes* the operands (e.g., + a b). Here are some examples of prefix expressions and their meaning in infix notation:

   ```
   + 3 * 6 2    = 3 + (6 * 2)
   * + 1 2 3    = (1 + 2) * 3
   + * 2 4 * 6 8 = (2 * 4) + (6 * 8)
   ```

4.3 Exercises

(a) Write a context-free grammar for prefix expressions. A prefix expression is either a number (terminal symbol number) or begins with the operator "+" or "*", followed by two prefix expressions (use recursion). The precedence rules between "+" and "*" can be ignored because they are implicit in the prefix notation.

(b) Turn your grammar into an attributed grammar so that the value of a prefix expression is returned as an output attribute. The value of number can be taken from t.numVal.

7. *Scripting language for Boolean expressions.* The following grammar describes a little language that can be used to calculate the values of Boolean expressions, store them in variables, and print them:

```
Program    = { Statement }.
Statement  = ident "=" Expr ";"
           | "print" Expr ";".
Expr       = Term { "||" Term }.
Term       = Factor { "&&" Factor }.
Factor     = "true" | "false" | ident | "(" Expr ")" | "!" Factor.
```

Turn this grammar into an attributed grammar so that the value of Boolean expressions can be calculated and stored in variables or printed. Keep the variables and their values in a global hash table (HashMap). An example program might look like this:

```
big = true;
small = ! big;
ready = false;
print (big || small) && ready || big && ! ready;
```

8. *Translation from XML to Json.* Both XML (*Extensible Markup Language*) and JSON (*JavaScript Object Notation*) are notations for describing labeled data sets. An XML data set consisting of several XML elements

```
<person>
  <name>Miller</name>
  <city>London</city>
</person>
<person>
  <name>Smith</name>
  <city>Paris</city>
</person>
```

is represented in JSON as follows:

```
[
  person: {
    name: Miller,
    city: London
  },
```

```
    person: {
      name: Smith,
      city: Paris
    }
  ]
```

We will use a simplified XML grammar in this example:

```
XML     = { Element } .
Element = "<" ident ">"
          ( ident
          | { Element }
          )
          "</" ident ">".
```

Turn this grammar into an attributed grammar that transforms an XML data set into a JSON data set. Also check that the tag names in <ident> and </ident> match.

Symbol Table 5

The symbol table is one of the central data structures of a compiler and has the following tasks:

- Management of all declared names and their properties, such as:
  - their data type
  - for constants, their value
  - for variables, fields, and methods, their address
  - for methods, their parameters

  Each time a name is used in the program, it is looked up in the symbol table and its properties (type, value, address, parameters) are returned.

- **Management of data types**. Simple data types (int and char) are denoted by a type code. For structured data types (arrays and classes), their structure must be stored.
- **Management of scopes**. Names are associated with the scope in which they were declared. For example, they can be local, global, or belong to a class.

We implement the symbol table as a class Tab with methods such as insert() to insert names and find() to look up names. The symbol table is a dynamic data structure consisting of three types of nodes:

- *Object nodes*:   store information about declared names
- *Structure nodes*: store information about data types
- *Scope nodes*:   manage scopes

A variety of data structures could be used such as a linear list, a binary tree, or a hash table. Binary trees and hash tables have the advantage that searching in them is efficient, but the disadvantage that the declaration order of the names is lost. Therefore, in our MicroJava compiler, where the programs are short and there are just a few declarations, we use linear lists, which are simpler and preserve the declaration order.

The Symbol Table as a Linear List

In our implementation, as discussed above, all the declared names are stored in a linked list. Given the following MicroJava declarations:

```
final int n = 10;
class T { ... }
int a, b, c;
void m() { ... }
```

an object node is created for each declared name and added to the list. This results in the data structure shown in Fig. 5.1.

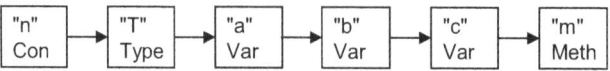

Fig. 5.1 Symbol table as a linear list of object nodes

Linear lists are easy to manage and as there are usually only a few declarations in MicroJava programs, these lists are short and searching is efficient. As you can see, the declaration order of the names is retained, which is convenient for the consecutive assignment of addresses for variables.

We will now look at the different types of nodes in the symbol table, their contents, and how they are managed.

5.1 Object Nodes

For each declared name, the compiler creates an object node and enters it into the symbol table. In MicroJava, there are the following kinds of objects, which are distinguished by a numeric code:

```
static final int    // object kinds
     Con  = 0,   // constant
     Var  = 1,   // variable or class field
     Type = 2,   // type
     Meth = 3,   // method
     Prog = 4;   // program
```

Depending on the kind of object, the following properties must be stored for it:

- For all objects: name, object kind, type
- For constants: value
- For variables: address, declaration level (local or global)
- For types: – (nothing; properties are stored in structure nodes)
- For methods: address, number of parameters, list of formal parameters
- For the program: – (nothing)

Since there are different kinds of object nodes, it would make sense to use a class hierarchy with a general superclass Obj and subclasses for the different object kinds (Fig. 5.2).

5.1 Object Nodes

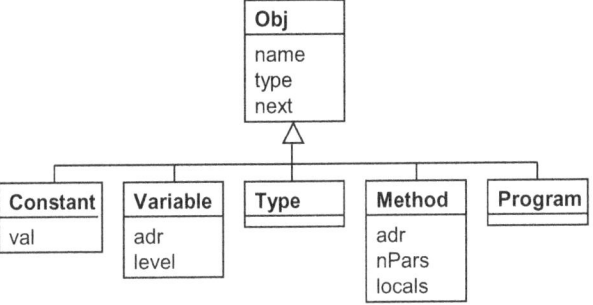

Fig. 5.2 Possible class hierarchy for object nodes

However, such an object-oriented design would be awkward to use due to constantly needing to perform type checks and casts, for example:

```
Obj obj = Tab.find("someVar");
if (obj instanceof Variable) {
   Variable v = (Variable) obj;
   v.adr = ...;
   v.level = ...;
}
```

If we look up a name in the symbol table, an object of the general type Obj is returned, which then usually has to be converted to the type of the actual object for further use. Type checks and casts cost run time and degrade the readability of the code.

Therefore, we choose a "flat" structure in the MicroJava compiler and declare all fields in a single class Obj. Depending on the object kind, only the fields relevant to this kind of object are used:

```
class Obj {
    static final int Con = 0, Var = 1, Type = 2, Meth = 3, Prog = 4;
    int      kind;    // object kind: Con, Var, Type, Meth, Prog
    String   name;    // object name
    Struct   type;    // object type (see later)
    Obj      next;
    int      val;     // for Con: value
    int      adr;     // for Var and Meth: address
    int      level;   // for Var: 0 = global, 1 = local
    int      nPars;   // for Meth: number of parameters
    Obj      locals;  // for Meth: list of parameters and local objects
}
```

Let's look at the following global MicroJava declarations again:

```
final int n = 10;
class T { ... }
int a, b, c;
void m (int x) { ... }
```

An Obj node is created for each declared name, resulting in the following list (Fig. 5.3):

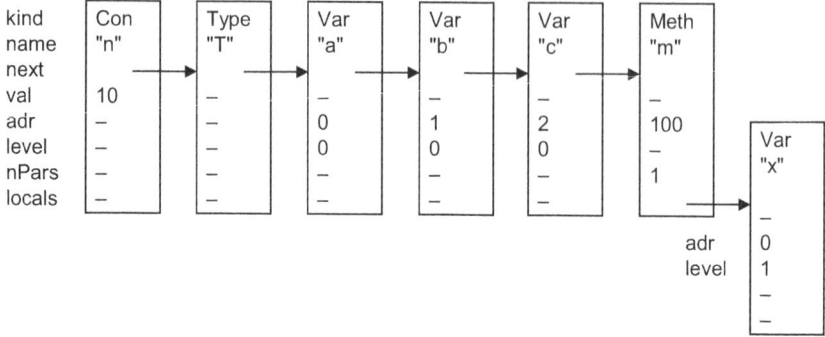

Fig. 5.3 Symbol table with the contents of the object nodes

We see that the field val is only used for constants, and the field adr only for variables and methods. The addresses of variables refer to their locations in memory. They are assigned consecutively, which we will look at in more detail in the next section. The addresses of methods refer to their positions in the code. In this example, we assume that method m() has the address 100. The field level denotes the declaration level of variables. Assuming that the above declarations are global, level is 0. Method m() has a single parameter, which is reflected by the field nPars. The field locals points to the formal parameters of the method, which again form a list of object nodes. In methods, the address assignment for parameters and local variables starts at 0 again, so adr is 0. The declaration level of the parameter x is 1 (local).

In MicroJava, there are global and local variables that are stored in different memory areas. We will now take a closer look at these areas.

5.1.1 Global Variables

At run time, global variables are stored in the *global data area* of the MicroJava VM. Each variable occupies 1 word (4 bytes). The addresses are assigned consecutively in declaration order. They are word numbers relative to the beginning of the data area. Figure 5.4 shows an example of global variables and how they are stored in the global data area.

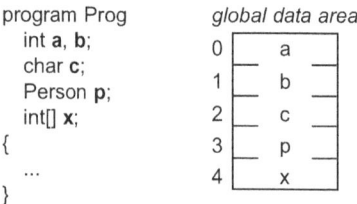

Fig. 5.4 Global variables and their allocation in the global data area

Variables of type char are also stored in a full word, as are variables that contain a reference to an object of a class (e.g., Person) or to an array.

5.1.2 Local Variables

Local variables are stored in the so-called *stack frame* of their method at run time. Each time a method is called, a new stack frame is allocated to store its local variables. When the method returns, it is released again. Thus, stack frames are managed dynamically in a stack-like way. Figure 5.5 shows an example of local variables and how they are stored in the stack frame of their method.

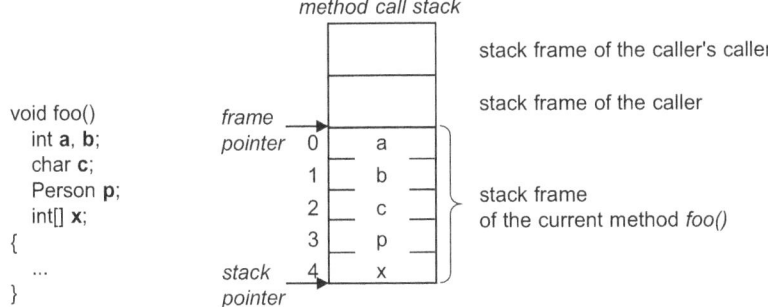

Fig. 5.5 Local variables and their allocation in the stack frame of their method

Stack frames are allocated on the *method call stack* of the MicroJava VM. The frame of the currently running method is delimited by two registers of the VM: the *frame pointer* (fp) points to the beginning of the frame, and the *stack pointer* (sp) points to its end, which is also the current end of the stack. Above the stack frame of the currently running method there is the stack frame of its caller and above that there is the stack frame of the caller's caller, up to the topmost method main().

In each stack frame, the local variables of the corresponding method are stored in the order in which they were declared. Each variable occupies exactly one word (4 bytes). The addresses are word numbers relative to the frame pointer.

5.1.3 Inserting Names into the Symbol Table

Whenever a name is declared, it is added to the symbol table by calling Tab.insert():

    Obj obj = Tab.insert(kind, name, type);

The parameter kind denotes the object kind of the name (Con, Var, Type, Meth, Prog), and type is the data type of the name. The insert() method creates a new object node with the values of the parameters, checks whether the name has already been declared, and then appends the node to the end of the list. Consecutive addresses are assigned to variables and fields, and the declaration level (global or local) is set for variables. The object node is finally returned so that it can be further processed in the caller. The following attributed grammar shows how variable declarations are processed:

```
VarDecl                  (. Struct type; String name; .)
= Type <↑type>
  ident <↑name>          (. Tab.insert(Obj.Var, name, type); .)
  { "," ident <↑name>    (. Tab.insert(Obj.Var, name, type); .)
  } ";" .
```

The kind parameter of insert() has the value Obj.Var, because these are variable declarations. The data type of the variables is supplied by the nonterminal symbol Type. It is an object of type Struct that contains type information (see Sect. 5.3).

5.1.4 Predeclared Names

In every programming language, there are names with a predefined meaning. For MicroJava, these are:

- Predeclared types: int, char
- Predeclared constants: null
- Predeclared methods: ord(ch), chr(i), len(arr)

These names are considered predeclared and are entered into the symbol table at the beginning of the compilation (see Fig. 5.6). They are known right from the start, so to speak. If they appear later in the source code, they are looked up in the symbol table and the corresponding object node is returned. Predeclared names do not differ from user-declared names in their use. The only difference is that they were predeclared at the beginning of the compilation.

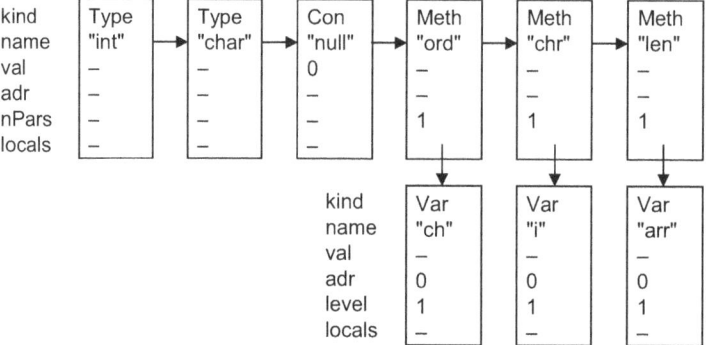

Fig. 5.6 Predeclared names in the symbol table

Alternatively, predeclared names could also be regarded as keywords. However, this would require special treatment in the compiler: if a type name is a keyword, it has to be associated with a predefined type, whereas if it is a user-declared name, its type must be looked up in the symbol table:

```
Type <↑type>
= ident <↑name>   (. Obj obj = Tab.find(name);  // type name – look it up
                   type = obj.type; .)
| "int"           (. type = Tab.intType; .)      // keyword – assign predefined type
| "char"          (. type = Tab.charType; .) .   // keyword – assign predefined type
```

It is therefore easier to treat predeclared and user-declared names in the same way, as shown in the following attributed grammar, in which both kinds of type names are simply represented by ident:

```
Type <↑type>
= ident <↑name>   (. Obj obj = Tab.find(name); type = obj.type; .) .
```

5.2 Scope Nodes

Each declared name is only visible in a certain range (*scope*) of the program. In MicroJava, for example, there are global names that are visible in the entire program, local names that are only visible in the method in which they were declared, and field names that are only visible in their class. Finally, predeclared names belong to a special scope called the "universe". So we have the following scopes:

- Program scope: contains global names
- Method scope: contains local names
- Class scope: contains fields
- Universe: contains predeclared names

Figure 5.7 shows an example of a MicroJava program and the scopes to which the declared names belong.

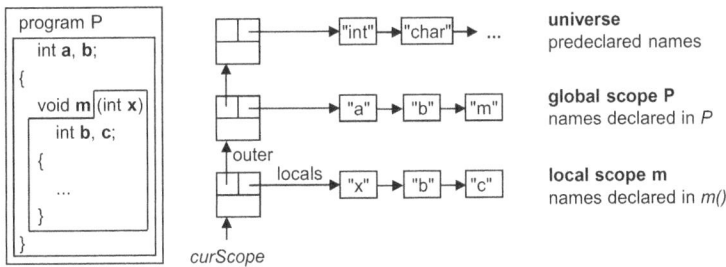

Fig. 5.7 Sample program with scopes and their contents

As you can see, the symbol table consists of several sublists—one for each scope. When the compiler passes through the source program and is in the method m(), the current scope (curScope) is that of m(); it contains object nodes for the local variables x, b, and c. The next outer scope is that of the program P with object nodes for the global variables a and b as well as for the method m(). Finally, the outermost scope is the "universe," which contains object nodes for all predeclared names. For each scope, there is a Scope node that points to the local objects of that scope (locals) and to the next outer scope (outer).

If the compiler encounters the use of a name, it searches for it in all open scopes. The search always starts in the current scope (curScope) and continues by following the outer pointers to the next outer scopes. For example, if the name b is searched in Fig. 5.7, it will already be found in the scope of m(). This is also the expected behavior: the local variable b hides the global variable b. If the name a is searched, it will not be found in the scope of m(), but will be found in the scope of P. Finally, if the name int is searched, it is not found in the scope of m() nor in the scope of P, but in the universe. The sublists are connected by scope nodes that look like this:

```
class Scope {
  Scope  outer;   // to next outer scope
  Obj    locals;  // to local objects of this scope
  int    nVars;   // number of variables declared in this scope
}
```

When a new scope starts (at the beginning of the program, a method, or a class), the method openScope() is called, which creates an empty scope and links it to the existing scopes. The new scope becomes the current scope (curScope) and the declaration level curLevel is incremented. curScope and curLevel are global variables of the class Tab.

```
static void openScope() {
  Scope s = new Scope();
  s.outer = curScope;
  curScope = s;
  curLevel++;
}
```

At the end of the program, a method, or a class, the current scope is closed again by calling the method closeScope(). curScope then points to the next outer scope again and curLevel is decremented. In other words, scopes are managed in a stack-like way.

```
static void closeScope() {
  curScope = curScope.outer;
  curLevel--;
}
```

The openScope() and closeScope() methods, like insert() and find(), belong to the class Tab. The insert() method always enters names into the current scope (curScope).

The following attributed grammar shows where openScope() and closeScope() are called in method declarations.

```
MethodDecl         (. Struct type; String name; .)
= Type <↑type>
  ident <↑name>    (. curMethod = Tab.insert(Obj.Meth, name, type);
                      Tab.openScope(); .)
  "(" ... ")"
  "{"              (. curMethod.locals = Tab.curScope.locals; .)
  ...
  "}"              (. Tab.closeScope(); .) .
```

5.2 Scope Nodes

The name of the method is entered into the program scope (using Meth as its kind) before a new scope is opened. The parameters and local variables of the method already go into this new scope when they are declared. Before the statements of the method begin, the list of local variables is linked to curMethod.locals so that it is not lost when the scope is closed at the end of the method. The global variable curMethod refers to the method that the compiler is currently working on.

To illustrate this, let's take a step-by-step look at how the program in Fig. 5.7 is processed. At the start of the compilation, the universe is created, which forms the current scope (Fig. 5.8).

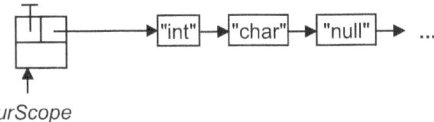

curScope

Fig. 5.8 Symbol table at the start of the compilation (containing the predeclared names of the universe)

After the keyword program and the program name P, openScope() is called and the two global variables a and b as well as the method m() are inserted into the new scope (Fig. 5.9).

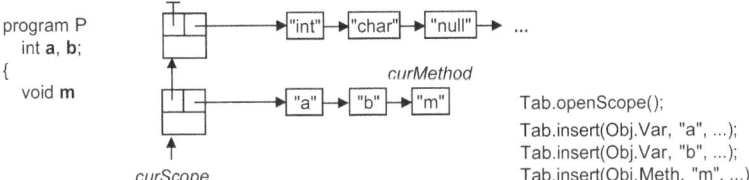

Fig. 5.9 Symbol table after the declarations of a, b and m()

After the declaration of the method name m, openScope() is called again and the parameter x as well as the two local variables b and c are inserted into the new scope. At the beginning of the statements of m(), the objects of the current scope are linked to curMethod.locals so that they do not become inaccessible when the scope is later closed (Fig. 5.10).

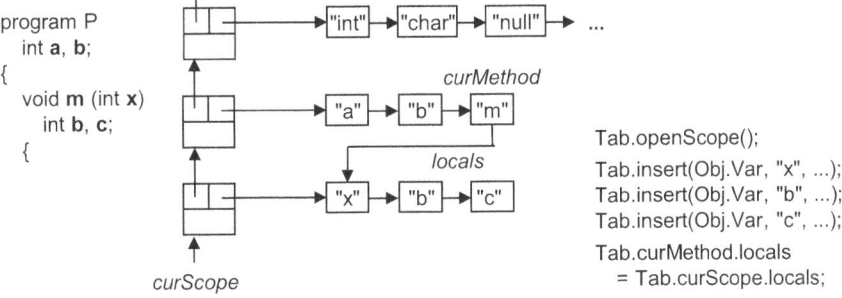

Fig. 5.10 Symbol table when reaching the statements of m()

At the end of the method m(), the current scope is closed using closeScope(). curScope now points to the scope of P again. However, the local objects of m() are still accessible via curMethod.locals (Fig. 5.11).

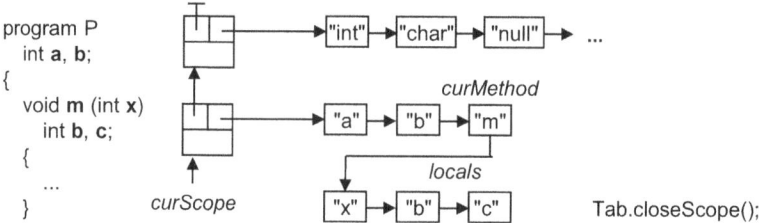

Fig. 5.11 Symbol table after the end of m() was reached

If another method declaration were to follow, a new scope would be opened and then closed again at the end of this method. In other words, the scopes are managed in a stack-like manner. In our example, however, there are no further method declarations, and the program's end is encountered. Therefore, the scope of P is closed by calling closeScope(), and we are back to the state shown in Fig. 5.8.

5.2.1 Inserting Names into the Current Scope

Now that we know how scopes are managed, let's look at the implementation of the insert() method, which enters names into the current scope when they are declared.

```
public static Obj insert (int kind, String name, Struct type) {
    //--- create and initialize object node
    Obj obj = new Obj(kind, name, type);
    if (kind == Obj.Var) {
        obj.adr = curScope.nVars; curScope.nVars++;
        obj.level = curLevel;
    }
    //--- insert object node into current scope
    Obj p = curScope.locals, last = null;
    while (p != null) {
        if (p.name.equals(name)) error(name + "declared twice");
        last = p; p = p.next;
    }
    if (last == null) curScope.locals = obj; else last.next = obj;
    return obj;
}
```

An object node is created and initialized with the object's kind (Con, Var, Type, Meth, Prog), the object's name, and its type. Variables are assigned an address that corresponds to the current number of variables in the current scope (curScope.nVars). So the first variable gets the address 0, the second gets the address 1, and so on. In addition, the declaration level of variables is set to curLevel, which is incremented in openScope() and decremented in closeScope().

The object node is then inserted into the current scope (curScope). To do this, the list of objects is traversed and checked for duplicate declarations. The object node is then appended to the end of the list and returned to the caller for further processing.

5.2.2 Searching Names in Scopes

Each time a name appears in the source program, it is searched in all open scopes using the method find().

```
Obj obj = Tab.find(name);
```

The search starts in the current scope (curScope). If the name is not found there, the search continues in the next outer scope (see Fig. 5.7).

```
public static Obj find (String name) {
    for (Scope s = curScope; s != null; s = s.outer) {      // for all open scopes
        for (Obj p = curScope.locals; p != null; p = p.next) { // for all objects in this scope
            if (p.name.equals(name)) return p;
        }
    }
    error(name + " is undeclared");
    return noObj;
}
```

If the name is not found in any of the scopes, an error object (noObj) is returned instead of null. This contributes to the robustness of the compiler, as otherwise it would always have to check for null when accessing this object later in order to avoid invalid accesses. The error object is initialized in such a way that subsequent accesses are unlikely to cause follow-up errors. For example, Obj.Var is chosen as its object kind, "$none" as its name (a name that cannot occur in MicroJava programs) and int as its type.

5.3 Structure Nodes

Structure nodes store information about the type of a name, in particular its structure: for classes, the fields are recorded, for arrays, the element type. In MicroJava, there are the following kinds of types, which are denoted by a type code:

```
static final int
    None  = 0,   // used for void methods
    Int   = 1,   // int (primitive type)
    Char  = 2,   // char (primitive type)
    Arr   = 3,   // array (structured type)
    Class = 4;   // class (structured type)
```

This leads to the following class for structure nodes:

```
class Struct {
    static final int None = 0, Int = 1, Char = 2, Arr = 3, Class = 4; // type kinds
    int      kind;         // None, Int, Char, Arr, Class
    Struct   elemType;     // for Arr: element type
    int      nFields;      // for Class: number of fields
    Obj      fields;       // for Class: list of fields
}
```

Again, individual fields of Struct are only used for certain kinds of types: the field elemType is only used for arrays, the fields nFields and fields only for classes. For the following (global) MicroJava declarations:

```
int a, b;
char c;
```

Figure 5.12 shows the structure nodes for the types int and char:

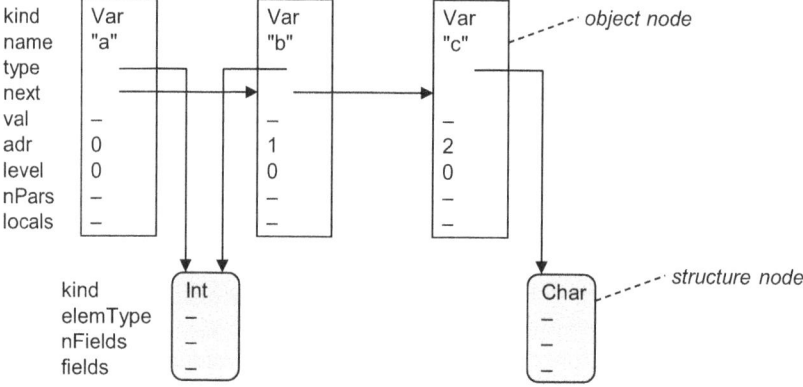

Fig. 5.12 Structure nodes for int and char

For each type, there is just a single structure node in the entire symbol table (also for int and char). All object nodes that refer to this type point to this unique structure node.

Figure 5.13 shows the structure nodes for arrays resulting from the following (global) MicroJava declarations:

```
int[] a;
int b;
```

5.3 Structure Nodes

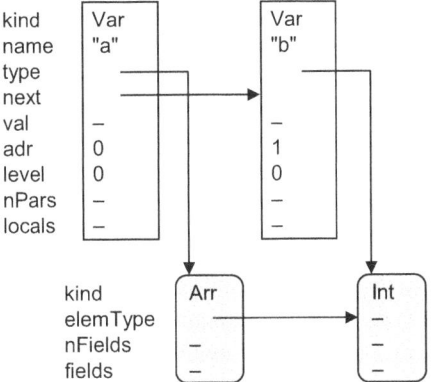

Fig. 5.13 Structure nodes for arrays

The variable a is of type "array of int", while b is only of type int. Again, you can see here that there is just a single structure node for int. In MicroJava (as in Java), the length of arrays is not known at compile time. It is only determined at run time and dynamically stored in the array objects on the heap.

Finally, Fig. 5.14, shows the structure nodes of classes for the following (global) declarations:

```
class C {
    int x, y, z,
}
C obj;
```

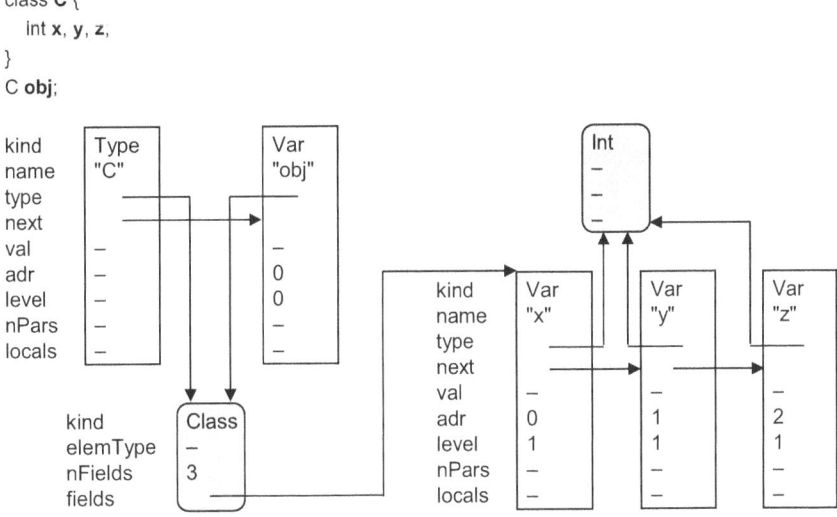

Fig. 5.14 Structure nodes for classes

The type of C is a class with three fields, which again form a list of object nodes. The addresses of fields start at 0 and the declaration level is 1. All three fields here are of type int and therefore point to the same structure node for int. The type of the variable obj is C, so the object node of obj points to the Class node of C.

Note that named types such as C are represented by two nodes in the symbol table: an *object node* that describes the name "C", and a *structure node* that describes the structure of C.

5.4 Type Checking

One of the tasks of a compiler is to perform type checks for assignments, parameter passing, expressions, and other operations to ensure that the types of the operands are compatible. This raises the question of when types are considered to be equivalent. There are two approaches here: *name equivalence* and *structural equivalence*. We will now review these two approaches and compare their advantages and disadvantages.

5.4.1 Name Equivalence

With name equivalence, two types are considered to be the same if they are denoted by the same *type name*. In the following declarations:

```
class T { ... }
T x;
T y;
```

x and y are both of type T. They have the same type name and therefore also the same type. Figure 5.15 shows that the object nodes of x and y point to the same structure node (the structure node of type T). Checking whether x and y have the same type can therefore be done by a pointer comparison objx.type == objy.type, which is simple and efficient.

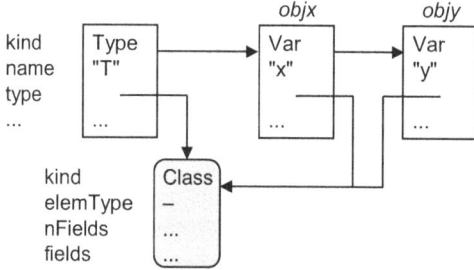

Fig. 5.15 Name equivalence—type check: objx.type == objy.type

5.4.2 Structural Equivalence

With structural equivalence, two types are considered to be the same if they have the same *structure* (for classes, the same number of fields of the same type; for arrays, the same element type). In the following declarations:

5.4 Type Checking

```
class T1 { int a, b; }
class T2 { int c, d; }
T1 x;
T2 y;
```

the types of x and y are (structurally) the same. Although they do not have the same name, they do have the same structure, namely a class each with two int fields (Fig. 5.16).

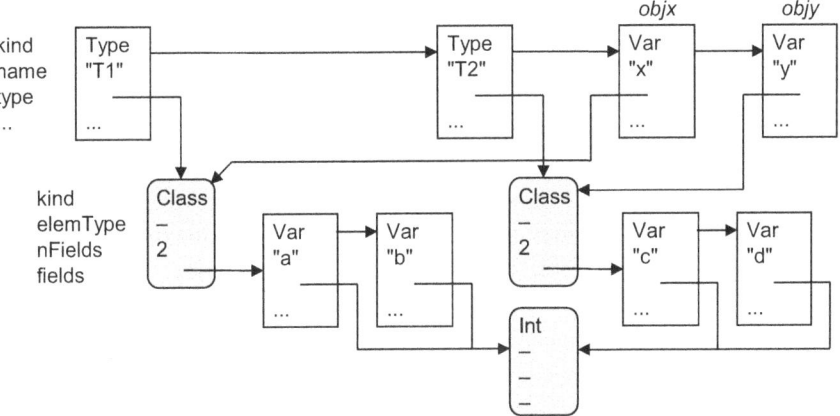

Fig. 5.16 Structural equivalence—type check: objx.type.structEquivalentTo(objy.type)

Checking for structural equivalence is much more complex than checking for name equivalence. If you want to check whether the types of x and y in Fig. 5.16 are structurally equivalent, it is necessary to check whether the structure nodes are of the same kind and whether (for classes) they have same number of fields with structurally equivalent types or (for arrays) whether the element types are structurally equivalent. This check may have to be done recursively and is expensive.

Therefore, most programming languages use name equivalence (e.g., Pascal, C/C++, C# and Java). Only few languages use structural equivalence such as Algol68 or Modula-3. In MicroJava, we also use name equivalence with a single exception, namely for array types, where structural equivalence is used. For the arrays

```
int[] x;
int[] y;
```

the variables x and y do not have the same type name, so their object nodes point to different structure nodes (see Fig. 5.17). Nevertheless, arrays with the same element type are considered equivalent in MicroJava (and also in Java).

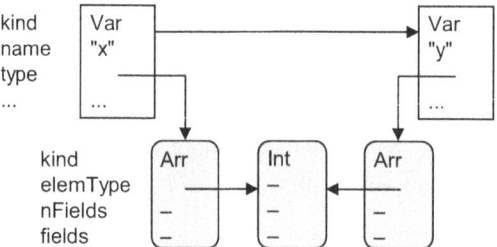

Fig. 5.17 Structural equivalence for arrays with the same element type

5.4.3 Variants of Type Compatibility

MicroJava requires different kinds of type compatibility in different places. For arithmetic operations, the operand types must be *the same*, for assignments, the right-hand side must be *assignable* to the left-hand side, and for comparisons, the operand types must be *comparable*. Therefore, we declare different methods in the Struct class to check these kinds of type compatibility. The equals() method checks whether two types are the same (structural equivalence for arrays, otherwise name equivalence).

```
public boolean equals (Struct other) { // checks if this.equals(other)
    if (this.kind == Arr)
        return other.kind == Arr & other.elemType == this.elemType;
    else
        return other == this;
}
```

For assignments, the assignableTo() method checks whether the right-hand side is assignable to the left-hand side. This is the case if the types of the left and right sides are the same, if the right-hand side is null and the left-hand side is of a reference type (class or array), or if both sides are arrays and the element type of the left-hand side is the special type Tab.noType.

The last case of assignableTo() requires an explanation: the predeclared method len(arr) returns the length of an array and should be applicable to arrays of any element type. Therefore, the formal parameter of len() is defined in the symbol table as if it had the type "array of noType". Since assignableTo() allows the assignment of any array to "array of noType", len() can be called for any array.

```
public boolean assignableTo (Struct dest) { // checks if this.assignableTo(dest)
    return this.equals(dest)
        || this == Tab.nullType && dest.isRefType()
        || this.kind == Arr & dest.kind == Arr & dest.elemType == Tab.noType;
}

public boolean isRefType() {
    return this.kind == Class || this.kind == Arr;
}
```

5.5 Resolving LL(1) Conflicts Using the Symbol Table

For comparison operations, the compatibleWith() method checks whether the types of the two operands are comparable. This is the case if the two types are the same, or if one of the two operands is null and the other is of a reference type.

```
public boolean compatibleWith (Struct other) { // checks if this.compatibleWith(other)
    return this.equals(other)
    || this == Tab.nullType && other.isRefType()
    || other == Tab.nullType && this.isRefType();
}
```

5.5 Resolving LL(1) Conflicts Using the Symbol Table

The syntax of methods is somewhat unconventional in MicroJava, as the declaration of local variables must come before the statement block:

```
void foo()
    int a;
{   a = 0; ...
}
```

It would be more familiar to declare methods like in Java:

```
void foo() {
    int a;
    a = 0; ...
}
```

However, this would lead to an LL(1) conflict, because a block could then contain both declarations and statements:

Block = "{" { VarDecl | Statement } "}".

Both VarDecl and Statement can start with an ident, so that the parser would not be able to decide whether a declaration or a statement begins if it sees an ident. This conflict is hard to eliminate by transforming the grammar—the grammar would become quite difficult to understand for the reader.

However, we can resolve the conflict using semantic information available from the symbol table. Declarations start with a type name, but statements start with a variable or method name. We can therefore write a helper method in the parser that checks if the lookahead symbol sym denotes a type name:

```
private static boolean nextTokenIsType() {
    if (sym != ident) return false;
    Obj obj = Tab.find(la.val);      // look up ident in the symbol table ...
    return obj.kind == Obj.Type;     // ... and return true if it denotes a type
}
```

The parser can now call this method to distinguish between declarations and statements in the Block() method (in pseudocode):

```
private static void Block() {
  check(lbrace);
  for (;;) {
    if (nextTokenIsType()) VarDecl();
    else if (sym ∈ First(Statement)) Statement();
    else if (sym ∈ {rbrace, eof}) break;
    else {
      error("invalid declaration or statement");
      while (sym ∉ First(Statement) - {ident} ∪ {rbrace, eof}) scan(); // synchronization
      errDist = 0;
    } // else
  } // for
  check(rbrace);
}
```

If there is a type name, the parser calls VarDecl(), if there is a valid start of a statement, it calls Statement(), if the parser encounters a closing curly brace or eof, it exits the loop, otherwise an error is reported and synchronization takes place.

As you can see, LL(1) conflicts can sometimes be solved by using semantic information which has become available during compilation. This makes it possible to analyze almost any grammar using recursive descent, even if it is not originally LL(1).

5.6 Initializing the Symbol Table

At the beginning of a compilation, the symbol table must be initialized with the predeclared names, which is best done in the static constructor of the Tab class. In other words, the "universe" scope must be built. Its form is as shown in Fig. 5.18.

5.6 Initializing the Symbol Table

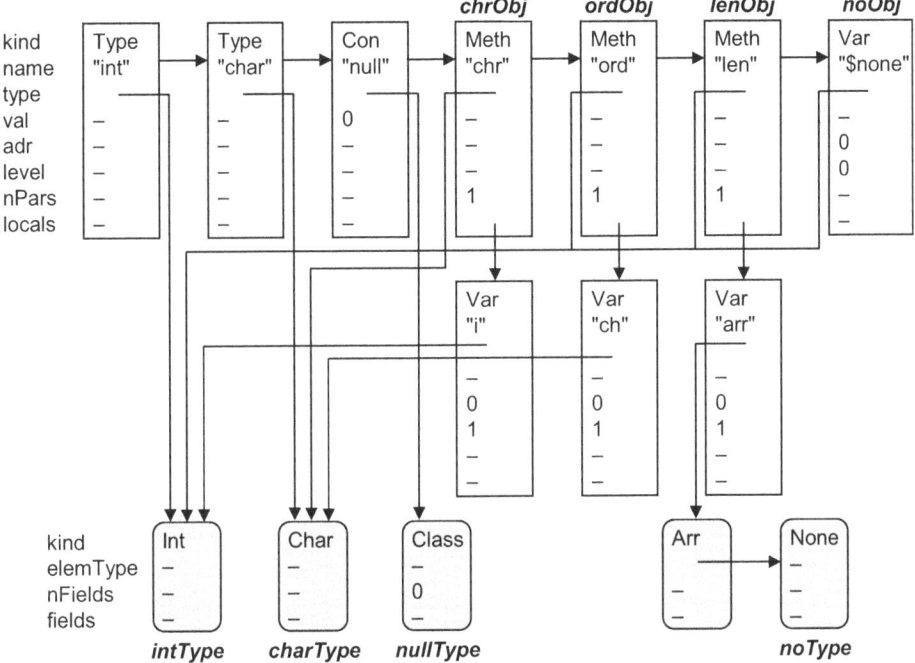

Fig. 5.18 Initialization of the universe

Some of the object and structure nodes are exported under a special name (e.g., chrObj, intType, ...), resulting in the following interface of the symbol table class:

```
public class Tab {
    public static Scope  curScope;    // current scope
    public static int    curLevel;    // nesting level of current scope
    public static Struct intType, charType, nullType, noType;   // predeclared types
    public static Obj    chrObj, ordObj, lenObj, noObj;   // predeclared objects
    public static Obj    insert (int kind, String name, Struct type) { ... }
    public static Obj    find (String name) { ... }
    public static Obj    findField (String name, Struct type) { ... }
    public static void   openScope() { ... }
    public static void   closeScope() { ... }
}
```

5.7 Exercises

1. *Symbol table with simple types.* Given the following program:

   ```
   program P
     final int a = 16;
     char b;
   {
     void foo (int c, int d)
       char e;
     { ... // <== 1
     }
     void bar()
       int f, g;
     { ... // <== 2
     }
   }
   ```

   (a) Draw the symbol table (like in Fig. 5.7) at the point in time when the compiler is at position 1 (in foo()). Draw all scopes with their object and structure nodes. For the universe, it is sufficient to draw a few example nodes. Also specify the values of the fields in object and structure nodes.

   (b) Draw the symbol table at the point in time when the compiler is at position 2 (in bar()).

2. *Symbol table with arrays.* Given the following method:

   ```
   void foo()
     int[] a, b;
     int c;
     char[] d, e;
   { ... // <== 1
   }
   ```

   Draw the symbol table at the point in time when the compiler is at position 1. You just need to draw the scope of the foo() method.

3. *Symbol table with classes.* Given the following program:

   ```
   program P
     class C1 { int f, g; }
     class C2 { int h; char ch; }
   {
     void foo()
       C1 a, b;
       C2 c;
     { ... // <== 1
     }
   }
   ```

Draw the symbol table at the point in time when the compiler is at position 1. Draw the scopes of P and foo(). You don't need to draw the scope of the universe.

4. *Object and structure nodes*. Why is there both an object node and a structure node for named types such as int or Person? What information is stored in the object node and what information is stored in the structure node?
5. *Type checking*. Explain in your own words the difference between name equivalence and structural equivalence in type checks. Why does Java (and MicroJava) use name equivalence in most cases, but structural equivalence for arrays?
6. *Implementation of structural equivalence*. Implement the method t1.equals(t2) in the Struct class so that it checks whether a type t1 is structurally equivalent to a type t2.
7. *Parameters*. Why is the list of parameters stored in a method's object node, and why is it retained after the method's scope has been closed?
8. *Indirect recursion*. MicroJava supports direct recursion, where a method can call itself. However, it does not support indirect recursion, where, for example, a method foo() calls a method bar() and that method calls foo() again. Why is indirect recursion not supported by MicroJava?
9. *Implementation of the symbol table*. Implement the symbol table class Tab for the MicroJava compiler along with the classes Obj for object nodes, Struct for structure nodes, and Scope for scope nodes, according to the description in this chapter and the interfaces of these classes (see Appendix B).

Code Generation

6

We now come to the final phase of the compilation process—code generation. It is the most complex and time-consuming phase and far less systematic than lexical analysis or syntax analysis. This is partly due to the target machines and their instruction sets, which are usually full of details and often quite irregular. For our compiler, however, we use the *MicroJava virtual machine* (μJVM) as a simple and regular target machine. As a result, much of the complexity is avoided. The most important tasks of code generation are:

- **Generation of machine instructions**. For each source-level operation, the appropriate machine instructions must be selected to achieve the required behavior. Sometimes an operation can be realized by different instructions, which may vary in efficiency. In addition, the appropriate addressing modes must be chosen for accessing the operands. For example, a memory cell can be accessed with an absolute address, relative to a base address, or with indexing.
- **Translation of branches and loops into jumps**. The target machine does not have source language constructs such as if or while statements. Thus, the control flow must be expressed using jump instructions.
- **Management of stack frames for local variables**. Each method has its own local variables. When a method is called, a new stack frame must therefore be allocated for its local variables and released at the end of the method. This is done by means of special instructions that the compiler has to generate.
- **Possible optimizations**. Optimizations are a comprehensive topic. They are usually performed in a separate phase before code generation and work on an intermediate representation of the program (e.g., an abstract syntax tree). In the MicroJava compiler, however, we deliberately refrain from extensive optimizations and only perform a few simple ones that can be done "on the fly" during code generation. For more extensive optimizations, see for example [ALSU06, Appe02, Coop22, FCL09, Much97].

- **Output of the object file**. At the end of the compilation, the generated machine code must be written to a file, which can then be executed. The format of this file can be quite complex but we will see that for MicroJava it is very simple. If errors are detected during compilation, no object file is created.

The general procedure for implementing a code generator is as follows:

1. **Study the target machine**. First of all, you have to fully understand the target machine and its design. To do this, take a look at the technical manual of the target machine: What registers are available and for what purposes can they be used? Which data formats are supported (integers, floating point numbers, bits, etc.)? What addressing modes can be used? What instructions are there and how are they encoded?
2. **Define the run-time data structures**. The layout of stack frames, global data, or heap objects is not determined by the target machine, but can be defined by the compiler engineer, although interoperability with other software running on the same machine may influence this.
3. **Manage the code area**. The machine code is not immediately written to a file, but is first kept in a code area, since the target addresses of jump instructions are sometimes only known later and can only be inserted then. Managing the code area also includes the encoding of instructions in binary format.
4. **Register allocation**. Register machines have a set of registers that have to be managed efficiently. However, the MicroJava VM is a *stack machine* that uses an *expression stack* instead of registers. Therefore, register allocation is not required in the MicroJava compiler.
5. **Generate code**. This is usually done bottom-up in the following order:
   - Loading variables and constants onto the expression stack
   - Processing object fields and array elements (e.g., x.y or a[i])
   - Processing expressions (e.g., a + 2 * b)
   - Managing jumps and labels
   - Processing statements
   - Processing methods and parameters

We will stay with this ordering and start by studying the target machine, i.e., the MicroJava VM, with its memory areas and its instruction set. The design of the MicroJava VM is based on a simplified version of the Java VM. By studying this VM, you will gain valuable insights into the general operation of virtual machines.

6.1 The MicroJava VM

The MicroJava VM (μJVM) is a *virtual machine*, i.e., a CPU implemented in software that lies between the actual hardware (e.g., an Intel CPU) and the MicroJava program (Fig. 6.1).

6.1 The MicroJava VM

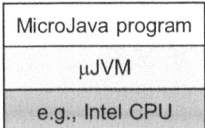

Fig. 6.1 The µJVM as a layer between the hardware and the MicroJava program

The µJVM has its own instruction set with an interpreter. MicroJava programs are translated into these instructions and executed by the µJVM interpreter.

The advantage of inserting a VM between the hardware and the application layer is that programs can run on any hardware, as long as there is an implementation of the corresponding VM there. This is why many modern programming languages such as Java and Python use a VM as an execution environment.

How the µJVM Works

The µJVM is a *stack machine*, i.e., it has no registers, but rather an *expression stack* (*EStack*) onto which the values of operands must be loaded before they can be processed. Instructions fetch their operands from the EStack and store their result back on the EStack. In effect, the EStack is used like a stack of pseudo registers.

Let's look at an example involving two local variables i and j. As will be seen later, these are located at addresses (0 and 1 in our case) in the *frame* of the current method on the method call stack (*MStack*). For illustration, we assume that at run time, i and j have the values 3 and 4, respectively (Fig. 6.2).

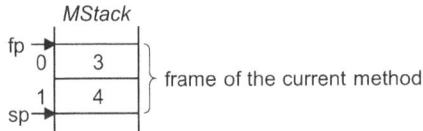

Fig. 6.2 Frame of the current method

The MicroJava statement

i = i + j * 5;

is translated into the following series of instructions (see also Sect. 6.1.2), which are shown in Fig. 6.3 together with their effect on the EStack at run time:

instruction	EStack	explanation
load0	3	load local variable from address 0 (i.e., variable i)
load1	3 | 4	load local variable from address 1 (i.e., variable j)
const5	3 | 4 | 5	load constant 5
mul	3 | 20	multiply the two topmost stack elements
add	23	add the two topmost stack elements
store0		store the topmost stack element to address 0

Fig. 6.3 Execution of the instruction i = i + j * 5;

The first three instructions load the local variables i and j as well as the constant 5 onto the EStack. The mul instruction multiplies the two topmost stack elements 4 and 5 and puts the result 20 back on the EStack. The add instruction adds the two topmost stack elements 3 and 20 and puts the result 23 back on the EStack. Finally, the instruction store0 stores the topmost stack element to address 0, i.e., to the local variable i.

As you can see, the EStack is only used to hold operands *during calculations* and is empty again at the end of each statement. The cells on the EStack take on the role of registers in register machines, so to speak.

6.1.1 Memory Areas

The μJVM has memory areas for data and code, which we will look at now.

Global Variables

Global variables are stored in a fixed-size array of 32-bit words and persist throughout program execution (Fig. 6.4). The size of the array is determined by the compiler from the number of global variables.

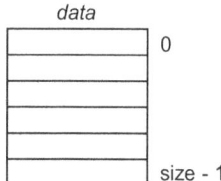

Fig. 6.4 Global variables

Each variable occupies exactly one word (32 bits). Variables are addressed by word numbers. For example, the instruction getstatic 2 loads the global variable at word address 2 from the global data area (data) onto the EStack.

Local Variables

Local variables are stored in the *stack frame* of their method. Each time a method is called, a new frame is allocated on the *method call stack* (*MStack*) and released again at the end of the method. In other words, frames are managed in a stack-like manner (Fig. 6.5).

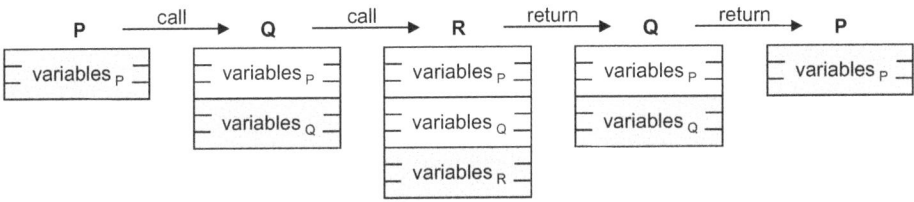

Fig. 6.5 Stack-like management of frames for local variables

Figure 6.6 shows the layout of the method call stack.

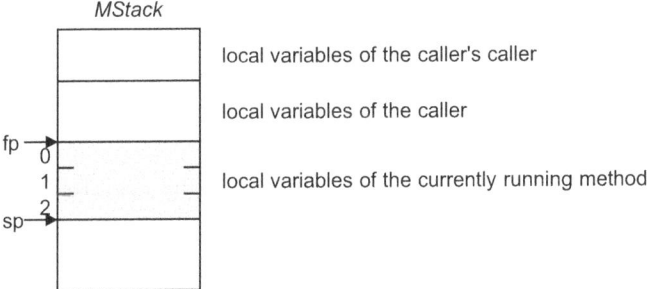

Fig. 6.6 Layout of the method call stack (MStack)

The frame of the currently running method is delimited by the *frame pointer* (fp) and the *stack pointer* (sp). The latter also marks the current end of the MStack. Each frame contains the local variables of its method, with each variable occupying exactly 1 word (4 bytes). The addresses are word numbers relative to fp. For example, the instruction load0 loads the local variable at address 0 from the frame of the currently running method onto the EStack.

Heap

The heap contains the dynamically allocated objects of classes and arrays. It is a fixed-size word array (see Fig. 6.7). New objects are allocated by the instructions new and newarray at the position free, and free is incremented accordingly. References to objects are word addresses relative to the beginning of the heap. In contrast to Java, there is no garbage collector in the μJVM. Objects on the heap therefore live for the entire execution of the program.

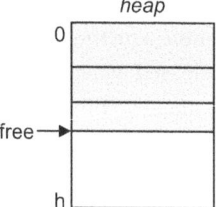

Fig. 6.7 Heap

Class objects. Figure 6.8 shows the layout of an object of a class C with three fields.

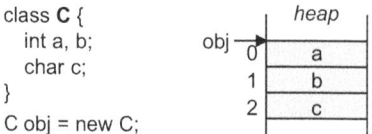

Fig. 6.8 Layout of class objects

Each field occupies exactly one word (4 bytes). Field addresses are word numbers relative to the beginning of the object.

Array objects. In array objects, the first word holds the length of the array, followed by the elements. Word arrays and char arrays differ in their layout (Fig. 6.9).

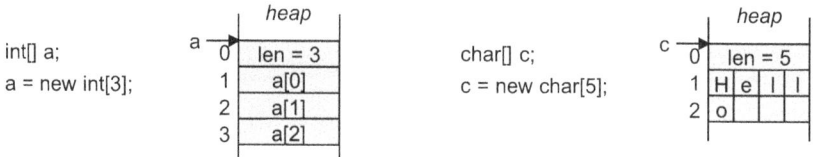

Fig. 6.9 Layout of array objects

In word arrays, each element occupies a word and is addressed by a word number. In char arrays, each element occupies a byte and is addressed by a byte number. However, the size of an array object is always a multiple of 4 bytes.

Code

The code area of the µJVM is a fixed-size byte array in which the instructions of the methods are stored in the order in which the methods are declared. The size of the code area is determined by the total size of the declared methods. The special register pc (*program counter*) of the VM always points to the instruction currently being executed. The main() method is at the address mainPc and is where the execution of the program begins (Fig. 6.10).

6.1 The MicroJava VM

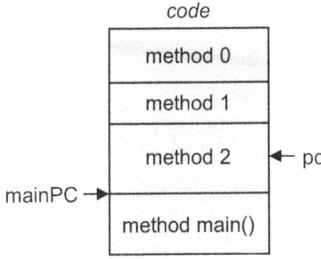

Fig. 6.10 Code area

6.1.2 Instruction Set

The μJVM has its own instruction set into which MicroJava programs are translated. It is based on the instruction set of the Java VM (JVM), but contains fewer and in some cases somewhat simplified instructions.

The instructions of the μJVM are extremely compact and often require just a single byte, which is why they are also referred to as *bytecode*. In contrast to the JVM, however, the instructions of the μJVM are untyped, i.e., the type of the operands is not encoded in the instructions (Fig. 6.11).

μJVM	JVM	
	for int	for float
load0	iload0	fload0
load1	iload1	fload1
add	iadd	fadd

Fig. 6.11 Untyped instructions of the μJVM versus typed instructions of the JVM

For example, to add two values, the JVM distinguishes whether they are of type int or float and uses different instructions accordingly. This is necessary because the JVM contains a *bytecode verifier* that checks whether the instructions are applied to operands of the correct type before they are executed. Although type checking has already been done by the compiler, the JVM checks the types again, since the bytecode may have been manipulated in the meantime. The μJVM does not perform this check for reasons of simplicity.

Instruction Format

The instruction format of the μJVM is much simpler than that of many other machines. A program consists of a sequence of instructions, all of which begin with one byte for the instruction code (opcode) and can have up to two operands of size 1, 2, or 4 bytes:

```
Code        = {Instruction}.
Instruction = opcode {operand}.
```

Examples of instructions with different numbers of operands are:

0 operands:	add	has two implicit operands on the EStack
1 operand:	load 7	loads the local variable from address 7
2 operands:	enter 1, 4	allocates a stack frame with 1 parameter and 4 local variables

Instructions without explicit operands (e.g., add) usually use implicit operands on the EStack.

Addressing Modes

The instructions access operands, which are addressed in different ways depending on the instruction. The μJVM supports six addressing modes, which are listed below together with examples. In each addressing mode the operands have a different meaning.

- **Immediate** const 7 *for constants*
  The operand is a constant and denotes itself.

- **Local** load 3 *for local variables on the MStack*
  The operand is the address of a local variable relative to fp.

- **Static** getstatic 3 *for global variables in* data
  The operand is the address of a global variable in data.

- **Stack** add *for loaded values on the EStack*
  There are no explicit operands, but implicit operands that are fetched from the EStack. For example, add expects two values on the EStack to be added.

- **Relative** getfield 3 *for fields of an object*
  The operand is the offset of an object field. The instruction expects the base address of the object on the EStack (see Fig. 6.12).

- **Indexed** aload *for elements of an array*
  The instruction expects as implicit operands the base address of an array and an index value on the EStack (see Fig. 6.12).

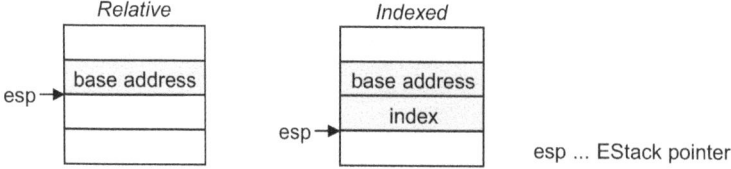

Fig. 6.12 EStack before executing an instruction with addressing mode Relative or Indexed

6.1 The MicroJava VM

The tables in the following sections show the instructions of the μJVM (second column) along with their instruction code (first column) and their effect (fourth column). The third column of the tables shows the contents of the EStack before and after the respective instruction. The format

    ..., val, val
    ..., val

means that the instruction fetches two values from the EStack and puts a new value on the EStack. The operands of the instructions have the following meanings:

    b   byte (8-bit, signed)
    s   short (16-bit, signed)
    w   word (32-bit, signed)

The push() and pop() operations refer to the EStack. local[b] means the local variable at address b in the current frame. and data[s] denotes the global variable at address s.

Loading and Storing Local Variables

The following instructions are available for accessing local variables:

1	load b	...	**Load local variable**
		..., val	push(local[b]);
2..5	load*n*	...	**Load local variable** (short form, n = 0..3)
		..., val	push(local[n]);
6	store b	..., val	**Store local variable**
		...	local[b] = pop();
7..10	store*n*	..., val	**Store local variable** (short form, n = 0..3)
		...	local[n] = pop();

Since most methods have only few local variables, low addresses are much more common than high addresses. Therefore, there are short forms of these instructions for the addresses 0 to 3 (load0, load1, load2, load3, store0, store1, store2, store3), which are encoded in a single byte. For higher addresses, the long form load b and store b must be used, where the address is encoded in an extra byte b. The long form therefore requires 2 bytes. Since the address of a local variable is encoded as a signed byte, up to 128 local variables can be addressed. Variables of type char are stored in the least significant byte of a word.

Loading and Storing Global Variables

The following instructions provide access to global variables:

11	getstatic s	...	**Load global variable**
		..., val	push(data[s]);
12	putstatic s	..., val	**Store global variable**
		...	data[s] = pop();

Since there are often more global variables than local ones, their address is encoded with two bytes.

Loading and Storing Object Fields

To access object fields, the following instructions are available:

13	getfield s	..., adr	**Load object field**
		..., val	adr = pop(); push(heap[adr+s]);
14	putfield s	..., adr, val	**Store object field**
		...	val = pop(); adr = pop();
			heap[adr+s] = val;

getfield and putfield expect the address of an object on the EStack, and putfield also expects the value to be stored. Figure 6.13 shows the translation of assignments between local and global variables as well as between object fields.

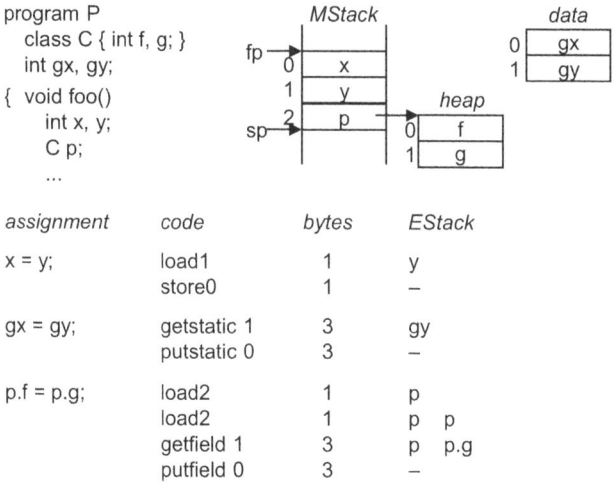

assignment	code	bytes	EStack
x = y;	load1	1	y
	store0	1	–
gx = gy;	getstatic 1	3	gy
	putstatic 0	3	–
p.f = p.g;	load2	1	p
	load2	1	p p
	getfield 1	3	p p.g
	putfield 0	3	–

Fig. 6.13 Examples of assignments between different kinds of variables

As you can see, an assignment between local variables takes only two bytes, while an assignment between global variables takes six bytes, and an assignment between object fields takes eight bytes. This is not uncommon and is a good reason for using local variables wherever possible.

Loading Constants

The following instructions are available for loading constants:

15..20	const$n$	...	**Load constant** (short form, n = 0..5)
		..., val	push(n);
21	const_m1	...	**Load minus one** (short form)
		..., -1	push(-1);
22	const w	...	**Load constant**
		..., val	push(w);

To load small constants (in the range 0–5), there are again short forms const0 to const5, which are encoded in a single byte, while to load large constants, the long form const w

6.1 The MicroJava VM

must be used, which takes 5 bytes. Since the constant −1 also occurs frequently, there is a short form const_m1 for loading the value −1.

Arithmetic

For arithmetic operations and shifts, there are the following instructions:

23	add	..., val1, val2 ..., val1+val2	**Add** push(pop() + pop());
24	sub	..., val1, val2 ..., val1-val2	**Subtract** push(-pop() + pop());
25	mul	..., val1, val2 ..., val1*val2	**Multiply** push(pop() * pop());
26	div	..., val1, val2 ..., val1/val2	**Divide** x = pop(); push(pop() / x);
27	rem	..., val1, val2 ..., val1%val2	**Remainder** x = pop(); push(pop() % x);
28	neg	..., val ..., − val	**Negate** push(-pop());
29	shl	..., val, x ..., val1	**Shift left** x = pop(); push(pop() << x);
30	shr	..., val, x ..., val1	**Shift right** (arithmetically) x = pop(); push(pop() >> x);
31	inc b1, b2	... ...	**Increment local variable** local[b1] = local[b1] + b2;

The instruction inc b1, b2 is used to increment a local variable (e.g., in x++;). The byte b2 is regarded as a signed value, which also allows decrement (x--;). Figure 6.14 shows some examples of arithmetic operations and their translation into bytecode.

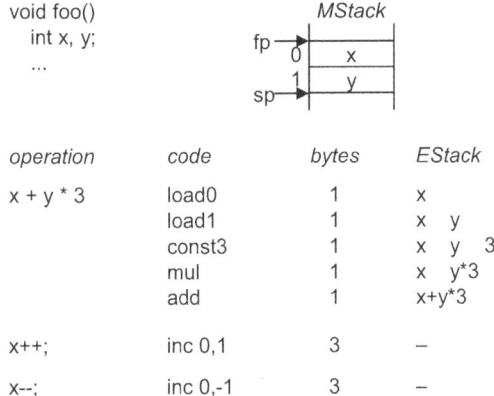

Fig. 6.14 Examples of arithmetic operations

Object Allocation

In MicroJava, there are objects of classes and arrays. They are allocated with the following instructions:

32	new s	..., adr	**New class object**
			allocate area of s words;
			initialize area to all 0;
			push(adr(area));
33	newarray b	..., len	**New array object**
		..., adr	len = pop();
			if (b==0)
			allocate array with len bytes (+ length word);
			else if (b==1)
			allocate array with len words (+ length word);
			initialize array to all 0;
			store len as the first word of the array object;
			push(adr(array));

When allocating a class object (new s), the desired size is given in words. When allocating an array object (newarray b), a switch b is provided to specify whether a word array or a byte array should be created. The length of the array is not encoded as an explicit operand of the instruction, but must be loaded onto the EStack beforehand, since the array length is often an expression whose value is not known at compile time. The array length is stored in the first word of the new array object and is used by the MicroJava VM for index checks on array accesses. Figure 6.15 shows examples of allocating class and array objects, both for word arrays and byte arrays.

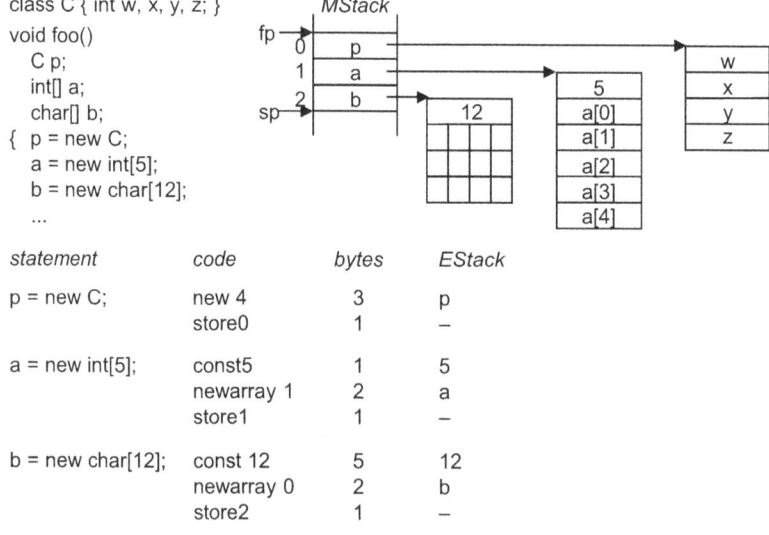

Fig. 6.15 Examples of allocating class and array objects

Array Access

To access arrays, the following instructions are available:

34	aload	..., adr, index	**Load array element**
		..., val	i = pop(); adr = pop();
			push(heap[adr+1+i]);
35	astore	..., adr, index, val	**Store array element**
		...	val = pop(); i = pop(); adr = pop();
			heap[adr+1+i] = val;
36	baload	..., adr, index	**Load byte array element**
		..., val	i = pop(); adr = pop();
			x = heap[adr+1+i/4];
			push(byte i%4 of x);
37	bastore	..., adr, index, val	**Store byte array element**
		...	val = pop(); i = pop(); adr = pop();
			x = heap[adr+1+i/4];
			set byte i%4 in x to val;
			heap[adr+1+i/4] = x;
38	arraylength	..., adr	**Get array length**
		..., len	adr = pop();
			push(heap[adr]);

The instructions aload and astore access elements of word arrays, while baload and bastore access elements of byte arrays. They expect the base address of the array and an index on the EStack, astore and bastore also expect the value to be stored. The index check is performed by the μJVM at run time based on the stored array length. The instruction arraylength returns the length of an array. Figure 6.16 shows an example of array accesses.

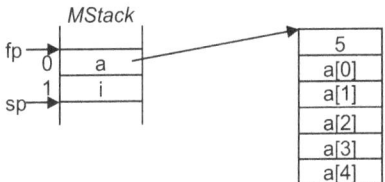

statement	code	bytes	EStack
a[i] = a[i+1];	load0	1	a
	load1	1	a i
	load0	1	a i a
	load1	1	a i a i
	const1	1	a i a i 1
	add	1	a i a i+1
	aload	1	a i a[i+1]
	astore	1	–

Fig. 6.16 Example of array accesses

As you can see, it is important that the operands of the instructions are loaded onto the EStack in the correct order. What looks like "magic" here will later turn out to be quite simple and systematic when we discuss code generation for array accesses in detail.

Expression Stack Manipulation

The following instructions manipulate the contents of the EStack:

39	pop	..., val	**Remove topmost stack element**
		...	dummy = pop();
40	dup	..., val	**Duplicate topmost stack element**
		..., val, val	x = pop(); push(x); push(x);
41	dup2	..., v1, v2	**Duplicate top two stack elements**
		..., v1, v2, v1, v2	y = pop(); x = pop();
			push(x); push(y); push(x); push(y);

The pop instruction is used, for example, to remove the return value of a function method from the EStack in case it is not used. An example of using dup2 is shown in Fig. 6.17 (variables are like in Fig. 6.16).

statement	code	bytes	EStack			
a[i]++;	load0	1	a			
	load1	1	a	i		
	dup2	1	a	i	a	i
	aload	1	a	i	a[i]	
	const1	1	a	i	a[i]	1
	add	1	a	i	a[i]+1	
	astore	1	–			

Fig. 6.17 Example of using dup2

Jumps

As on every computer, there are conditional and unconditional jumps for the μJVM, which are expressed by the following instructions:

42	jmp s		**Jump unconditionally**
			pc = pc + s;
43..48	j<cond> s	..., val1, val2	**Jump conditionally** (cond = eq, ne, lt, le, gt, ge)
		...	y = pop(); x = pop();
			if (x cond y) pc = pc + s;

An *unconditional jump* is always taken, whereas a *conditional jump* only happens if a previously evaluated condition is true. There are six variants of conditional jumps:

jeq	jump on equal
jne	jump on not equal
jlt	jump on less than
jle	jump on less or equal
jgt	jump on greater than
jge	jump on greater or equal

A conditional jump instruction expects two values on the EStack, which it compares according to its condition, and jumps when the condition is true. The jump distances for all jumps are relative to the program counter pc (i.e., to the start of the jump instruction) and can be positive or negative. Thus, forward and backward jumps are possible.

6.1 The MicroJava VM

Figure 6.18 shows an example of a conditional jump in an if statement. If the condition of the if statement is false, the program jumps over the if branch, otherwise the if branch is entered. We will take a closer look at this in Sect. 6.8.2. In this example, x and y are local variables at addresses 0 and 1.

statement	code	bytes	EStack	
if (x > y) y = x;	load0	1	x	
	load1	1	x	y
	jle 5	3	–	
	load0	1	x	
	store1	1	–	

Fig. 6.18 Example of a conditional jump (jump distance = 5 bytes relative to the jump)

Method Calls

The following instructions are used for calling and returning from methods, as well as for allocating and releasing the stack frame for the local variables of the invoked method. The operations PUSH() and POP() refer to the MStack, while push() and pop() refer to the EStack.

49	call s		**Call method**
			PUSH(pc+3); // return address
			pc = pc + s;
50	return		**Return**
			pc = POP();
51	enter b1, b2	..., params	**Enter method**
		...	psize = b1; lsize = b2; // in words
			PUSH(fp); fp = sp; sp = sp + lsize;
			initialize frame to 0;
			for (i = psize-1; i >= 0; i--) local[i] = pop();
52	exit		**Exit method**
			sp = fp; fp = POP();

The functionality of these instructions is somewhat complex and is therefore illustrated in Fig. 6.19.

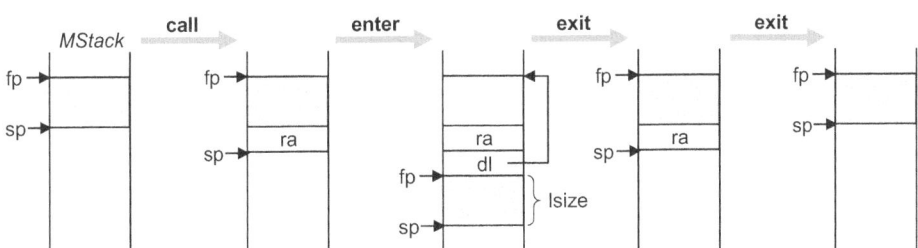

Fig. 6.19 Method call and allocation of a new stack frame for local variables

When calling a method, the caller executes a call instruction, which pushes the return address ra (= pc + 3) onto the MStack and jumps to the called method. The jump distance is relative to the start of the call instruction and can be positive or negative.

The first instruction of each method is enter. It pushes a pointer to the caller's stack frame onto the MStack. The µJVM uses this pointer, which is called the *dynamic link* (dl), to find its way back to the caller's frame when the method returns. Then fp is set to the end of the MStack and sp is incremented by the number of variables of the called method (lsize). This creates a new stack frame for the local variables of the callee. The content of the frame is cleared and any parameters (psize) are copied from the EStack to the beginning of the frame (see Sect. 6.9).

At the end of a method, exit is called, which releases the frame of the method and—following the dynamic link—sets fp back to the frame of the caller. Thus, the state before the execution of enter is restored.

The last instruction of a method is return. It fetches the return address via POP() and jumps back to this address, i.e., to the point after the call instruction. The MStack is now back in the same state as it was before the call instruction was executed.

Input/Output

The µJVM supports the input and output of integers and characters on the console. To this end, it offers the following instructions:

53	read	...	**Read integer**
		..., val	readInt(x); push(x);
54	print	..., val, width	**Print integer**
		...	width = pop(); writeInt(pop(), width);
55	bread	...	**Read character**
		..., val	readChar(ch); push(ch);
56	bprint	..., val, width	**Print character**
		...	width = pop(); writeChar(pop(), width);

The instructions print and bprint expect the value to be printed as well as a field width on the EStack. The value is output right-aligned with this field width on the console. If the field width is too small, the value is output with the minimum required field width.

Run-time Errors

The following instruction reports a run-time error and then aborts the program:

57	trap b		**Generate run time error**
			print error message depending on b;
			abort execution;

In MicroJava programs, there is only one place where a trap instruction is generated, namely when a function method reaches its end without having returned a value by means of a return statement.

Example

To conclude this section, we will look at a complete method and the code generated for it (Fig. 6.20). The method has four local variables that are located at addresses 0 to 3 in its frame. At the beginning of the method, this frame is allocated with a length of four words using the enter instruction. Since the method has no parameters, the first operand of the

6.2 Code Buffer

enter instruction is 0. As you can see, the if and while statements are translated into jumps. How the individual instructions are generated is then the subject of the following sections.

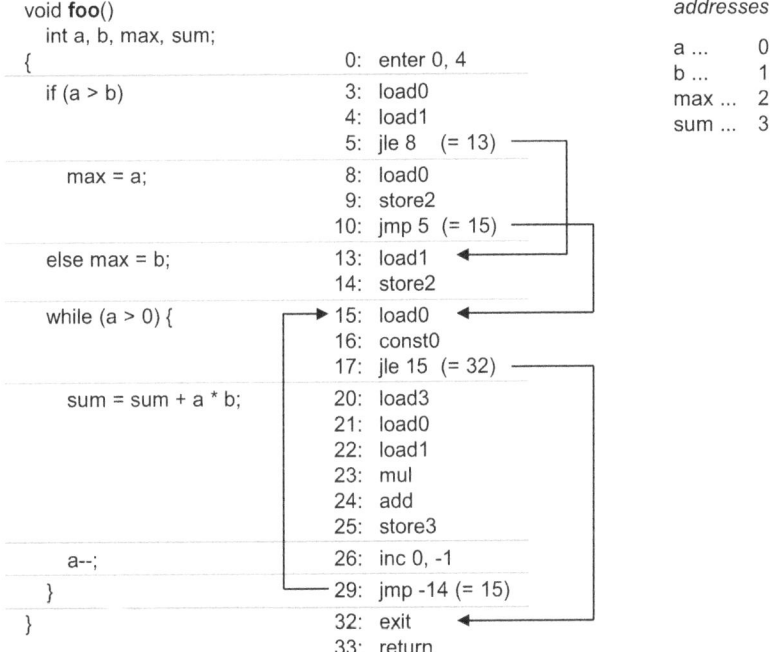

Fig. 6.20 Example of a method and the code generated for it

6.2 Code Buffer

The instructions generated by the compiler are not immediately written to a file, but to a code buffer, since some jump instructions still have to be patched later with the correct jump distances.

The code buffer is a byte array in the code generator (class Code). The variable pc points to the next free location in the code buffer. To emit the instructions, there are the methods put(), put2() and put4(), which append 1, 2 or 4 bytes to the code buffer.

```
class Code {
    static final int // instruction codes
        load = 1, load0 = 2, load1 = 3, load2 = 4, load3 = 5,
        store = 6, store0 = 7, store1 = 8, store2 = 9, store3 = 10,
        getstatic = 11, putstatic = 12, ...;
    private static byte[]  code = new byte[10000]; // code buffer
    public static int   pc = 0;
    public static void put (int x) { code[pc++] = (byte) x; }
    public static void put2 (int x) { put(x >> 8); put(x); }
    public static void put4 (int x) { put2(x >> 16); put2(x); }
    ...
}
```

Due to the simple instruction format of the μJVM, emitting the instructions is also simple. For example, the instructions load0, store 7, getstatic 2 and const 10 can be emitted as follows:

```
Code.put(Code.load0);                              // load0
Code.put(Code.store); Code.put(7);                 // store 7
Code.put(Code.getstatic); Code.put2(2);            // getstatic 2
Code.put(const); Code.put4(10);                    // const 10
```

6.3 Operands of Code Generation

We now come to the actual code generation and start with a concept that is essential to a systematic approach: the *operand descriptors*. If we want to generate code for a specific operation, we need certain information about its operands. For example, to add two values, the general code pattern is:

> ... load operand 1 ...
> ... load operand 2 ...
> add

But what instructions should be generated to load the operands? Of course, this depends on the kinds of operands; for different operand kinds different load instructions will be needed:

operand kind	required load instruction
constant c	const c
local variable at address a	load a
global variable at address a	getstatic a
field at offset a	getfield a
array element	aload
value on the EStack	– (nothing)
function method at address a	call a

So a descriptor is needed to tell us the kind of operand (and thus its addressing mode) as well as other information such as its address (for variables), its value (for constants), and so on. The following list shows the information needed for each kind of operand (see also the description of the addressing modes in Sect. 6.1.2):

operand kind	denoted by	required information
constant	Con	constant value
local variable	Local	address in the stack frame
global variable	Static	address in data
field	Fld	offset relative to the start of the object
array element	Elem	– (information is on the EStack)
value on the EStack	Stack	– (information is on the EStack)
method	Meth	address in the code, method object

6.3 Operands of Code Generation

This information is defined in a class Operand:

```
class Operand {
    static final int     // operand kinds
        Con = 0, Local = 1, Static = 2, Stack = 3, Fld = 4, Elem = 5, Meth = 6;
    int     kind;        // Con, Local, Static, Stack, Fld, Elem, Meth
    Struct  type;        // type of the operand
    int     val;         // for Con: constant value
    int     adr;         // for Local, Static, Fld, Meth: address
    Obj     obj;         // for Meth: method object with formal parameters
}
```

As with the symbol table in Chap. 5, individual fields are only used for certain kinds of operands: for example, val is only used for constants, obj only for methods.

Operand descriptors usually obtain their data from objects in the symbol table. When the compiler sees a name in the program, it looks it up in the symbol table and creates an operand descriptor from the found object node using the following constructor.

```
public Operand (Obj obj) {
    type = obj.type; val = obj.val; adr = obj.adr;
    switch (obj.kind) {
        case Obj.Con:   kind = Con; break;
        case Obj.Var:   if (obj.level == 0) kind = Static; else kind = Local; break;
        case Obj.Meth:  kind = Meth; this.obj = obj; break;
        case Obj.Type:  error("a type is not a valid operand"); break;
        case Obj.Prog:  error("the program cannot be used as an operand"); break;
    }
}
```

There is another constructor that can be used to create an operand descriptor from an integer constant:

```
public Operand (int val) {
    kind = Con; type = Tab.intType; this.val = val;
}
```

If operand descriptors are created from object nodes anyway, why cannot we just use object nodes instead of operand descriptors? There are two reasons for this: Firstly, operands can also represent designators such as a[i] or x.f and not just simple names as stored in the symbol table; Secondly, operands describe items whose location can change during code generation. For example, a local variable is initially located on the MStack. After it has been loaded, however, it is on the EStack. So the location has changed, which is expressed by a changed operand descriptor (see Fig. 6.21). Object nodes in the symbol table, on the other hand, never change.

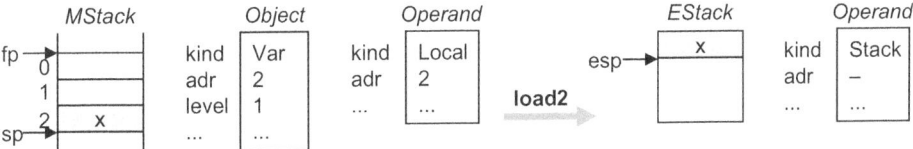

Fig. 6.21 Variable x on the MStack and after loading it onto the EStack

Operand descriptors are created during code generation and describe the kind and location of operands. Most parser methods return an operand descriptor as a result of their translation. This descriptor is then used for code generation in the caller of the parser method and may lead to a new operand descriptor that is again returned by the corresponding parser method. Figure 6.22 shows the call hierarchy of parser methods and the operand descriptors they return for the assignment

x = y + z * 3;

where x, y, and z are local variables at the addresses 0, 1, and 2.

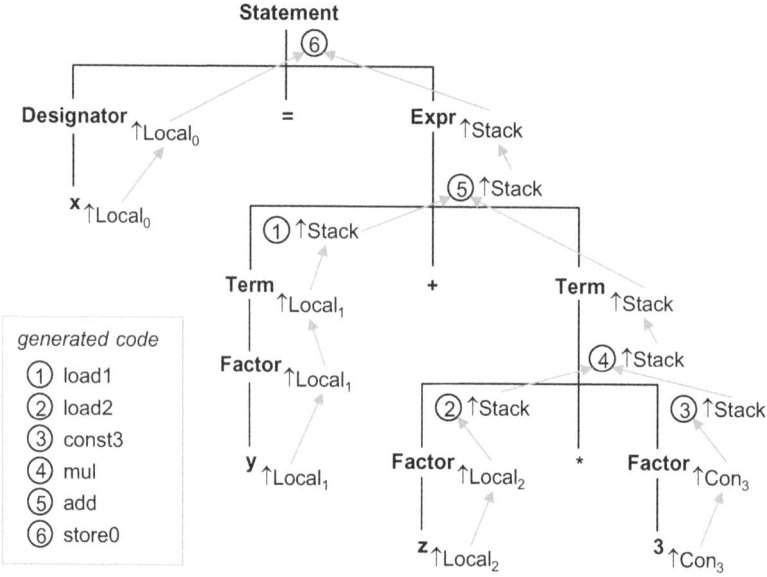

Fig. 6.22 Call hierarchy of parser methods and the operands they return

Statement calls Designator, which recognizes the name x, looks it up in the symbol table, and converts the found object into an operand descriptor of kind Local with the address 0 (Local0). This operand is returned by Designator. The parser then continues, recognizes "=", calls Expr, and then Term and Factor. Factor recognizes the name y and creates an operand descriptor Local1, which is returned by Factor and Term. Before the parser continues, it generates the instruction load1 at the location ① to load the operand Local1 onto the EStack, and changes its operand kind to Stack.

Now the parser recognizes "+", calls Term, and this calls Factor. Factor recognizes the name z and creates an operand descriptor Local2 for it. Before the parser continues, it generates the instruction load2 at location ② to load the operand Local2 onto the EStack, again creating a Stack operand. Then it recognizes "*" and calls Factor. Factor detects the constant 3 and creates an operand descriptor Con3 for it, which is loaded onto the EStack at the location ③ using const3.

Both factors are now on the EStack, so that they can be multiplied by mul at the position ④. The result of the multiplication is on the EStack, so Term returns an operand of kind Stack. Both terms are now on the EStack, so that they can be added at the location ⑤ using add. The result of the addition is again on the EStack, so Expr returns an operand of kind Stack. Since Designator has provided an operand Local0, the compiler knows that it has to assign the value on the EStack to the local variable at the address 0 via store0 at the location ⑥.

As you can see, the operand descriptors provide the compiler with all the information it needs to generate the appropriate instructions. This is the general principle of code generation, which we will use in the sections that follow.

6.4 Loading Values

Before values can be processed by the µJVM, they must be loaded onto the EStack. The following method load() from the class Code takes an operand of arbitrary kind and generates an instruction to load it onto the EStack.

```
public static void load (Operand x) { // in class Code
    switch (x.kind) {
        case Operand.Con:
            if (0 <= x.val && x.val <= 5) put(const0 + x.val);
            else if (x.val == -1) put(const_m1);
            else { put(const); put4(x.val); }
            break;
        case Operand.Static:
            put(getstatic); put2(x.adr);
            break;
        case Operand.Local:
            if (0 <= x.adr && x.adr <= 3) put(load0 + x.adr);
            else { put(load); put(x.adr); }
            break;
        case Operand.Fld: // assert: object base address is on the EStack
            put(getfield); put2(x.adr);
            break;
        case Operand.Elem: // assert: array base address and index are on the EStack
            if (x.type ==Tab.charType) put(baload); else put(aload);
            break;
        case Operand.Stack: break; // nothing (already loaded)
        case Operand.Meth: error("cannot load a method");
    }
    x.kind = Operand.Stack; // the operand has been loaded and is now on the EStack
}
```

It is typical for code generation that instruction selection leads to numerous case distinctions. For example, the load() method makes a first choice according to the kind of the operand. If it is a constant, the method has further choices between constants in the range

0–5, which can be loaded by a short form (const0 to const5), the constant −1, for which there is the special load instruction const_m1, and other constants that are loaded by the long form (const w). The situation is similar for the other kinds of operands. Note that no code is generated for operands of kind Stack because they are already loaded. At the end of the load() method, the operand is considered to be loaded, so its kind is set to Stack.

The load() method is very helpful. We can now use it to load operands of any kind without having to worry about the details of the necessary load instructions.

6.4.1 Loading Variables

Variables occur in expressions, more specifically in factors. So let's take a look at an attributed grammar of Factor to see how variables are loaded.

```
Factor <↑x>       (. String name; .)
=  ident <↑name>  (. Obj obj = Tab.find(name);        // obj.kind = Var | Con
                     Operand x = new Operand(obj);    // x.kind = Local | Static | Con
                     Code.load(x); .)                 // x.kind = Stack
|  ... .
```

The name is looked up in the symbol table and its object node obj is converted into an operand x, which is then loaded. Figure 6.23 shows this using a local variable v at address 2 as an example.

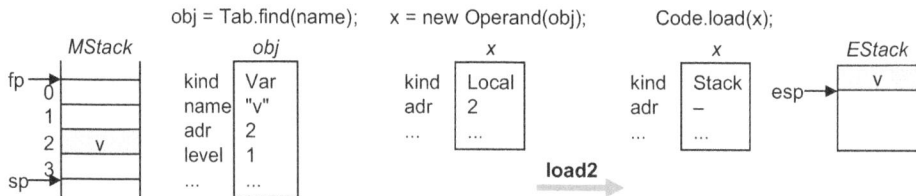

Fig. 6.23 Loading a variable

6.4.2 Loading Constants

Like variables, constants occur in the production Factor. Let's look at how constants are loaded there.

```
Factor <↑x>       (. int val;.)
=  ...
|  number <↑val>  (. Operand x = new Operand(val);    // x.kind = Con
                     Code.load(x); .) .                // x.kind = Stack
```

The number's value val is converted to an operand, which is then loaded. Figure 6.24 visualizes this process.

6.4 Loading Values

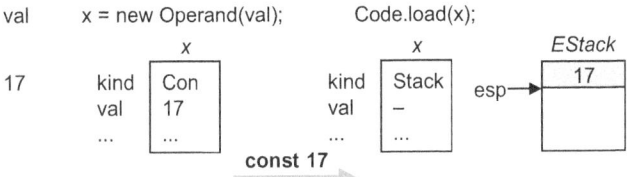

Fig. 6.24 Loading a constant

6.4.3 Loading Object Fields

Accesses to object fields such as var.f are described in the production of Designator. To load such fields, we first need to check the corresponding context conditions (see Appendix A):

Designator$_0$ = Designator$_1$ "." ident.
- The type of Designator$_1$ must be a class. (context condition 1)
- ident must be a field of Designator$_1$. (context condition 2)

Again, we describe the loading process with an attributed grammar.

```
Designator <↑x>         (. String name, fname; .)
= ident <↑name>          (. Obj obj = Tab.find(name);
                            Operand x = new Operand(obj); .)
{ "." ident <↑fname>     (. if (x.type.kind == Struct.Class) { // context condition 1
                                Code.load(x);
                                Obj fld = Tab.findField(fname, x.type); // checks also cc 2
                                x.kind = Operand.Fld; // change operand to kind Fld
                                x.adr = fld.adr;
                                x.type = fld.type;
                            } else error(name + " is not an object"); .)
| ...
}.
```

For the designator var.f, the name var is looked up in the symbol table and converted to an operand x. If a field name (e.g., .f) follows, we first have to check that the type of var is a class (context condition 1). Then var is loaded, because the base address of the object must be on the EStack before the field is loaded later. Then the field name is looked up in var's class using Tab.findField(), which returns the corresponding object node fld. The method findField() is similar to find(), but only searches in the fields of the specified type. If the field is not found, findField() reports an error. This corresponds to the check of the second context condition.

Finally, the operand descriptor x is set to be of kind Fld; its address and type are taken from the object node fld. If errors are detected and reported, it doesn't matter what code is generated. It will be discarded later anyway.

Now further field accesses could follow (e.g., var.f.g). In that case, the process would be repeated as described in the attributed grammar. If no further field accesses follow, Designator returns the Fld operand x as its result. If x were to be loaded later, a getfield instruction would be generated. Note that the base address of the object is already on the EStack in preparation for this. Figure 6.25 visualizes the loading of object fields and shows the sequence of operand descriptors created in the process.

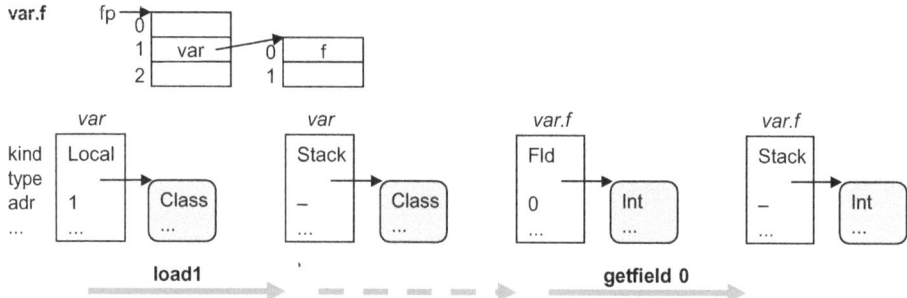

Fig. 6.25 Loading an object field—sequence of operand descriptors

6.4.4 Loading Array Elements

Next, we look at loading an array element a[i]. There are again context conditions to be checked (see also Appendix A):

Designator$_0$ = Designator$_1$ "[" Expr "]".
- The type of Designator$_1$ must be an array. (cc 1)
- The type of Expr must be int. (cc 2)

We describe the process by an attributed grammar:

```
Designator <↑x>      (. String name; Operand x, y; .)
= ident <↑name>      (. Obj obj = Tab.find(name); Operand x = new Operand(obj); .)
    { ...
    | "["            (. Code.load(x); // array address
                        if (x.type.kind != Struct.Arr) error(name + " is not an array"); .) // cc 1
      Expr <↑y>      (. if (y.type != Tab.intType) error("index must be of type int"); // cc 2
                        Code.load(y); // index
                        x.kind = Operand.Elem; // change operand kind to Elem
                        x.type = x.type.elemType; .)
      "]"
    }.
```

The array name a is looked up in the symbol table and converted to an operand x. If an index bracket follows, x is loaded, since the address of the array must be on the EStack for array accesses. We also check that x represents an array (context condition 1). The index expression returns an operand y, the type of which must be int (context condition 2). The index is then also loaded. The address of the array and the index are now on the EStack. The kind of x is set to Elem, and the type of x is set to the element type of the array. If x were to be loaded later, an aload or a baload instruction would be generated.

6.4 Loading Values

Figure 6.26 visualizes this process and shows the sequence of operand descriptors that are created.

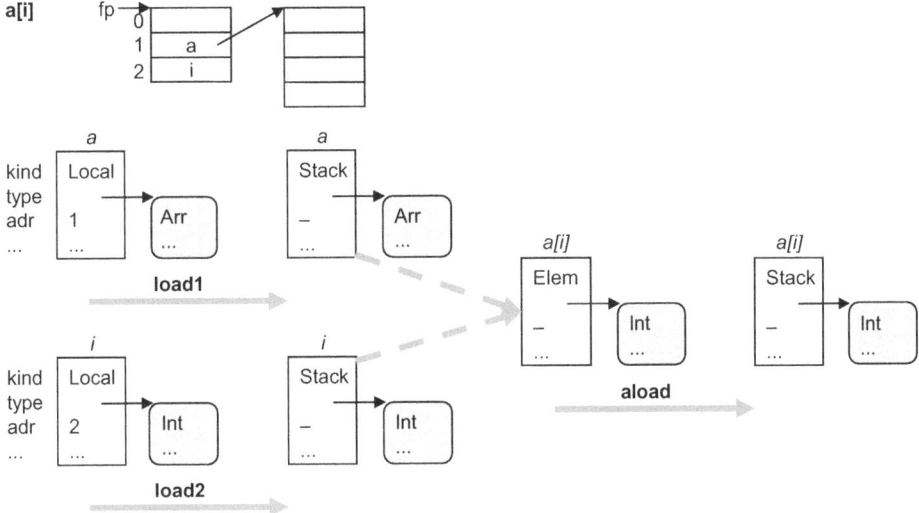

Fig. 6.26 Loading an array element—sequence of operand descriptors

Of course, array and field accesses can also be combined for example as in a[i].f, provided that a[i] points to an object with a field f. Figure 6.27 shows the operand descriptors that arise in this process (in an alternative way of visualization).

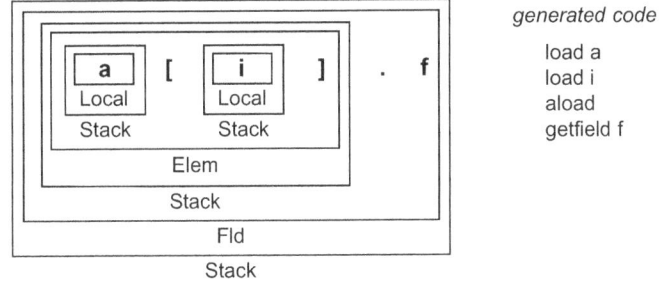

Fig. 6.27 Operand descriptors for loading a[i].f

The variable a is represented by an operand of kind Local, which is loaded onto the EStack (load a) and thus becomes a Stack operand. The same happens to i (load i). The two Stack operands are then combined to form an Elem operand, which is also loaded (aload) and thus becomes a Stack operand. This is the base address of an object. Together with the field f it is turned into a Fld operand, which is eventually loaded as well (getfield f).

6.5 Expressions

Now that we can load simple and structured variables as well as constants, let's turn to code generation for arithmetic expressions. On a stack machine such as the µJVM, the operands of an expression must always be loaded before generating the instruction for the operator. For example, the pattern for calculating x + y is:

```
... load x ...
... load y ...
add
```

Expressions are described by the Expr production, for which the following context conditions must be checked:

Expr = "–" Term.
- Term must be of type int. (context condition 1).

Expr$_0$ = Expr$_1$ AddOp Term.
- Expr1 and Term must both be of type int. (context condition 2)

Code generation for Expr is described by the following attributed grammar:

```
Expr <↑x>           (. Operand x, y; int op; .)
= (   Term <↑x>
    | "-" Term <↑x> (. if (x.type != Tab.intType) // context condition 1
                          error("operand must be of type int");
                       if (x.kind == Operand.Con) x.val = – x.val;
                       else {
                          Code.load(x); Code.put(neg);
                       } .)
  )
  {   ( "+"         (. op = Code.add; .)
      | "-"         (. op = Code.sub; .)
      )             (. Code.load(x); .)  // load first operand
      Term <↑y>     (. Code.load(y);     // load second operand
                       if (x.type != Tab.intType || y.type != Tab.intType) // context condition 2
                          error("operands must be of type int");
                       Code.put(op); .)
  } .
```

The two terms provide the operands x and y. If there is a "–" in front of the first term, the term must be negated. If the term is a constant, the negation can be done at compile time, otherwise the operand x must be loaded and negated by a neg instruction. This is one of the few optimizations we do in the MicroJava compiler.

The first term can be followed by other terms combined by the operators "+" or "–". We remember the instruction (add or sub) that must be emitted later for the operator and store it in the variable op. Before the second term is parsed, the first term must be loaded, because we have to put the terms onto the EStack in the right order. So the first term must be loaded before code is possibly generated during the parsing of the second term. Finally, we also load the second term y and emit the remembered instruction for the operator.

6.5 Expressions

Next, let's look at code generation for terms. Again, there is a context condition:

Term$_0$ = Term$_1$ MulOp Factor.
- Term1 and Factor must both be of type int.

Code generation for Term is described by the following attributed grammar:

```
Term <↑x>              (. Operand x, y; int op; .)
= Factor <↑x>
  { ( "*"              (. op = Code.mul; .)
    | "/"              (. op = Code.div; .)
    | "%"              (. op = Code.rem; .)
    )                  (. Code.load(x); .)
    Factor <↑y>        (. Code.load(y);
                          if (x.type != Tab.intType || y.type != Tab.intType) // context condition
                             error("operands must be of type int"); Code.put(op); .)
  }.
```

The processing is similar to that of Expr. The two factors provide the operands x and y, which are loaded onto the EStack. We keep the instruction (mul, div or rem) to be emitted for the operator in the variable op and emit it after loading the second factor.

The only thing missing now is the code generation for factors. For the time being, we will ignore function calls, which are also factors and are discussed in Sect. 6.9. The following context conditions must be checked:

Factor = "new" ident.
- ident must denote a class. (cc 1)

Factor = "new" ident "[" Expr "]".
- ident must denote a type. (cc 2)
- The type of Expr must be int. (cc 3)

The attributed grammar then looks as follows:

```
Factor <↑x>            (. Operand x; int val; String name; Struct type; .)
= Designator <↑x>      // for function calls see later
| number <↑val>        (. x = new Operand(val); .)
| charCon <↑val>       (. x = new Operand(val); x.type = Tab.charType; .)
| "(" Expr <↑x> ")"
| "new" ident <↑name>  (. Obj obj = Tab.find(name); type = obj.type; .)
  ( "[" Expr <↑x> "]"  (. if (obj.kind != Obj.Type) error ("type expected"); // cc 2
                          if (x.type != Tab.intType)
                             error("array size must be of type int"); // cc 3
                          Code.load(x); // array length
                          Code.put(Code.newarray);
                          if (type = Tab.charType) Code.put(0); else Code.put(1);
                          type = new Struct(Struct.Arr, type); .)
  |                    (. if (obj.kind != Obj.Type || type.kind != Struct.Class) // cc 1
                             error("class type expected")
                          Code.put(Code.new_); Code.put2(type.nFields); .)
  )                    (. x = new Operand(); x.kind = Operand.Stack; x.type = type; .) .
```

This grammar is a bit more complicated than the previous ones. But first, let's take a look at the first four alternatives, which are still simple: Designator returns an operand of the kind Local, Static, Fld or Elem. For field and array accesses, code has already been generated in Designator. number and charCon return a constant value val that is converted to an operand. Expr also returns an operand. The operand resulting from these four alternatives is simply returned by Factor.

Now for the fifth alternative, which describes the allocation of array and class objects. The name in new ident is looked up in the symbol table, and its type is stored in the variable type. This can be followed by either a length expression or nothing.

If a length expression follows, this is the allocation of an array object. We have to check whether ident denotes a type (cc 2) and whether the specified array length is of type int (cc 3). The array length is then loaded, and newarray 0 or newarray 1 is emitted, depending on whether it is a byte array or a word array. The type of the allocated object is changed from type to "Arr of type".

If no length expression follows, this is the allocation of a class object. We have to check whether ident denotes not only a type, but also a class type (cc 1). Then, the instruction new is emitted, where the number of words to be allocated is taken from type.nFields.

In both cases, a new Stack operand with the appropriate type is created and returned by Factor.

We will now look at a summarizing example that shows the calls of parser methods during code generation for the expression var.f + 2 * var.g as well as the resulting operand descriptors (Fig. 6.28).

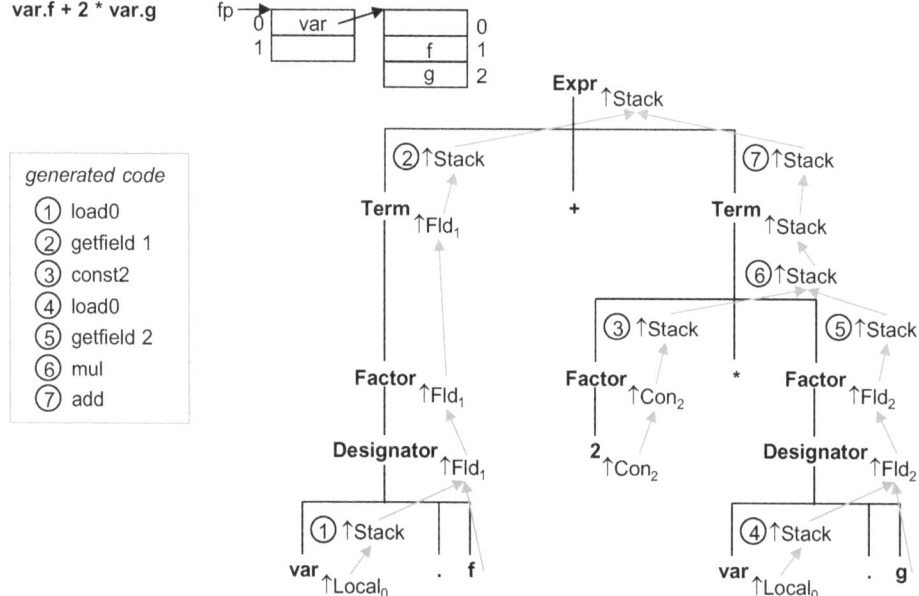

Fig. 6.28 Parser methods and operands when translating an expression

6.6 Assignments

Expr calls Term, Factor, and Designator, where var is recognized and made into a Local0 operand. This is loaded at the location ① because the address of the object must be on the EStack for the subsequent field access. The field f is looked up in var's class, and a Fld_1 operand is created (f has the offset 1), which is returned by Designator, Factor, and Term. Before proceeding with the operator "+" in Expr, the first term must be loaded at the location ②.

Now the second term is processed. Factor detects the constant 2 and turns it into a Con_2 operand, which is returned by Factor. Before Term proceeds with the operator "*", the first factor must be loaded at the location ③. Then the second factor is processed, which provides a Fld_2 operand for var.g similar to before. This is now also loaded (location ⑤). Since both factors are now on the EStack, a mul instruction is generated at the location ⑥. The result of the multiplication is on the EStack and is returned by Term as a Stack operand. At location ⑦, the two terms on the EStack are added using add, and Expr returns a Stack operand as the result of the addition.

Figure 6.28 also shows the code generated at each location. As can be seen from the example, code generation is carried out quite systematically in the parser methods, with the operand descriptors containing all the information required to generate the corresponding instructions.

6.6 Assignments

Next, we will turn to code generation for statements and start with the simplest kind of statement, namely assignments. Assignments have the form

   designator = expr;

Depending on the kind of the designator on the left-hand side (a local or global variable, an object field, or an array element), different instructions must be generated (Fig. 6.29).

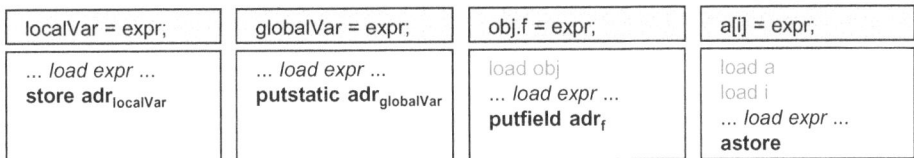

Fig. 6.29 Code variants for assignments depending on their left-hand side

In each of the four cases, the expression on the right-hand side of the assignment must first be loaded onto the EStack. Then, depending on the kind of the left-hand side, a store, putstatic, putfield, or astore instruction must be emitted. The shaded load instructions in the last two cases of Fig. 6.29 are already generated by Designator (see Sect. 6.4). Context conditions must also be checked:

Statement = Designator "=" Expr ";".
- Designator must denote variable, an array element, or an object field. (cc 1)
- The type of Expr must be *assignment compatible* with the type of Designator. (cc 2)

The following attributed grammar describes the translation of assignments:

```
Statement              (. Operand x, y; .)
= Designator <↑x>      // may already generate code
  "=" Expr <↑y>        (. Code.load(y);
                          if (y.type.assignableTo(x.type)) // cc 1
                              Code.assignTo(x); // x: Local | Static | Fld | Elem
                          else error("incompatible types in assignment"); .)
  ";" .
```

Assignment compatibility (cc 2) is checked in assignableTo() (see Sect. 5.4). The check of the first context condition and the generation of the appropriate assignment instruction occurs in the assignTo() method, which looks as follows:

```
public static void assignTo (Operand x) {
  // x denotes the left-hand side of an assignment; the right-hand side has already been loaded
  switch (x.kind) {
    case Operand.Local:
      if (x.adr <= 3) put(store0 + x.adr) else { put(store); put(x.adr); }
      break;
    case Operand.Static:
      put(putstatic); put2(x.adr);
      break;
    case Operand.Fld: // the base address of the object is already loaded
      put(putfield); put2(x.adr);
      break;
    case Operand.Elem: // the array address and the index are already loaded
      if (x.type == Tab.charType) put(bastore); else put(astore);
      break;
    default:
      error("invalid left-hand side in assignment");
  }
}
```

6.6.1 Increment and Decrement Statements

The increment statement x++; and the decrement statement x-- ; are a special form of assignment, as they correspond to the long forms x = x + 1; or x = x -1;. Again, there are context conditions to be checked:

Statement = Designator ("++" | "--") ";".
- Designator must denote variable, an array element, or an object field. (cc 1)
- Designator must be of type int. (cc 2)

The translation is as follows:

IncDecStatement	(. Operand x, y; .)
= Designator <↑x>	(. if (x.type != Tab.intType) error("type int expected"); // cc 2
	if (x.kind == Operand.Fld) Code.put(Code.dup);
	else if (x.kind == Operand.Elem) Code.put(Code.dup2);
	y = (Operand) x.clone();
	Code.load(y);
	Code.put(Code.const1); .)
("++"	(. Code.put(Code.add); .)
| "--"	(. Code.put(Code.sub); .)
)	(. Code.assignTo(x); .) // checks also cc1
";" .	

If Designator is an object field or an array element, parts of its address have already been loaded onto the EStack in Designator. These parts are now duplicated using dup or dup2. Then the duplicate is loaded and finally the value 1 is added or subtracted before the result is assigned to the designator using assignTo().

The statement a[i]++; would lead to the following code (a and i are local variables at addresses 0 and 1):

```
              EStack
load0         a
load1         a i
dup2          a i a i
aload         a i a[i]
const1        a i a[i] 1
add           a i a[i]+1
astore        –
```

Note that the above implementation did not make use of the µJVM's inc instruction, which can only be applied to local variables. However, this can easily be built in and is left as an exercise.

6.7 Jumps and Labels

Before we look at control flow structures such as if and while statements, we need to think about how we are going to implement jumps and labels. Like every machine, the µJVM has *unconditional jumps*, which always happen

    jmp offset

and *conditional jumps*, which only happen if a previously evaluated condition is true, for example:

    ... load operand1 ...
    ... load operand2 ...
    jeq offset   // if (operand1 == operand2) jmp offset

As mentioned above, there are six kinds of conditional jumps, which correspond to the six possible comparison operators (Fig. 6.30).

comparison operators (in class Code)	conditional jumps	

static final int
  eq = 0,
  ne = 1,
  lt = 2,
  le = 3,
  gt = 4,
  ge = 5;
	jeq
	jne
	jlt
	jle
	jgt
	jge
		jump on equal
		jump on not equal
		jump on less than
		jump on less or equal
		jump on greater than
		jump on greater or equal

Fig. 6.30 Comparison operators and conditional jumps

Unconditional jumps are generated by:

```
Code.put(Code.jmp);
Code.put2(offset);
```

Conditional jumps are generated by adding the comparison operator to the jeq instruction and thus selecting the appropriate jump instruction:

```
Code.put(Code.jeq + operator);
Code.put2(offset);
```

In both cases, the jump distance is an offset (2 bytes) relative to the beginning of the jump instruction.

6.7.1 Forward and Backward Jumps

The jump distance can be positive or negative, so jumps can be forward or backward. *Backward jumps* are easier to generate, because the jump target is already known due to sequential code generation, and the jump distance can be emitted immediately when the jump instruction is generated (Fig. 6.31).

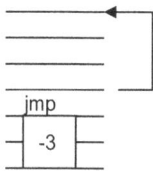

Fig. 6.31 Backward jumps

In *forward jumps,* the target of the jump is not yet known when the jump instruction is emitted. Therefore, the two bytes for the jump distance must be left empty and patched ("fixed up") later when the jump target becomes known (Fig. 6.32).

6.7 Jumps and Labels

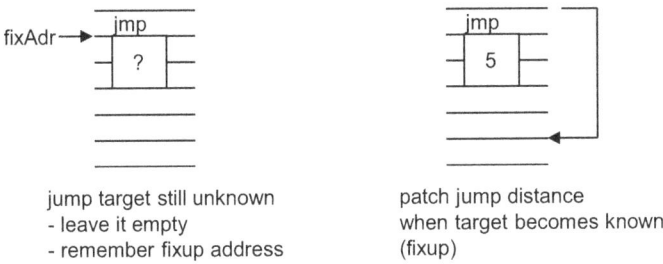

Fig. 6.32 Forward jumps

Sometimes, several forward jumps lead to the same jump target, for example, when a loop is exited by multiple break statements. Another example are compound Boolean expressions that are built with the operators && and ||. We will discuss them in Sect. 6.8.4.

If multiple forward jumps lead to the same jump target, the *fixup* addresses of those jumps must be collected in a list. As soon as the address of the jump target becomes known, the fixup list is resolved and the jump instructions are patched with the correct jump distances (Fig. 6.33).

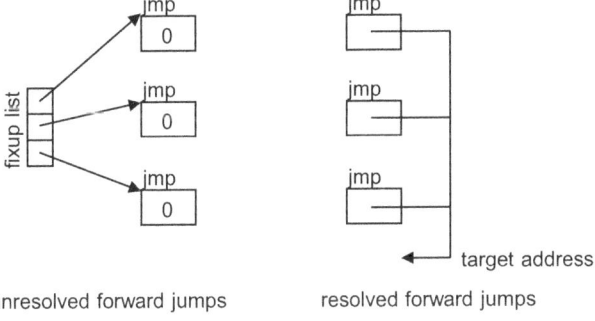

Fig. 6.33 Fixup list for multiple unresolved forward jumps

6.7.2 Labels

The target addresses of jumps are defined by labels, which are implemented as a class Label with the following two operations:

- label.here();   defines the label at the current pc position
- label.putAdr();   emits the jump distance to the label at the current pc position

These operations are used as follows:

```
Label label = new Label();   // creates a new and yet undefined label
...
Code.put(Code.jmp);          // forward jump to this label
label.putAdr();              // emits an empty cell and adds its address to the fixup list
...
label.here();                // defines label at the current pc position and resolves the fixup list
```

Each label has an address (which is negative if the label is still undefined) and a fixup list. Here is the implementation of the Label class:

```
public class Label {
    private int adr;                              // adr >= 0: label address (already defined)
                                                  // adr < 0: label still undefined
    private ArrayList<Integer> fixupList;         // list of fixup addresses

    public Label() {
        adr = -1;                                 // still undefined
        fixupList = new ArrayList<Integer>();     // empty list
    }

    public void putAdr() {
        if (adr >= 0) { // backward jump; label is already defined
            Code.put2(adr - (Code.pc - 1));
        } else { // forward jump; label is still undefined
            fixupList.add(Code.pc);
            Code.put2(0);
        }
    }

    public void here() {
        if (adr >= 0) error("label defined twice");
        for (Integer pos: fixupList) {
            Code.put2(pos, Code.pc - (pos - 1));
        }
        adr = Code.pc;
    }
}
```

The putAdr() method emits the jump distance to the respective label. In the case of backward jumps, the label is already defined (adr >= 0), so the distance from the beginning of the jump instruction (Code.pc - 1) to the label's address adr is emitted. For forward jumps, a two-byte cell with the value 0 is emitted and the address of the cell is added to the fixup list (Fig. 6.34).

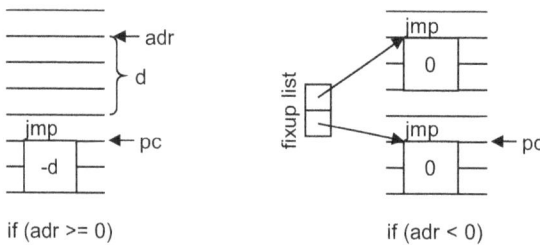

Fig. 6.34 Effect of putAdr()

The here() method resolves the fixup list by entering the distance between the beginning of the jump instruction (pos - 1) and the current pc position in each fixup cell. The label is then defined at the current pc position (Fig. 6.35).

6.7 Jumps and Labels

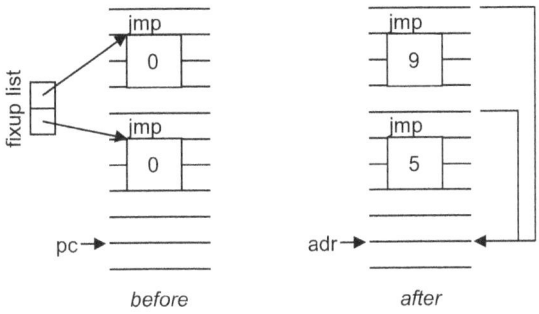

Fig. 6.35 Effect of here()

6.7.3 Conditions

In if and while statements, conditions are checked such as

if (a > b) ...

If the condition is true, the program will enter the if branch, otherwise it will jump over it. This requires the following code pattern:

... load a ...
... load b ...
jle ...

There is a small problem here: The µJVM has no explicit comparison instructions, but comparisons are carried out as part of conditional jumps. Therefore, the information about the comparison to be performed must be transferred to the jump instruction.

We solve this problem by making the nonterminal symbol Condition, which handles conditions, provide a new kind of operand—a Cond operand that contains not only the comparison operator used in the condition, but also two target labels for unresolved forward jumps that lead out of the condition (note that this is rather tricky and requires careful reading). The class Operand is therefore extended by the following elements (in bold):

```
class Operand {
    static final int Con = 0, Local = 1, Static = 2, Stack = 3, Fld = 4, Elem = 5, Meth = 6, Cond = 7;
    ...
    int     op;         // for Cond: operator of condition
    Label   tLabel;     // for Cond: target label for "true jumps"
    Label   fLabel;     // for Cond: target label for "false jumps"
}
```

The labels tLabel and fLabel are only used for compound Boolean expressions that contain the operators || or &&. For simple conditions, they are unused. Figure 6.36 shows how the fields of the Cond operand are set for a compound Boolean expression (see Sect. 6.8.4). The field op is the operator of the last comparison in the condition. The fields fLabel and tLabel are targeted by *false jumps* and *true jumps*.

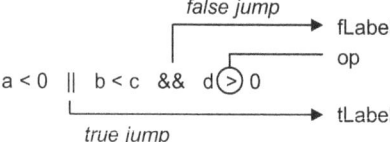

Fig. 6.36 Fields of a Cond operand for a compound Boolean expression

A *true jump* happens if the previous comparison was true, a *false jump* happens if it was false.

If the first operand of an expression x || y is already true, the whole expression is true; the second operand no longer needs to be evaluated. This is called *short-circuit evaluation* (see Sect. 6.8.4). Therefore, a *true jump* happens at the position of the operator || in the Boolean expression in Fig. 6.36: if a < 0, the program jumps to tLabel. Similarly, if the first operand of an expression x && y is already false, the entire expression is false. Therefore, in Fig. 6.36, a *false jump* happens at the position of the operator &&: If b < c is false, the program jumps to fLabel.

To be able to initialize Cond operands when they are created, we declare another constructor in the Operand class:

```
public Operand (int kind, int val, Struct type) {
  this.kind = kind; this.val = val; this.type = type;
  if (kind == Cond) {
    op = val;
    tLabel = new Label();  // still undefined
    fLabel = new Label();  // still undefined
  }
}
```

We also declare some helper methods in the class Code for creating unconditional and conditional jumps.

```
public class Code {
  private static final int eq = 0, ne = 1, lt = 2, le = 3, gt = 4, ge = 5;
  private static int inverse[] = {ne, eq, ge, gt, le, lt};  // inverse of eq, ne, lt, le, gt, ge
  ...
  public static void jump (Label label) {  // unconditional jump
    put(jmp); label.putAdr();
  }
  public static void tJump (int op, Label label) {  // conditional true jump
    put(jeq + op);  // jeq, jne, jlt, jle, jgt, jge
    label.putAdr();
  }
  public static void fJump (int op, Label label) {  // conditional false jump
    put(jeq + inverse[op]);  // jne, jeq, jge, jgt, jle, jlt
    label.putAdr();
  }
}
```

6.8 Control Flow Structures

The following example shows the use of the fJump() method in a (simplified) if statement, where Condition returns a Cond operand x. A *false jump* is generated, which jumps to x.fLabel depending on x.op. The label x.fLabel is set at the end of the if branch and the jump is resolved (i.e., fixed up) there.

```
IfStatement                 (. Operand x; .)
= "if" "(" Condition <↑x> ")"   (. Code.fJump(x.op, x.fLabel); .)
    Statement               (. x.fLabel.here(); .) .
```

6.8 Control Flow Structures

Now that we know how to deal with jumps, let's look at control flow structures such as if and while statements that are implemented using jumps. The simplest control flow structure is the while statement, which we will look at first.

6.8.1 While Statement

A while statement executes a loop as long as a condition is satisfied, which is checked at the beginning of each loop iteration.

Whenever we want to generate code for a specific language construct, it is helpful to first compare the construct schematically in the source code and in the target code. Figure 6.37 shows this for the while statement.

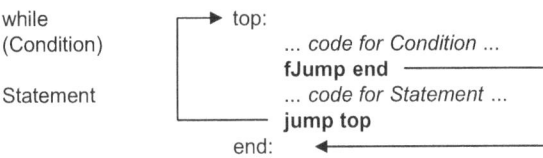

Fig. 6.37 Scheme for translating while statements

At the beginning of the loop, a label top is set that is the destination of a jump from the end of the loop. If the condition at the beginning of the loop is false, a *false jump* happens to a label end, which is set after the end of the loop. For Condition and Statement, code is generated that is part of this scheme but does not affect the control flow. The scheme can be implemented by the following attributed grammar:

```
WhileStatement              (. Operand x; .)
=   "while"                 (. Label top = new Label();
                               top.here(); .)
    "(" Condition <↑x> ")"  (. Code.fJump(x.op, x.fLabel); .)
    Statement               (. Code.jump(top);
                               x.fLabel.here(); .) .
```

Condition returns a Cond operand x. Code.fJump() then jumps to x.fLabel depending on the operator x.op. This label corresponds to the label end in Fig. 6.37. It is set by x.fLabel.here() after the backward jump to the label top. Figure 6.38 shows a simple while loop and the code generated for it.

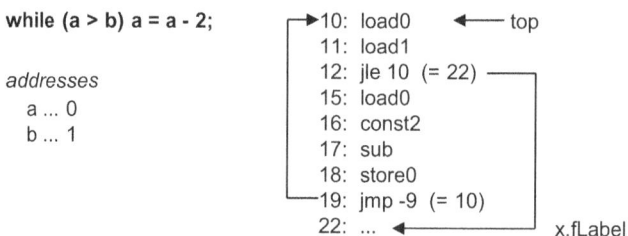

Fig. 6.38 Example of a while loop and the code generated for it

Since the condition is a > b, a jle instruction is generated as a *false jump*, i.e., it jumps if a <= b. As this is a forward jump, the jump distance will only be entered when the jump target x.fLabel is defined after the loop. Remember: the jump distance is the difference between the jump target (here 22) and the start of the jump instruction (here 12).

6.8.2 If Statement

The if statement is more complicated than the while statement, as it can come in two variants: with and without an else branch. Let's look at the two variants schematically again before we implement the code generation for them (Fig. 6.39).

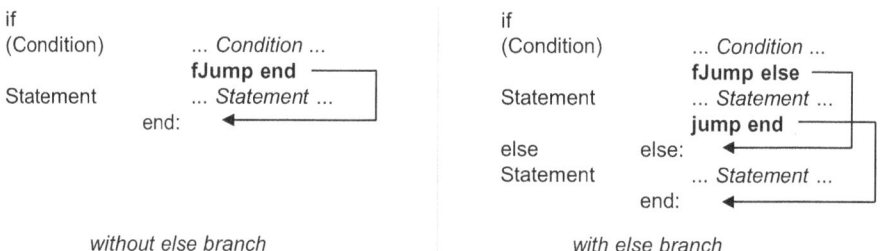

Fig. 6.39 Scheme for translating if statements (without and with else branch)

If the condition is false, we must jump over the if branch, either to the end of the statement or to the else branch. If there is an else branch, an unconditional jump across the else branch must be created at the end of the if branch. We therefore have two (intertwined) forward jumps that need to be resolved in the right place.

We show the implementation of the if statement for both variants (with and without else branch) using an attributed grammar.

6.8 Control Flow Structures

```
IfStatement                     (. Operand x; Label end; .)
= "if"
  "(" Condition <↑x> ")"        (. Code.fJump(x.op, x.fLabel); .)
  Statement
  ( "else"                      (. end = new Label(); Code.jump(end);
                                   x.fLabel.here(); .)
    Statement                   (. end.here(); .)
  |                             (. x.fLabel.here(); .)
  ) .
```

The optional else branch is expressed by two alternatives, with the second alternative being empty and consisting only of a semantic action.

Condition again returns a Cond operand x. Depending on x.op, there is a *false jump* to the label x.fLabel. If there is an else branch, this label is set before the statements of the else branch (i.e., the jump leads to the else branch), otherwise it is set in the empty else branch (i.e., the jump leads to the end of the if statement).

At the beginning of the else branch, an unconditional jump to the label end (i.e., to the end of the else branch) is generated, because when the program gets to this point, it has already executed the if branch and must skip the else branch. Figure 6.40 shows a simple if statement and the code generated for it.

```
if (a > b) max = a; else max = b;    10: load0
                                     11: load1
addresses                            12: jle 8  (= 20)
                                     15: load0
a ...  0                             16: store2
b ...  1                             17: jmp 5  (= 22)
max ... 2                            20: load1                x.fLabel
                                     21: store2
                                     22: ...                  end
```

Fig. 6.40 Example of an if statement and the code generated for it

You can see the two forward jumps: the *false jump* over the if branch and the unconditional jump over the else branch.

6.8.3 Break Statement

The break statement is used in MicroJava to exit loops. The code generation for this is simple: a break is translated into an unconditional jump out of the enclosing loop. After the loop, we set a break label that is jumped to by the break statement.

However, there is a problem with nested loops: each loop must have its own break label, and we have to make sure that the break label of an inner loop does not override that of the outer loop. We solve this by using a global *label stack*.

| Label | **curBreakLab** = null; | // current break label |
| Stack<Label> | **breakLabs** = new Stack<>(); | // break labels of outer loops |

When the compiler gets to the beginning of a loop, it pushes the current break label onto the stack and pops it again at the end of the loop. This is shown in the following attributed grammar, which also describes the translation of the break statement.

```
Statement
= "while"                     (. breakLabs.push(curBreakLab);       // save outer break label
                                 curBreakLab = new Label();
   ... .)
  "(" Condition <↑x> ")"      (. ... .)
  Statement                   (. ...
                                 curBreakLab.here();                 // breaks lead to this location
                                 curBreakLab = breakLabs.pop(); .)   // restore outer break label
| "break" ";"                  (. if (curBreakLab == null) error("break outside of a loop");
                                 Code.jump(curBreakLab); .)
| ... .
```

In Java, loops can be tagged with a label name that can be referenced in a break statement (e.g., break outerLab;). As a result, outer loops can also be exited from an inner loop. If you wanted to implement this in MicroJava, you would have to store label names (e.g., outerLab) as objects in the symbol table, along with their address. If the program then references such a label name in a break statement, the compiler could look it up in the symbol table, get its address and jump to it.

6.8.4 Short-circuit Evaluation of Compound Boolean Expressions

We have already seen in Sect. 6.7 that Boolean expressions that are composed with || and && are evaluated in "short-circuit mode", i.e., the evaluation of the expression stops as soon as the result is known. In pseudocode, this can be expressed as follows:

```
a || b    ⇔    if (a) true else b
a && b    ⇔    if (!a) false else b
```

If a is already true in a || b, the whole expression is true. If a is already false in a && b, the whole expression is false.

Short-circuit evaluation can be implemented by inserting *true jumps* and *false jumps* at the positions of the operators || and && (see Fig. 6.41; the letters a to f stand for comparisons such as x > y).

6.8 Control Flow Structures

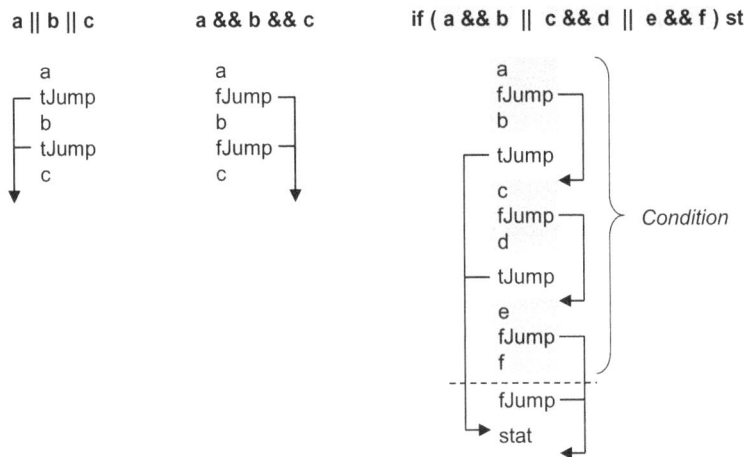

Fig. 6.41 Short-circuit evaluation of Boolean expressions

As you can see, a tJump is generated for each || operator, and an fJump for each && operator. If you combine || and &&, the interlocked structure shown on the far right in Fig. 6.41 is created. In this scenario, the fJumps of the && operators lead behind the tJumps of the || operators.

The dashed line indicates the end of the Condition in the if statement. As you can see, there can be two open fixup lists at this point—one for *true jumps* and one for *false jumps*. After the Condition, a fJump is generated in the if statement that jumps over the if branch. This is added to the fJump list. Any existing tJumps are made to lead to the position right after this fJump, since the if branch now begins, which should be executed if Condition returns true. The fJumps lead to the position after the if branch.

Since there can be *true jumps* in a condition, we need to take this into account in the attributed grammar of the while and if statements. These *true jumps* must lead to the beginning of the loop body or the if branch:

```
WhileStatement          (. Operand x; .)
= "while"               (. Label top = new Label();
                           top.here(); .)
  "(" Condition <↑x> ")" (. Code.fJump(x.op, x.fLabel);
                           x.tLabel.here(); .)  // true jumps from Condition lead to here
  Statement             (. Code.jump(top);
                           x.fLabel.here(); .) .
```

Compound Boolean expressions are defined by the following grammar:

```
Condition  = CondTerm {"||" CondTerm}.
CondTerm   = CondFactor {"&&" CondFactor}.
CondFactor = Expr RelOp Expr.
RelOp      = "==" | "!=" | ">" | ">=" | "<" | "<=".
```

We will now take a look at the code generation for Boolean expressions, with the following context conditions for CondFactor:

CondFactor = Expr RelOp Expr.
- The types of both expressions must be *compatible*. (cc 1)
- Classes and arrays may only be checked for equality and inequality. (cc 2)

The attributed grammar for CondFactor is:

```
CondFactor <↑x>      (. Operand x, y; int op; .)
= Expr <↑x>          (. Code.load(x); .)
  RelOp <↑op>
  Expr <↑y>          (. Code.load(y);
                        if (! x.type.compatibleWith(y.type)) error("type mismatch"); // cc 1
                        if (x.type.isRefType() && op != Code.eq && op != Code.ne) // cc 2
                          error("invalid compare");
                        x = new Operand(Operand.Cond, op, null); .) .
```

The two expressions are loaded, but the comparison will take place only later in the jump instruction. CondFactor therefore returns a Cond operand x, where x.op contains the comparison operator and the labels x.tLabel and x.fLabel are still undefined. CondTerm then implements the && operation:

```
CondTerm <↑x>        (. Operand x, y; .)
= CondFactor <↑x>
  { "&&"             (. Code.fJump(x.op, x.fLabel); .)
    CondFactor <↑y>  (. x.op = y.op; .)
  } .
```

For each && operator, a fJump is generated. Again, CondTerm returns a Cond operand x, where x.op always contains the operator of the last CondFactor and there may be some fJumps to x.fLabel stored in the label's fixup list. Condition is finally implemented as follows:

```
Condition <↑x>       (. Operand x, y; .)
= CondTerm <↑x>
  { "||"             (. Code.tJump(x.op, x.tLabel);
                        x.fLabel.here(); .)
    CondTerm <↑y>    (. x.op = y.op;
                        x.fLabel = y.fLabel; .)
  } .
```

For each || operator, a tJump is generated, and a possibly existing *false jump* list is resolved to lead to the position right after it. Condition returns a Cond operand x, which can contain open *true jump* and *false jump* lists. x.op is the last operator in the last CondTerm and x.fLabel is the possible *false jump* list leading out of the last CondTerm. Therefore, y.op and y.fLabel have to be copied to x.op and x.fLabel.

6.9 Methods

As the last part of code generation, we will now look at the implementation of methods, i.e., their invocation including parameter passing, their declaration, the management of frames for local variables, and the return statement.

6.9.1 Calling void Methods

Methods that are declared as void are called as statements. The call

    m(a, b);

results in the following code scheme:

    ... load a ...
    ... load b ...
    call m

The parameters are loaded onto the EStack before the call. Then comes the call instruction, which pushes the return address onto the MStack and jumps to the address m. The implementation is simple:

```
Statement                (. Operand x, y;   )
= Designator <↑x>
  ( ActPars <↓x>         (. Code.callMethod(x);
                            if (x.type != Tab.noType) Code.put(Code.pop); .)
  | "=" Expr <↑y>        (. .... .)
  ) ";"
  |   ... .
```

If a statement starts with a Designator, it can be a method call or an assignment. Method calls are followed by a parameter list and assignments by an assignment operator. ActPars loads the actual parameters onto the EStack, and callMethod() generates the call instruction (see below).

If the called method was not void (x.type != Tab.noType) but rather a function method, its return value (which is returned on the EStack) must be removed. In this case a pop instruction is generated.

6.9.2 Calling Function Methods

Function methods are invoked as part of expressions. The call

    c = m(a, b);

results in the following code scheme:

```
... load a ...
... load b ...
call m
... store c ...
```

The parameters are passed on the EStack. The return value is also returned on the EStack and can then be further processed or stored away. Function calls are implemented in the production Factor:

```
Factor <↑x>              (. Operand x; .)
= Designator <↑x>
  [ ActPars <↓x>         (. if (x.type == Tab.noType) error("void method called as a function");
                            Code.callMethod(x);
                            x.kind = Operand.Stack; .)
  ]
  | ... .
```

If a factor is a Designator with parameters, it denotes the call of a function method. ActPars loads the actual parameters onto the EStack. After checking that the method is not void, the call instruction is generated using callMethod(). Since a function method leaves a return value on the EStack, the operand x, which is returned by Factor, has its kind set to Operand.Stack.

The method callMethod() generates the call instruction. However, it also deals with the standard methods ord(), chr() and len(), for which no call is generated, but which are embedded "inline" into the code.

```
public static void callMethod (Operand m) {
    if (m.obj == Tab.ordObj || m.obj == Tab.chrObj) ; // nothing
    else if (m.obj == Tab.lenObj) // inline len() function
        put(arraylength);
    else { // emit call with relative offset
        put(call); put2(m.adr – (pc – 1));
    }
}
```

The processing of the standard methods requires an explanation: if, for example, ord('a') is called, ActPars will load the value 'a' onto the EStack. Since the function ord() is of type int, the operand x returned by Designator and later by Factor is also of type int. It is therefore sufficient to treat the loaded parameter 'a' as a value of type int. Thus, callMethod() does not need to do anything. Factor simply returns the already loaded parameter as Stack operand of type int. The same happens when calling chr(i): the parameter i is loaded, and Factor returns a Stack operand of type char.

When len(a) is called, ActPars loads the address of the array a onto the EStack. call-Method() then generates an arraylength instruction that loads the length of the array onto the EStack. Finally, Factor returns a Stack operand of type int (i.e., the type of the len() method), which corresponds to the array length.

6.9.3 Stack Frames

When a method is called, a stack frame must be allocated for its local variables and must be released again at the end of the method. The sequence of the instructions call—enter—exit—return, which has already been described in Fig. 6.19, is shown again in Fig. 6.42:

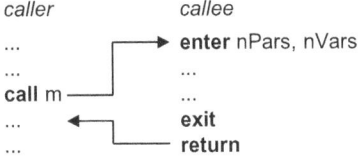

Fig. 6.42 Method call—instructions involved

The first instruction of each method is enter, which allocates a frame with nVars words and links it to the caller's frame via a *dynamic link*. The parameters (nPars) are moved from the EStack to the beginning of the MStack so that the EStack is empty at the beginning of the method (Fig. 6.43).

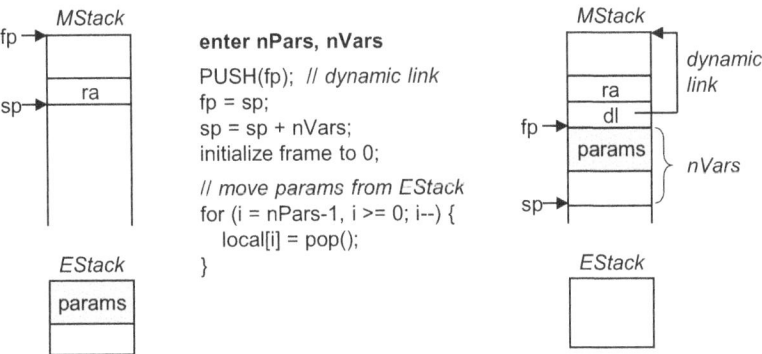

Fig. 6.43 Effect of the enter instruction

Before a method returns, it executes an exit instruction, which releases the current frame and resets fp and sp to the caller's frame. Thus, exit "undoes" enter. If the method is a function, its return value is returned on the EStack (Fig. 6.44).

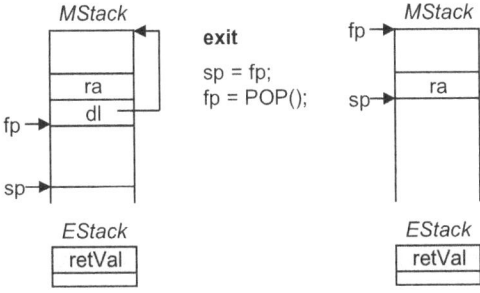

Fig. 6.44 Effect of the exit instruction

6.9.4 Method Declarations

A method is declared by its name and its formal parameters. It can contain local variables for which a new scope is created in the symbol table and a frame is allocated on the MStack. Finally, a method also has statements that are translated to instructions in the code buffer. The following attributed grammar describes the processing a method declaration:

```
MethodDecl              (. Struct type; String name; int n; .)
= (   Type <↑type>      (. if (type.isRefType()) error("methods may only return int or char"); .)
  |   "void"            (. type = Tab.noType; .)
  )
  ident <↑name>         (. curMethod = Tab.insert(Obj.Meth, name, type);
                           Tab.openScope(); .)
  "(" FormPars <↑n> ")" (. curMethod.nPars = n;
                           if (name.equals("main")) {
                              Code.mainPc = Code.pc;
                              if (curMethod.type != Tab.noType) error("main must be void");
                              if (curMethod.nPars != 0) error("main must not have parameters");
                           } .)
  { VarDecl }           (. curMethod.locals = Tab.curScope.locals; // save this scope
                           curMethod.adr = Code.pc;
                           Code.put(Code.enter);
                           Code.put(curMethod.nPars);
                           Code.put(Tab.curScope.nVars); .)
  "{" { Statement } "}" (. if (curMethod.type == Tab.noType) {
                              Code.put(Code.exit);
                              Code.put(Code.return_);
                           } else { // end of function reached without a return statement
                              Code.put(Code.trap); Code.put(1);
                           }
                           Tab.closeScope(); .) .
```

A method declaration starts with a function type or void. In MicroJava, functions may only return int or char values. The type of void methods is Tab.noType.

The name of the method is entered into the current scope (i.e., the program scope), then a new scope is opened into which the parameters and the local variables are entered. At the end of the method, this scope is closed again.

The address of the main() method is stored in Code.mainPc and later written to the object file. We also have to check the context conditions that the main() method must be a parameterless void method (see Appendix A).

Before the statements of the method begin, the method's address is stored in curMethod. adr and an enter instruction is generated. At the end of the statements, we emit an exit and a return instruction for void methods. For function methods, if they reach their end without returning a value by means of a return statement (see below), a trap instruction is emitted that reports this error and aborts the program.

6.9.5 Formal Parameters

Formal parameters are treated as local variables and are entered into the scope of their method. In addition, they are counted.

```
FormPars <↑n>          (. int n = 0; .)
= [ FormPar            (. n++; .)
    { "," FormPar      (. n++; .)
    }
  ].
FormPar                (. Struct type; String name; .)
= Type <↑type>
  ident <↑name>        (. Tab.insert(Obj.Var, name, type); .) .
```

6.9.6 Actual Parameters

The actual parameters of a method must be loaded onto the EStack. For each actual parameter, we also have to check whether it is *assignment compatible* with the corresponding formal parameter. Finally, we must check that the number of actual and formal parameters match. This is implemented by the following attributed grammar:

```
ActPars <↓m>           (. Operand m, ap; .)
= "("                  (. if (m.kind != Operand.Meth) {
                             error("not a method");
                             m.obj = Tab.noObj;
                         }
                         int aPars = 0;              // number of actual parameters
                         int fPars = m.obj.nPars;    // number of formal parameters
                         Obj fp = m.obj.locals; .)   // first formal parameter
  [ Expr <↑ap>         (. Code.load(ap); aPars++;    // load and count actual parameter
                         if (fp != null && !ap.type.assignableTo(fp.type))
                             error("parameter type mismatch"); .)
    { "," Expr <↑ap>   (. Code.load(ap); aPars++;    // load and count actual parameter
                         fp = fp.next;               // next formal parameter
                         if (fp != null && !ap.type.assignableTo(fp.type))
                             error("parameter type mismatch"); .)
    }
  ]                    (. if (aPars > fPars)         // check number of parameters
                             error("too many actual parameters");
                         else if (aPars < fPars)
                             error("too few actual parameters"); .)
  ")" .
```

The number of formal parameters (fPars) is taken from m.obj.nPars, the number of actual parameters (aPars) is counted. The variable fp runs through the formal parameters, and the attribute ap through the actual parameters. For each actual parameter, we check whether it is *assignment compatible* with the corresponding formal parameter and load it onto the EStack. At the end, we check whether the number of actual and formal parameters match. Figure 6.45 visualizes this process for a method declared as:

```
void foo (int a, char b) { ... }
```

and its call:

```
foo(3, 'x');
```

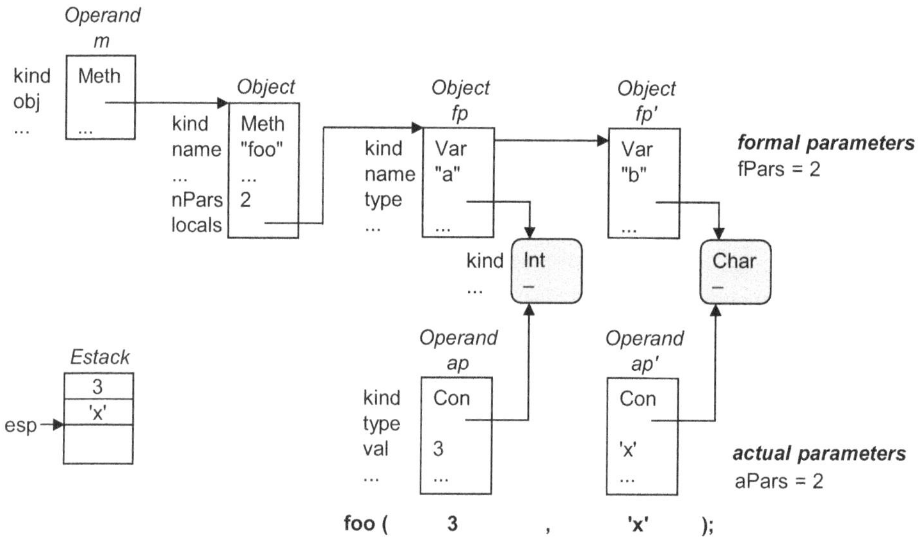

Fig. 6.45 Processing and checking actual parameters

6.9.7 Return Statement

The return statement exists in two variants. In function methods, it returns a value that must be loaded onto the EStack and checked whether it is *assignment compatible* with the function type of the current method. In void methods, the return statement does not return a value.

In both cases, an exit and a return instruction are generated, since the method must return to the caller here. The following attributed grammar implements this process:

```
Statement      (. Operand x; ... .)
=  ...
|  "return"
   (  Expr <↑x>  (. Code.load(x); // load return value
                    if (curMethod.type == Tab.noType)
                       error("void method must not return a value");
                    else if (!x.type.assignableTo(curMethod.type))
                       error("type of return value must match method type"); .)
```

```
        |                   (. if (curMethod.type != Tab.noType) error("return value expected"); .)
        )                   (. Code.put(Code.exit);
                               Code.put(Code.return_); .)
";"  .
```

6.10 Object File

The last task of code generation is to output the object file. In addition to the code buffer, the following information that is required by the loader of the μJVM is written to the beginning of the object file:

- Code size (in bytes), which results from the length of the code buffer.
- Size of the global data area (in words), which results from the number of global variables that is kept in the nVars field of the global scope.
- Address of the main() method, which is kept in Code.mainPc.

Figure 6.46 shows the contents of the object file. The first two bytes are always "MJ" and can be used to verify that it is a MicroJava object file.

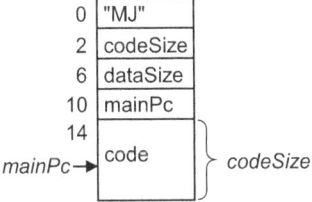

Fig. 6.46 Contents of the object file

When the object file is loaded, the μJVM will allocate memory areas for the code, the global data, the method call stack, and the heap. It will then load the code into the code area and start interpreting it at the address mainPc.

MicroJava's object file format is extremely simple. In product compilers, an object file usually contains much more information and is typically based on the common object file format of a specific operating system such as Windows or Linux. Such object files may contain also the following information:

- *List of exported names with their addresses.* If programs consist of multiple files, the linker needs this information to resolve external references to names in other files.
- *List of imported names.* If a name that is declared in some other file is used in the source code, the linker must resolve the external reference to that name by inserting the address of that name.
- *Meta information for the debugger.* A debugger needs information about the names, addresses, and types of all declared program elements so that it can display the binary machine state (stack and heap) in a human-readable form.

6.11 Exercises

1. *Operands of code generation (1)*. Similar to Fig. 6.25, show which operands are created when compiling the expression 3 + p.f and which code is generated in the process. p is a local variable at address 0 that points to an object in which the field f has the offset 1.

2. *Operands of code generation (2)*. Similar to Fig. 6.25, show which operands are created when compiling the expression a[2*i] + i and which code is generated in the process. a is a local variable at address 0 pointing to an int array, i is a local variable at address 1.

3. *Control flow structures (1)*. Specify the MicroJava bytecode for the following piece of code:

   ```
   while (x > 0) {
      sum = sum + x; x--:
   }
   ```

   sum and x are local int variables at addresses 0 and 1.

4. *Control flow structures (2)*. Specify the MicroJava bytecode for the following piece of code:

   ```
   if (x > 0) y = 1;
   else if (x < 0) y = -1;
   else y = 0;
   ```

   x and y are local int variables at addresses 0 and 1.

5. *Compound Boolean expressions*. Specify the MicroJava bytecode for the following piece of code:

   ```
   if (a == 10 || 0 < a && a < b) a = 0; else a = 1;
   ```

   a and b are local variables at addresses 0 and 1. Pay attention to the short-circuit evaluation in the compound Boolean expression.

6. *Method call*. Consider the following method declaration:

   ```
   void foo (char ch, int n)
      int x;
      { ... }
   ```

   (a) Specify the MicroJava bytecode for this method (enter, exit and return), where the method body can be expressed by ....

   (b) Specify the MicroJava bytecode for the method call foo('x', i+1);, where i is a local int variable at address 0.

6.11 Exercises

7. *Function call.* Consider the following declaration of a function method:

   ```
   int max (int a, int b) {
       if (a > b) return a; else return b;
   }
   ```

   (a) Specify the MicroJava bytecode for this method.
   (b) Specify the MicroJava bytecode for the function call sum = max(x, 10);, where sum and x are local int variables at addresses 0 and 1.

8. *Increment and decrement statement.* In Sect. 6.6 we discussed the code generation for the increment and decrement statement (x++; and x--;), but without using the inc instruction of the μJVM. Write an attributed grammar for these statements that generates code using the inc instruction (see Sect. 6.1.2). To do this, write a method Code.inc(x, val) that increments a designator described by the operand x by the value val (1 or −1). Also note the context conditions (see Appendix A) as well as the fact that the inc instruction can only be used for local variables.

9. *Language extension: special while loop.* Extend MicroJava's while statement so that a loop can have multiple loop headers and multiple loop bodies, for example:

   ```
   while (n % 2 == 0)    // loop header 1
       n = n / 2;
   || (n % 3 == 0)       // loop header 2
       n = n − 1;
   ```

   The first loop header begins with while, the others with ||. The loop conditions are checked sequentially. If any of them is true, the corresponding statement is executed; after this statement, the program jumps back to the beginning of the loop. The loop terminates if none of the loop conditions is true. The context-free grammar for this looks as follows:

   ```
   WhileStat = "while" "(" Condition ")" Statement { "||" "(" Condition ")" Statement } .
   ```

   Turn this grammar into an attributed grammar so that the correct jump instructions are generated. To do this, use the helper methods for labels and jumps described in Sect. 6.7 (Code.jump(), Code.fJump(), and label.here()). Note that Condition returns a Cond operand.

10. *Language extension: enumeration types.* What changes would be necessary in the compiler if there were enumeration types in MicroJava? The declaration

    ```
    enum Color {RED, BLUE, GREEN}
    ```

    would define an enumeration type with three enumeration constants represented internally by the values 0, 1, and 2. Using an attributed grammar, show how the declaration of enumeration types and the access to enumeration constants (e.g., Color.RED) are handled. Changes are required in the scanner, the parser, the symbol table and the code generator.

11. *Language extension: data type boolean.* What changes would be necessary in the compiler if MicroJava had a data type boolean with the values true and false? It should also be possible to store the result of a Boolean expression in a boolean variable, for example:

    boolVar = a < b && b < c;

    Boolean variables should be usable in conditions and as operands of Boolean expressions, for example:

    if (boolVar) ...
    if (boolVar || a < b) ...

    Finally, it should also be possible to output Boolean expressions using the print statement.

12. *Implementation of the code generator.* Implement the code generator of the MicroJava compiler as a class Code, along with a class Operand for operand descriptors and a class Label for managing jump labels, as described in this chapter and in the interfaces of these classes (see Appendix B).

The Compiler Generator Coco/R 7

In the previous chapters, you have learned how to implement a simple compiler "manually" (i.e., without tools). This manual implementation is perfectly adequate for small compilers or for compiler-like tools. However, you have probably noticed that many compiler construction techniques (especially in lexical analysis and syntax analysis) are very systematic and can be applied almost mechanically. It is therefore not surprising that these techniques and processes can be automated.

Tools that generate parts of a compiler from a compact specification are called *compiler generators*. Most of them generate a scanner and a parser, while the remaining compiler parts have to be written by hand. There are also tools for code generation and optimization, but we will not discuss them here. Our focus is on the generation of scanners and parsers (Fig. 7.1), as they are present in all compilers.

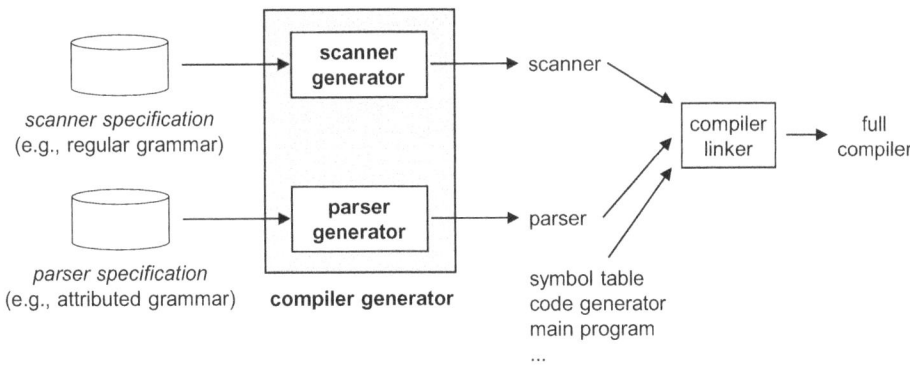

Fig. 7.1 Operation and components of a compiler generator

© The Author(s), under exclusive license to Springer Nature Switzerland AG 2025
H. Mössenböck, *Compiler Construction*,
https://doi.org/10.1007/978-3-031-84813-1_7

A *scanner generator* generates a scanner as a source code class from a scanner specification (e.g., from a regular grammar of the terminal symbols). A *parser generator* generates a parser from a parser specification (e.g., from an attributed grammar)—also as a source code class. The programmer still needs to add further hand-written classes (e.g., for symbol table handling and for code generation).

The individual classes are then compiled and linked, resulting in a full compiler. In most cases, the scanner generator and the parser generator are combined into a single tool, which is then called a *compiler generator*, although it only generates parts of a compiler.

There are numerous such generators, most of which are also available free of charge. Among the oldest are the scanner generator *Lex* and the parser generator *Yacc* [LMB92], which produce compiler parts in C, but there are also versions for other languages. Among the most well-known compiler generators today are *ANTLR* [Parr13] and *JavaCC* [Cope20], which generate both a scanner and a parser (JavaCC in Java, ANTLR in various languages).

Coco/R

In this book, we will use the compiler generator *Coco/R* [Coco], which can generate scanners and parsers in various languages. "Coco" stands for "compiler compiler" (another name for compiler generator). The suffix "R" means that it generates parsers in recursive descent (but there are also other versions of Coco that produce table-driven parsers). Coco/R can handle LL(*) grammars, i.e., grammars for top-down parsing with arbitrarily far lookahead. Figure 7.2 shows the parts generated by Coco/R.

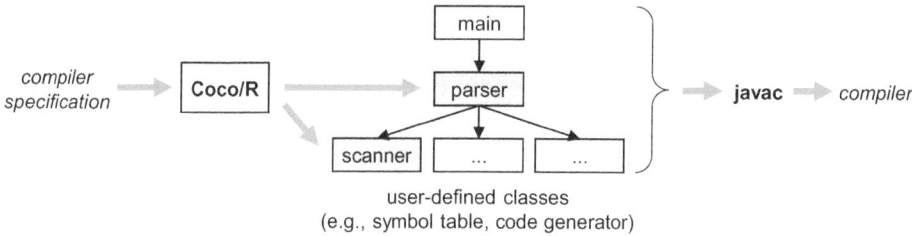

Fig. 7.2 Compiler parts generated by Coco/R

Coco/R generates a scanner and a parser in Java[1] from a compiler specification. The scanner is implemented as a finite automaton and is generated from a regular grammar of the terminal symbols. The parser is generated from an attributed grammar and is implemented using recursive descent parsing.

The scanner and the parser form the core of the generated compiler. The user must add further classes, such as a symbol table handler and a code generator in order to obtain a complete compiler.

---

[1] There are also versions for C#, C++, VB.NET, Delphi, Modula-2, and other languages. See *https://ssw.jku.at/Coco/*.

CoCo/R is available for free under the open source GPL license and can be downloaded from *https://ssw.jku.at/Coco/*.

Example of a Compiler Specification

To get an idea of what a compiler specification for Coco/R looks like, let's start with a simple example. We want to write a "compiler" that parses a constant expression (e.g., 2 * (3 + 5)), calculates its value, and prints it. The compiler specification for this looks as follows and should be easy to understand for the readers of this book:

```
COMPILER Calc
CHARACTERS
  digit = '0' .. '9'.
TOKENS
  number = digit {digit}.
COMMENTS FROM "/*" TO "*/" NESTED
PRODUCTIONS
  Calc                      (. int x; .)
  = "CALC" Expr <out x>     (. System.out.println(x); .) .

  Expr <out int x>          (. int y; .)
  = Term <out x>
    { '+' Term <out y>      (. x = x + y; .)
    } .

  Term <out int x>          (. int y; .)
  = Factor <out x>
    { '*' Factor <out y>    (. x = x * y; .)
    } .

  Factor <out int x>
  = number                  (. x = Integer.parseInt(t.val); .)
  | '(' Expr <out x> ')' .
END Calc .
```

The first part defines the character sets, terminal symbols, and comments of the language. The second part is an attributed grammar of the language to be translated and should be easy to understand.

From this specification, Coco/R generates a scanner and a parser. For this simple example, we don't need a symbol table or a code generator, but just a small main program, which in the simplest case would look like this:

```
class Calc {
  public static void main (String[] arg) {
    Scanner scanner = new Scanner(arg[0]);
    Parser parser = new Parser(scanner);
    parser.Parse();
    System.out.println(parser.errors.count + " errors detected");
  }
}
```

The main program creates a scanner and passes it the name of the input file (arg[0]). Then it creates a parser, connects it to the scanner and starts it (parser.Parse()). The parser now analyzes the input (e.g., CALC 2 * (3 + 5)), calculates the value of the expression (16) and prints it. Note that the scanners and parsers generated by Coco/R are objects, not classes with static methods, as was the case in the previous chapters of this book.

From this example, it should already be reasonably clear how to use Coco/R. Nevertheless, we will now take a closer look at the individual parts of the compiler specification, but without going into too much detail. A more detailed documentation can be found at [Coco].

Structure of a Compiler Specification

The structure of a compiler specification for Coco/R is:

```
CompilerSpecification
  = [ImportClauses]
    "COMPILER" ident
    [GlobalFieldsAndMethods]
    ScannerSpecification
    ParserSpecification
    "END" ident "." .
```

It starts with the keyword COMPILER and a name that also denotes the start symbol of the grammar. It ends with the keyword END and the same name. The COMPILER line can be preceded by Java import clauses, for example:

```
import java.util.ArrayList;
import java.io.*;
```

After the COMPILER line, arbitrary fields and methods can be declared, which will become fields and methods of the generated parser, for example:

```
int sum;
void add (int x) {
   sum = sum + x;
}
```

These fields and methods can be accessed in the semantic actions of the attributed grammar. They are global to the whole grammar rather than being local to a specific production.

The most important parts of the compiler specification are the description of the scanner and the parser, which we will explain in the following sections.

7.1 Scanner Specification

The scanner specification describes the lexical structure of the language to be compiled. It defines the terminal symbols, but also the sets of characters that make up the terminal symbols. It finally also defines comments and other characters to be ignored. We will now take a closer look at the individual parts of the scanner specification.

7.1.1 Character Sets

Terminal symbols consist of characters (e.g., letters or digits). However, we have to define which characters we consider to be letters or digits. In other words, we need to specify the character sets used. Here are some examples of how this can be done:

```
CHARACTERS
    digit    = "0123456789".          // the set of all digits
    letter   = 'A' .. 'Z'.            // the set of all upper-case letters
    hexDigit = digit + "ABCDEF".      // the set of all hexadecimal digits
    eol      = '\n'.                  // the set of an end-of-line character
    noDigit  = ANY – digit.           // the set of all characters that are not digits
```

A character set can be defined either by a string (e.g., "0123456789"), by a range (e.g., 'A' .. 'Z') or by a single character (e.g., '\n'). Character sets can also be combined using + and – (e.g., digit + "ABCDEF"). An interesting feature is the keyword ANY, which means "all characters" and can be used to define *complementary sets*. For example, ANY – digit denotes all characters that are not digits.

Coco/R supports the Unicode character set (UTF-8) and also allows the usual escape sequences such as '\n' for "newline" or \u03c0' for the character π.

7.1.2 Terminal Symbols

Terminal symbols can be *literals* or *terminal classes*. Literals such as "if", "while", '+' or ">=" do not need to be declared, but can simply be used in the productions of the attributed grammar. Terminal classes such as ident or number, of which there can be several instances, must be declared in the TOKENS section, for example:

```
TOKENS
    ident  = letter {letter | digit | '_'}.
    number = digit {digit}
           | "0x" hexDigit hexDigit hexDigit hexDigit.
    float  =   digit {digit} '.' digit {digit} ['E' ['+' | '-'] digit {digit}].
```

Each terminal class is declared by a regular EBNF production, where only literals or names of character sets may be used on the right-hand side.

Note that the two alternatives of number can start with the same character. The first alternative starts with digit (which contains '0') and the second alternative with '0'. This conflict is automatically resolved by Coco/R. First, a non-deterministic finite automaton is created, which is then transformed into a deterministic automaton in which there is only one transition with each character in each state.

Coco/R also offers the option to generate only a parser and to write the scanner by hand. In this case, the terminal symbols are only declared by their names (see the user manual [Coco]).

7.1.3 Pragmas

Pragmas are a concept we have not encountered so far. They are terminal symbols that are recognized and semantically processed by the scanner, but are not passed on to the parser. This can be used, for example, to process compiler options, which may occur at any point in the source code. For example, the option $ABC could be used to set certain compiler switches. Pragmas are not part of the syntax of the language and are therefore not forwarded to the parser just as comments are not forwarded. Nevertheless, they must be processed. Here is an example of a pragma declaration:

```
PRAGMAS
    option = '$' {letter}. (. for (char ch: la.val.toCharArray()) {
                                if (ch == 'A') ... set compiler switch A ...
                                else if (ch == 'B') ... set compiler switch B ...
                                ...
                            } .)
```

Pragmas, like terminal symbols, are described by an EBNF production, which is followed by a semantic action to process the pragma. In our example, the pragma string la.val (e.g., "$ABC") is analyzed, and the letters in it are used to set certain compiler switches.

In addition to compiler options, pragmas can also be used to process preprocessor commands (e.g., #ifdef), documentation comments (e.g., as in *javadoc* [JavaDoc]) or end-of-line characters. End-of-line characters are usually treated as whitespace and are ignored. However, there are also languages in which line endings have a special meaning. In such languages, they can be declared as pragmas and processed by a semantic action when they occur.

7.1.4 Comments

Comments are not part of a language's syntax. They provide explanations for human readers, but are ignored by the compiler. Therefore, comments are not declared like terminal symbols, but in a separate section. Also, nested comments, unlike terminal symbols, cannot be described by a regular grammar.

Comments are declared by specifying the strings with which they can start and end. If they can be nested, this is specified by the suffix NESTED. There can be multiple kinds of comments in a scanner specification, for example:

```
COMMENTS FROM "/*" TO "*/" NESTED
COMMENTS FROM "//" TO "\r\n"
```

7.1.5 Characters to Be Ignored

In most languages, there are characters that can occur between terminal symbols but are ignored by the compiler (*whitespace*). Blanks are always regarded as whitespace. For other characters, such as line endings or tabs, you have to specify this if desired. The directive

    IGNORE '\r' + '\n' + '\t'

specifies that the generated compiler should ignore line endings ('\r' and '\n') and tab characters ('\t') in addition to blanks.

7.1.6 Case Sensitivity

By default, Coco/R generates compilers in which case is significant (i.e., Foo and foo are regarded as different names). If you do not want this, you can write

    IGNORECASE

at the beginning of the scanner specification (before the character sets). This has the effect that all letters in terminal symbols are accepted as both upper-case and lower-case letters. Thus, keywords such as while, While and WHILE or the constants 3.14e0 and 3.14E0 are considered to be the same. However, the token value t.val of terminal symbols such as ident or string is retained with characters in their original case.

7.1.7 Interface of the Generated Scanner

From the scanner specification Coco/R generates a class Scanner, which has the following interface:

```
public class Scanner {
    public Scanner (String fileName) { ... }
    public Scanner (InputStream s) { ... }
    public Token   Scan() { ... }
    public Token   Peek() { ... }
    public void    ResetPeek() { ... }
}
```

The first constructor receives the name of an input file as a parameter. The scanner is supposed to read the program's source text from that file. The second constructor takes an already opened input stream of type InputStream as a parameter.

The most important method is Scan()[2]. It is called repeatedly by the parser and returns the next recognized token on each call. The Peek() method can be used to look ahead in the source code without removing the read tokens from the input stream. This can be used to

---

[2] Scan() corresponds to the next() method from Chap. 2.

resolve LL(1) conflicts by looking ahead by more than one symbol (see Sect. 7.4). ResetPeek() resets the peek position so that you can look ahead several times from the same position in different ways. The tokens returned by Scan() and Peek() have the following type:

```
public class Token {
    public int      kind;  // token kind (I.e., token code)
    public String   val;   // token value
    public int      pos;   // token position in the source text (starting at 0)
    public int      col;   // token column (starting at 1)
    public int      line;  // token line (starting at 1)
}
```

The field val contains the token value (for names, the text of the name; for numbers, the string of digits, etc.). The fields col and line denote the column and line number of the token and are used for error messages. There is also a field pos that specifies the textual position of the token relative to the start of the input stream.

Note that for numbers, val does not contain their numerical value, but a digit string, which must be converted to a numerical value if required.

7.2 Parser Specification

The parser specification is an attributed grammar of the language to be compiled. It consists of productions, semantic actions, and attributes from which Coco/R generates a recursive descent parser. Let's look at the individual parts of the parser specification.

7.2.1 Productions

The productions form a context-free grammar in EBNF. They may be declared in any order, but there must be exactly one production for each nonterminal symbol. In particular, there must be a production for the start symbol of the grammar whose name was specified after the keyword COMPILER. Here is an example (lighter printed parts belong to the scanner specification):

```
COMPILER Expr
CHARACTERS
    ident   = ...
    number  = ...
    ...
PRODUCTIONS
    Expr    = Term {AddOp Term}.  // production of the start symbol
    Term    = Factor {MulOp Factor}.
    Factor  = ident | number | '(' Expr ')' | '-' Factor.
    AddOp   = '+' | '-'.
    MulOp   = '*' | '/' | '%'.
END Expr.
```

7.2.2 Semantic Actions

Semantic actions are arbitrary pieces of Java code that are written between the brackets (. and .) and are executed by the generated parser at the position where they appear in the grammar. For example:

```
IdentList         (. int n; .)
= ident           (. n = 1; .)
  { ',' ident     (. n++; .)
  }               (. System.out.println(n); .) .
```

The semantic actions are copied into the generated parser without being checked by Coco/R. Any syntax or semantic errors in the Java code are only detected when the generated parser is compiled. It is important that such errors are corrected in the attributed grammar and not in the code of the generated parser, so that the changes are not lost when the parser is regenerated.

Each production can declare its own local variables (e.g., the variable n in the example above). Global declarations as well as any required import clauses are specified after (respectively before) the line with the keyword COMPILER, for example:

```
// imports
import java.io.*;
COMPILER Sample
  // global declarations
  FileWriter w;
  void open (String path) {
     w = new FileWriter(path);
  }
CHARACTERS
...
TOKENS
...
PRODUCTIONS
  Sample = ...   (. open("in.txt"); .) .
  ...
END Sample.
```

Global declarations become fields and methods of the generated parser and are not checked by Coco/R. They can be accessed in the semantic actions of grammar.

7.2.3 Attributes

Terminal symbols do not have explicit attributes, but their values can be accessed in semantic actions via the following global variables of the parser:

```
public Token t;    // most recently recognized token
public Token la;   // lookahead token (not yet recognized)
```

For example, the value of a number token can be obtained as follows:

```
Factor = number   (. int numVal = Integer.parseInt(t.val); ) .
```

t.val is the digit string of the previously recognized number token, which can be converted into a number with Integer.parseInt().

Nonterminal symbols can have any number of input attributes, but at most one output attribute. Attributes are written in angle brackets (<...>) after the respective nonterminal symbol. We distinguish between formal and actual attributes.

Formal attributes, if required, are specified on the left-hand side of a production and are declared with their type. An output attribute is prefixed by the keyword out and must be the first attribute in an attribute list:

```
A <int n, char c> = ... .   // formal input attributes n and c
B <out int x, int y> = ... .   // formal output attribute x, formal input attribute y
```

Actual attributes are specified when a nonterminal symbol appears on the right-hand side of a production. No type is specified here, but output attributes must again be prefixed with the keyword out:

```
... A <y, 'a'> ...   // actual input attributes y and 'a'
... B <out z, 3> ...   // actual output attribute z, actual input attribute 3
```

Actual input attributes can be constants, variables, or expressions. Actual output attributes must be variables, because they are assigned a value in the production of the nonterminal symbol. Of course, formal and actual attributes must match in their number and types.

7.2.4 Translation into Parser Methods

From each production of the attributed grammar, Coco/R generates a parser method. Attributes become parameters or function return values and semantic actions are inserted in the appropriate place. For example, from the production

```
Expr <out int n>      (. int n1; .)
= Term <out n>
  {  '+'
     Term <out n1>   (. n = n + n1; .)
  } .
```

Coco/R generates the following parser method (attributes and semantic actions are lightly printed; the method Get() corresponds to the method scan() from Chap. 3):

```
int Expr() {
  int n; int n1;
  n = Term();
  while (la.kind == 3) {
    Get();
    n1 = Term(); n = n + n1;
  }
  return n;
}
```

7.2 Parser Specification

The generated code is deliberately not very readable (e.g., token codes are represented by numbers instead of by named constants) so as not to tempt programmers to edit it. Any errors in the semantic actions should be corrected in the attributed grammar and not in the parser code generated from it.

7.2.5 The Symbol ANY

We have already seen the symbol ANY in the scanner specification, where it means the set of all characters. However, ANY can also be used in the parser specification, where it means all terminal symbols that are not an alternative to this ANY.

This can be used to implement *fuzzy parsing*, i.e., a form of syntax analysis in which only certain parts of the syntax are checked and other parts are covered by ANY. A simple example is a parser that counts how often the type name int occurs in a program, while all other primitive types are ignored. This can be expressed as follows:

```
Type
=  "int"      (. intCounter++; .)
|  ANY .
```

In this context, ANY means all terminal symbols except the keyword int, because only int is an alternative to ANY. A slightly more interesting example is a parser that analyzes an attributed grammar and determines the length of semantic actions. We only show the production of SemAction here.

```
SemAction <out int len>
=  "(."       (. int beg = t.pos + 2; .)
   {ANY}
   ".)"       (. len = t.pos – beg; .) .
```

ANY here means all terminal symbols except ".)", because only ".)" is an (implicit) alternative to this ANY. All symbols within the semantic action are covered by ANY and skipped, which eliminates the need for precise syntax analysis of the Java statements in semantic actions.

Finally, let's look at an even more sophisticated example: a parser that counts the number of statements that are terminated with a semicolon in a Java program. This is done in the production Block which processes statements and includes them in the count:

```
Block <out int statements>   (. int n; .)
=  "{"                       (. statements = 0; .)
   {  ";"                    (. statements++; .)
   |  Block <out n>          (. statements += n; .)
   |  ANY
   }
   "}" .
```

The alternatives of this ANY are ";", the terminal start symbols of Block (i.e., "{"), and the terminal successors of the iteration (i.e., "}"). So ANY matches all symbols here that are not ";", "{", or "}". Only the semicolons are processed and counted; other symbols in statements are covered by ANY (*fuzzy parsing*). Nested blocks provide the number of semicolons they contain, which are also counted.

7.2.6 Generation of the Scanner and the Parser

Coco/R generates a scanner and a parser as Java classes. However, these classes are not created from scratch, only the relevant parts are generated (the automaton of the scanner and the methods of the parser) and inserted into *frame files* (Fig. 7.3).

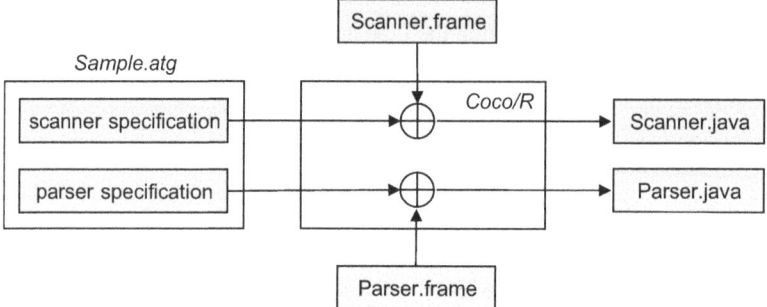

Fig. 7.3 Generation of the scanner and the parser from frame files

The frame files contain placeholders that are marked by "-->..." and are replaced with the parts generated by Coco/R. Here is a snippet of the frame file Scanner.frame:

```
public class Scanner {
  static final int EOL = '\n';
  static final int eofSym = 0;
-->declarations
  ...
  static {
    start = new StartStates(); literals = new HashMap();
-->initializations
  }
}
```

Coco/R inserts generated declarations at "-->declarations", initialization statements at "-->initializations", and so on.

The frame files are ordinary text files that can be edited. Thus, you can adapt the source code of the generated scanner and parser to a certain degree. However, care must be taken to ensure that the functionality of the scanner and parser is not impaired. In general, it is not necessary to modify the frame files.

The frame files must be in the same directory as the compiler specification, which usually has the extension *.atg.

7.2.7 Interface of the Generated Parser

From the parser specification and the frame file Parser.frame, Coco/R generates a class Parser with the following interface:

```
public class Parser {
    public Scanner    scanner;                          // scanner connected to this parser
    public Errors     errors;                           // error message stream
    public Token      t;                                // most recently recognized token
    public Token      la;                               // lookahead token (not yet recognized)
    public Parser (Scanner scanner) { ... }             // constructor; connects the parser with a scanner
    public void Parse() { ... }                         // entry point; starts parsing
    public void SemErr (String msg) { ... }             // for error messages
}
```

To start the parser, you must connect it to a scanner and then call the Parse() method. The compiler's main() method should look something like this:

```
public static void main (String[] arg) {
    Scanner scanner = new Scanner(arg[0]); // arg[0] is the input file name
    Parser parser = new Parser(scanner);
    parser.Parse();
    System.out.println(parser.errors.count + " errors detected");
}
```

Errors are reported and counted via the class Errors, which is also generated (see next section). The number of errors detected during compilation can be obtained via parser.errors.count.

7.3 Error Handling

Error handling in the generated compilers includes the output of error messages and the recovery after syntax errors. Both are largely automated but require some intervention by the compiler engineer to improve error messages and enable recovery after syntax errors.

7.3.1 Syntax Error Messages

For syntax errors, the parser automatically generates error messages with line and column numbers. If an expected *terminal symbol* is not recognized, this is reported as follows:

```
production:      S = a b c.
input:           a x c
error message:   -- line ... col ...: b expected
```

If none of the alternatives in an *alternative list* match, the parser reports that the nonterminal symbol to which the alternative list belongs is invalid:

production: S = a (b | c | d) e.
input: a x e
error message: -- line ... col ..: invalid S

To make such error messages more specific, the alternative list can be made into a separate nonterminal symbol:

production: S = a T e.
                T = b | c | d.
input: a x e
error message: -- line ... col ..: invalid T

If a descriptive name is chosen for T, a sufficiently good error message will be printed.

7.3.2 Syntax Error Recovery

Once a syntax error occurs, the erroneous input stream must be synchronized with the grammar so that the parser can proceed and find further errors. The parsers generated by Coco/R use the technique of *specific anchors* for syntax error recovery (see Sect. 3.4.3): the synchronization occurs only in a few places where particularly "safe" terminal symbols are expected that do not occur anywhere else in the grammar. Appropriate places are the beginning of statements (where keywords such as if or while are expected) or the beginning of declarations (where keywords such as void or public are expected). However, these places cannot be determined automatically by Coco/R and so need to be identified and marked in the grammar, as they are language-dependent. The keyword SYNC is used to do this as shown in the following example:

```
Statement
= SYNC
  (   Designator ('=' Expr | '(' ActPars ')') SYNC ';'
  |   "if" '(' Expr ')' Statement ["else" Statement]
  |   "while" '(' Expr ')' Statement
  |   ...
  ).
```

If a syntax error is detected, the parser reports it and then continues to run until it reaches the next synchronization point marked by SYNC (follow-up error messages are suppressed). At the synchronization point, the parser skips terminal symbols until it finds one that is expected there:

```
while (la.kind is not expected here) {
    Get(); // get next token from the scanner
}
```

7.3.3 Semantic Error Messages

Semantic errors are detected in semantic actions and must be reported by calling the method SemErr(). For example:

```
Expr <out Struct type>       (. Struct type1; .)
= Term <out type>
  { '+' Term <out type1>     (. if (type != type1) SemErr("incompatible types"); .)
  } .
```

SemErr() is a method of the generated parser that augments the error message with the line and column number of the most recent token and forwards it to the SemErr() method of the Errors class:

```
public void SemErr (String msg) {
    errors.SemErr(t.line, t.col, msg);
}
```

During syntax error recovery, terminal symbols may have been skipped and certain semantic actions may not have been executed. Thus, you must be aware that certain variables may not have the value expected. This can be countered with defensive programming, e.g., by including plausibility checks on individual values.

7.3.4 Class Errors

To manage error messages, Coco/R also generates a class Errors with the following interface:

```
public class Errors {
    public int count = 0;                                    // number of errors detected
    public PrintStream errorStream = System.out;             // error message stream
    public String errMsgFormat = "-- line {0} col {1}: {2}"; // 0 = line, 1 = column, 2 = msg
    public void SynErr (int line, int col, int n) { ... }
    public void SemErr (int line, int col, String msg) { ... }
}
```

Syntax errors are reported by the parser using SynErr(), and semantic errors are reported using SemErr(). Both methods write an error message to errorStream and increment the error counter count.

The default output stream is the console, but you can assign a different value to errorStream so that the error messages go to a file, for example. By changing the variable errMsgFormat you can also adapt the format of the error messages (e.g., for messages in some language other than English).

7.4 LL(1) Conflicts

Perhaps the greatest benefit of Coco/R is that it checks if a grammar is well-formed. It verifies that all nonterminal symbols are declared and that there are no circular dependencies between productions (see Sect. 3.3). In particular, it checks the grammar for any LL(1) conflicts and reports these so that they can be eliminated by transforming the grammar.

If you take a grammar from the Internet or from a language description, it is usually not LL(1). Finding and resolving LL(1) conflicts in non-trivial grammars is complicated and error-prone. Coco/R helps you with this and ensures that the grammar is suitable for recursive descent parsing. For example, for the grammar

```
PRODUCTIONS
  Sample    = {Statement} .
  Statement = Qualident '=' number ';'
            | Call
            | "if" '(' ident ')' Statement ["else" Statement] .
  Call      = ident '(' ')' ';' .
  Qualident = [ident '.'] ident .
```

Coco/R reports the following LL(1) conflicts:

```
LL1 warning in Statement: ident is start of several alternatives
LL1 warning in Statement: "else" is start & successor of deletable structure
LL1 warning in Qualident: ident is start & successor of deletable structure
```

The first conflict comes from the fact that the first two alternatives of Statement start with Qualident and Call, and these in turn start with ident. So both alternatives can start with ident, and the parser cannot decide which one to choose. The conflict must therefore be resolved by transforming the grammar.

The second conflict is the well-known problem of the *dangling else* (see Sect. 3.3). The keyword else can be both the start of the optional else branch and a successor of the option (and thus of Statement). As we have seen, however, this conflict can be ignored. The parser always chooses the first suitable alternative, which in this case is the optional else branch. This is the desired behavior in if statements.

The third conflict occurs in the production of Qualident, which contains an option. Both the start and the successor of this option is ident, so the parser cannot decide whether to enter or skip the option. This conflict must also be eliminated by transformation.

This grammar is not particularly complicated, so the LL(1) conflicts would probably have been found also without the help of Coco/R. However, with large or complex grammars, discovering such conflicts can become quite difficult and time-consuming.

LL(1) conflicts can usually be eliminated by transforming the grammar, which is necessary for the first and third conflicts of our example. The second conflict can be ignored (effectively, it is just a warning in this case). The transformed grammar looks like this:

7.4 LL(1) Conflicts

```
Sample    = {Statement} .
Statement = ident ( ['.' ident] '=' number ';'
                  | '(' ')' ';'
                  )
          | "if" '(' ident ')' Statement ["else" Statement] .
```

The conflicts here were resolved by factorization. ident has been extracted from Qualident and Call, and only afterwards do the alternatives separate. However, such a transformation is not always possible, and even if it is possible, as here, it does not really make the grammar more readable or easier to understand. Therefore, Coco/R offers also other ways for resolving LL(1) conflicts.

7.4.1 Conflict Resolution by Multi-symbol Lookahead

The following grammar

```
A = ident {',' ident} ':' ...
  | ident {',' ident} ';' .
```

is not LL(1), but can easily be transformed by factorization into:

```
A = ident {',' ident} ( ':' ... | ';' ) .
```

However, if different semantic actions are to be performed in both alternatives, such as in

```
A = ident (. x = 1; .) {',' ident (. x++; .) } ':' ...
  | ident (. foo(); .) {',' ident (. bar(); .) } ';' .
```

this factorization is no longer possible. Coco/R therefore offers the option of placing a so-called *conflict resolver* before the first of the conflicting alternatives. A conflict resolver has the form:

```
IF (BooleanExpr)
```

The alternative is then only chosen if the Boolean expression is true. Our grammar can thus be written as follows:

```
A = IF (followedByColon())
    ident (. x = 1; .) {',' ident (. x++; .) } ':' ...
  | ident (. foo(); .) {',' ident (. bar(); .) } ';' .
```

The method followedByColon() resolves the conflict by looking ahead in the token stream to see whether there is a ':' after the list of identifiers. In this case, it returns true, otherwise false. If it returns true, the parser enters the alternative annotated with the resolver, otherwise it continues with the next alternative.

We implement the method followedByColon() in the global declarations of the compiler specification and use the scanner's Peek() method for looking ahead. On each call, Peek() returns the next token, without removing these tokens from the input stream so that they are delivered again later during regular scanning. So Peek() allows us to look ahead arbitrarily far.

```
boolean followedByColon() {
  Token x = la; // start with the lookahead token
  while (x.kind == _ident || x.kind == _comma) { // read beyond identifiers and commas
    x = scanner.Peek();
  }
  return x.kind == _colon;
}
```

The names _ident, _comma and _colon are automatically generated by Coco/R for all declared tokens. To make this work, however, we must explicitly declare the symbols ',' and ':' as tokens, in addition to their use as literals in the grammar:

```
TOKENS
  ident = letter {letter | digit}.
  comma = ',' .
  colon = ':' .
  ...
```

Coco/R then generates constant declarations for them:

```
static final int
  _ident = 1,
  _comma = 2,
  _colon = 3,
  ...
```

7.4.2 Conflict Resolution by Semantic Information

Conflict resolvers can resolve LL(1) conflicts not only by lookahead, but also by using semantic information. Let's consider the following grammar:

```
Factor = '(' ident ')' Factor   // type cast
       | '(' Expr ')'            // nested expression
       | ident
       | number.
```

The first alternative describes a type cast, the second a nested expression. Both alternatives start with '(', so the grammar is not LL(1). But it is not LL(2) either, because Expr can start with ident, so even a lookahead of 2 tokens does not help. Even if we look ahead for 3 tokens, we cannot resolve the conflict because '(' ident ')' can be both a type cast and a nested expression.

A lookahead or a transformation of the grammar do not help here, but we can again place a conflict resolver in front of the first alternative, which checks whether ident denotes a type. In this case, it must be a type cast; otherwise it's a nested expression.

```
Factor = IF (isCast())
           '(' ident ')' Factor    // type cast
         | '(' Expr ')'            // nested expression
         | ident
         | number.
```

Here is how we implement the resolver method:

```
boolean isCast() { // la contains _lpar, ident or number
  Token next = scanner.Peek();
  if (la.kind == _lpar && next.kind == _ident) {  // if we have '(' ident
    Obj obj = Tab.find(next.val);                 // look up the name in the symbol table
    return obj.kind == Obj.Type;                  // return true if the name denotes a type
  } else return false;
}
```

With conflict resolvers, it is possible to resolve LL(1) conflicts by multi-symbol lookahead or by semantic information. Coco/R can thus process grammars that are LL(*), i.e., grammars in which alternatives can be distinguished by (arbitrarily far) lookahead or by semantic information. This makes Coco/R a powerful tool.

7.5 Examples

We will now look at some examples that show how to use Coco/R in practice, deliberately choosing also examples that do not come from compiler construction in the strict sense. After all, this book is intended to show that the techniques presented here are also useful for applications outside of actual compiler construction.

7.5.1 Reading a Binary Tree

We start with a small but not trivial example. We want to develop a program that reads a textual representation of a binary tree in bracket notation and builds this binary tree in memory. This is not a compiler in the strict sense, but a program that processes a syntactically structured input and translates it into some other representation. Thus, we can apply the techniques of compiler construction.

Figure 7.4 shows the textual representation of the input (in bracket notation) and the corresponding binary tree.

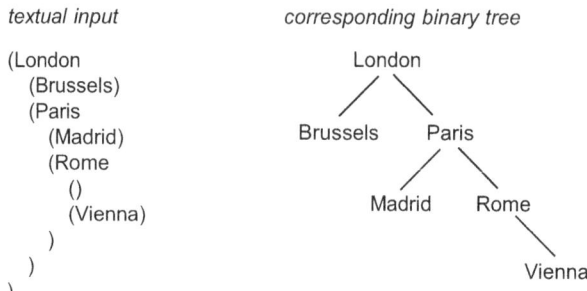

```
textual input
(London
  (Brussels)
  (Paris
    (Madrid)
    (Rome
      ()
      (Vienna)
    )
  )
)
```

Fig. 7.4 Binary tree in bracket notation

To be able to process the input by an attributed grammar, we first need to set up a context-free grammar for it. In doing so, it is helpful to think about the patterns that may appear in the input. A subtree can take one of the following three forms:

Subtree
= '(' ')'   // empty subtree
| '(' ident ')'   // subtree with a single leaf node
| '(' ident Subtree Subtree ')' .   // subtree with a root and two subtrees

These three alternatives can be combined by factorization to form the following grammar, which describes our input and is LL(1):

Subtree
= '(' [ident [Subtree Subtree]] ')' .

The nonterminal symbol Subtree should return as an output attribute the root of a binary tree with nodes of the following type:

```
class Node {
  String name;
  Node left, right;
  Node (String s) { name = s; }
}
```

The semantic actions should assemble new trees from their subtrees. Finally, to check that the whole tree was built correctly, it should be output again in bracket notation using the method print(). The compiler specification, which is stored in a file TreeReader.atg, has the following form:

```
COMPILER TreeReader
  class Node { ... } // see above
  static void print (Node n, int indent) { ... } // see below
CHARACTERS
  letter = 'A' .. 'Z' + 'a' .. 'z'.
TOKENS
  ident = letter {letter}.
IGNORE '\t' + '\r' + '\n'
```

7.5 Examples

PRODUCTIONS

TreeReader   (. Node n;.)
=   Subtree <out n>   (. print(n, 0); .).

Subtree <out Node n>
=   '('   (. n = null; .)
    [ident   (. n = new Node(t.val); .)
        [Subtree <out n.left>
            Subtree <out n.right>
        ]
    ]
    ')' .
END TreeReader.

The terminal symbols are ident as well as the literals '(' and ')', which do not have to be declared, but can be used directly in the attributed grammar. ident is declared as a sequence of letters. Line endings and tab characters should be ignored.

The attributed grammar consists of productions for the start symbol TreeReader and for the nonterminal symbol Subtree. Subtree returns a (possibly empty) subtree n and is recursively called to build the left and right subtrees, which are connected to n.left and n.right. Calling Subtree in TreeReader returns the entire tree, which is printed using print(). The parameter indent is used to control the indenting of subtrees in the output.

```
static void print (Node n, int indent) {
    for (int i = 0; i < indent; i++) System.out.print(' ');   // indent
    System.out.print('(');                                    // opening bracket
    if (n != null) {
        System.out.print(n.name);                             // node name
        if (n.left != null || n.right != null) {
            System.out.println();
            print(n.left, indent + 2);                        // left subtree with increased indent
            print(n.right, indent + 2);                       // right subtree with increased indent
            for (int i = 0; i < indent; i++) System.out.print(' ');
        }
    }
    System.out.println(')');                                  // closing bracket
}
```

Finally, we need a main program that starts the parser:

```
class TreeReader {
    public static void main (String[] arg) {
        Scanner.scanner = new Scanner(arg[0]);
        Parser parser = new Parser(scanner);
        parser.Parse();
        System.out.println(parser.errors.count + " errors detected");
    }
}
```

The compiler specification is now processed with Coco/R:

    java -jar Coco.jar TreeReader.atg

Coco/R generates the files Scanner.java and Parser.java, which must be compiled by the Java compiler along with the main program:

    javac Scanner.java Parser.java TreeReader.java

Our "compiler" can then be invoked with an input file input.txt:

    java TreeReader input.txt

input.txt contains a textual representation of a binary tree in the form shown in Fig. 7.4 on the left. The file is parsed, a binary tree is built in memory and finally printed out for control purposes.

7.5.2 Questionnaire Generator

Our second example illustrates a *domain-specific language*, i.e., a self-defined language for a specific domain. In our case, we want to design a language for creating questionnaires. The result should be a questionnaire that is displayed in an internet web browser and could look as shown in Fig. 7.5.

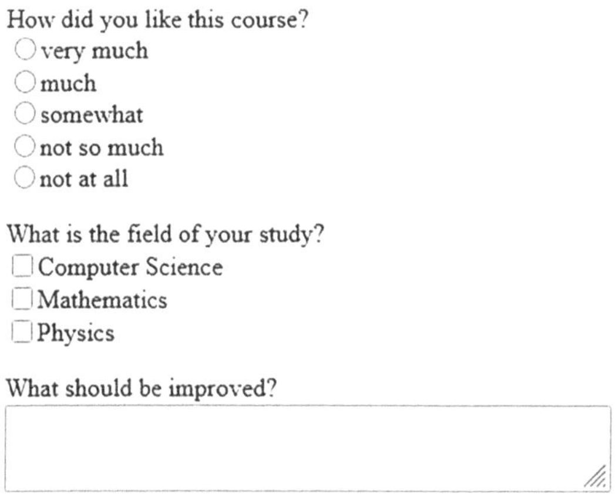

Fig. 7.5 Web questionnaire

Of course, we could write the user interface directly in the browser's hypertext markup language (HTML), but that would be tedious and error-prone. Instead, we want to design a small language that can be used to specify the content and structure of the questionnaire. The user interface can then be automatically created by processing the questionaire's specification.

7.5 Examples

The description of the questionnaire in our domain-specific language could look like this:

```
RADIO "How did you like this course?"
   ("very much", "much", "somewhat", "not so much", "not at all")
CHECKBOX "What is the field of your study?"
   ("Computer Science", "Mathematics", "Physics")
TEXTBOX "What should be improved?"
```

So how can we translate this input into an interactive questionnaire on the website? First, we need to describe the input by a context-free grammar. Then we need to consider which attributes the symbols should provide and which methods we want to call in the semantic actions to generate the equivalent in HTML. Finally, we can set up an attributed grammar and process it with Coco/R.

The input obviously consists of several queries that can take one of three forms (RADIO, CHECKBOX, TEXTBOX). The first two forms include a list of values defined as strings. So the context-free grammar is:

```
Queryform = {Query}.
Query     = "RADIO" Caption Values
          | "CHECKBOX" Caption Values
          | "TEXTBOX" Caption.
Caption   = string.
Values    = '(' string {',' string} ')'.
```

The nonterminal symbol Caption should return a string as an output attribute, the nonterminal symbol Values a list of strings. To output HTML code, we define the following methods, which we implement in a class HtmlGenerator:

- printHeader() creates the HTML header
- printFooter() creates the HTML footer
- printRadio(caption, values) creates a sequence of radio buttons
- printCheckbox(caption, values) creates a sequence of checkboxes
- printTextbox(caption) creates a text box

The terminal symbols of the grammar are string as well as the literals '(', ')' and ',', which we do not have to declare as tokens. Thus, we can implement the attributed grammar as follows:

```
import java.util.ArrayList;
COMPILER QueryForm
   HtmlGenerator html; // to emit the HTML code
CHARACTERS
   noQuote = ANY - '"'.
TOKENS
   string = '"' {noQuote} '"'.
COMMENTS FROM "//" TO "\r\n"
IGNORE '\t' + '\r' + '\n'
```

```
PROUDUCTIONS
QueryForm =                              (. html.printHeader(); .)
{ Query }                                (. html.printFooter(); .) .
//-------------------------------------------------------------------------------------
Query                                    (. String caption; ArrayList values; .)
= "RADIO" Caption <out caption> Values <out values>
                                         (. html.printRadio(caption, values); .)
| "CHECKBOX" Caption <out caption> Values <out values>
                                         (. html.printCheckbox(caption, values); .)
| "TEXTBOX" Caption <out caption>
                                         (. html.printTextbox(caption); .) .
//-------------------------------------------------------------------------------------
Caption <out String s> = StringVal<out s>.
//-------------------------------------------------------------------------------------
Values <out ArrayList values>            (. String s; .)
= '(' StringVal <out s>                  (. values = new ArrayList(); values.add(s); .)
   { ',' StringVal <out s>               (. values.add(s); .)
   }
   ')'.
//-------------------------------------------------------------------------------------
StringVal <out String s>
= string                                 (. s = t.val.substring(1, t.val.length()-1); .) .
END QueryForm.
```

The grammar defines an additional nonterminal symbol StringVal, which returns the value of a string (without quotes) as an attribute. The attributes provided by Caption and Values are passed to the methods of the HTML generator, which generate the corresponding HTML code. The class HtmlGenerator looks like this:

```
import java.io.*;
import java.util.ArrayList;
class HtmlGenerator {
  PrintStream s;
  int itemNo = 0;  // current query number
  public HtmlGenerator(String fileName) throws FileNotFoundException {
    s = new PrintStream(fileName);
  }
  public void printHeader() {
    s.println("<html>");
    s.println("<head><title>Query Form</title></head>");
    s.println("<body>");
    s.println("  <form>");
  }
  public void printFooter() {
    s.println("  </form>");
    s.println("</body>");
    s.println("</html>");
    s.close();
  }
```

7.5 Examples

```
    public void printRadio(String caption, ArrayList values) {
      s.println(caption + "<br>");
      for (Object val: values) {
        s.print("<input type='radio' name='Q" + itemNo + "' ");
        s.print("value='" + val + "'>" + val + "<br>");
        s.println();
      }
      itemNo++; s.println("<br>");
    }
    public void printCheckbox(String caption, ArrayList values) {
      s.println(caption + "<br>");
      for (Object val: values) {
        s.print("<input type='checkbox' name='Q" + itemNo + "' ");
        s.print("value='" + val + "'>" + val + "<br>");
        s.println();
      }
      itemNo++; s.println("<br>");
    }
    public void printTextbox(String caption) {
      s.println(caption + "<br>");
      s.println("<textarea name='Q" + itemNo + "' cols='50' rows='3'></textarea><br>");
      itemNo++; s.println("<br>");
    }
  }
```

The printRadio() method, for example, outputs the following HTML code for the above input:

```
How did you like this course?<br>
<input type='radio' name='Q0' value='very much'>very much<br>
<input type='radio' name='Q0' value='much'>much<br>
<input type='radio' name='Q0' value='somewhat'>somewhat<br>
<input type='radio' name='Q0' value='not so much'>not so much<br>
<input type='radio' name='Q0' value='not at all'>not at all<br>
<br>
```

Finally, we need a main program, which reads the command line arguments, creates and initializes the scanner and the parser, and then starts the parser. It also creates an object of the class HtmlGenerator and assigns it to the global variable parser.html so that the attributed grammar can access it. The main program could look like this:

```
import java.io.*;
class MakeQueryForm {
  public static void main(String[] args) {
    String inFileName = args[0];
    String outFileName = args[1];
    Scanner scanner = new Scanner(inFileName);
    Parser parser = new Parser(scanner);
```

```
      try {
        parser.html = new HtmlGenerator(outFileName);
        parser.Parse();
        System.out.println(parser.errors.count + " errors detected");
      } catch (FileNotFoundException e) {
        System.out.println("-- cannot create file " + outFileName);
      }
    }
  }
```

We process our compiler specification again using Coco/R:

```
java -jar Coco.jar QueryForm.atg
```

and get the files Scanner.java and Parser.java, which we compile together with the files HtmlGenerator.java and MakeQueryForm.java:

```
javac Scanner.java Parser.java HtmlGenerator.java MakeQueryForm.java
```

Assuming our questionnaire description is in the file input.txt and the output should be written to the file output.html, our questionnaire generator can be invoked as:

```
java MakeQueryForm input.txt output.html
```

7.5.3 Abstract Syntax Trees

The last example comes from the core area of compiler construction. We want to develop a compiler that translates programs of a simple language called *Taste* into abstract syntax trees (ASTs). Abstract syntax trees (see Sect. 1.5) are a common intermediate representation of programs on which optimizations can be performed before machine code is generated. However, we will concentrate here on the mere generation of ASTs without optimizations and code generation.

Some compiler generators use special notations to generate abstract syntax trees. However, we want to show here that it is just as easy to use ordinary attributed grammars for this.

Remember: an AST is a tree whose leaves are operands and whose inner nodes are operators. Figure 7.6 shows what the assignment x = 3 * x + 1 looks like as an AST, where the assignment operator '=' is also regarded as an operator.

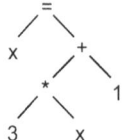

Fig. 7.6 AST for the assignment x = 3 * x + 1;

7.5 Examples

Basic Idea

The basic idea behind the generation of an AST is that each nonterminal symbol provides a sub-AST as an output attribute, which is then combined with other sub-ASTs to form a new AST. An example of this can be seen in the following production:

```
Expr <out Node e>                    (. Node e1, e2; .)
= Term <out e1> '+' Term <out e2>    (. e = new BinExpr(e1, Operator.PLUS, e2); .).
```

This results in the AST shown in Fig. 7.7.

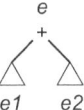

Fig. 7.7 AST generated from the Expr production

The nodes of the AST are objects of classes such as Expr or BinExpr that are derived from a common base class Node.

```
abstract class Node {}                      // base class of all nodes
abstract class Expr extends Node {}         // base class of nodes that form (sub)expressions
class BinExpr extends Expr {                // class describing binary expressions
    Operator op;
    Expr left;                              // left subexpression
    Expr right;                             // right subexpression
    BinExpr (Expr e1, Operator op, Expr e2) { this.op = op; left = e1; right = e2; }
}
enum Operator {ADD, SUB, MUL, DIV, ...}
```

In the following, we will first introduce our example language *Taste*, and then show how to build abstract syntax trees for expressions, statements, declarations, and procedures.

The Example Language Taste

Our example language *Taste* has a few simple kinds of statements as well as global variables and parameterless procedures with local variables. The only data types are int and bool. The language has been deliberately kept simple. However, readers should have no difficulties extending it with additional constructs. The context-free grammar of *Taste* is:

```
Taste    = "program" ident "{" { VarDecl | ProcDecl } "}".
VarDecl  = Type ident { "," ident } ";".
Type     = "int" | "bool".
ProcDecl = "void" ident "(" ")" Block.
Block    = "{" { Stat | VarDecl } "}".
Stat     = ident ( "=" Expr | "(" ")" ) ";"
         | "if" "(" Expr ")" Stat [ "else" Stat ]
         | "while" "(" Expr ")" Stat
         | "read" ident ";"
         | "write" Expr ";"
         | Block.
```

```
Expr     = SimExpr [ RelOp SimExpr ].
SimExpr  = Term { AddOp Term }.
Term     = Factor { MulOp Factor }.
Factor   = ident | number | "-" Factor | "true" | "false".
RelOp    = "==" | "<" | ">".
AddOp    = "+" | "-".
MulOp    = "*" | "/".
```

Abstract Syntax Trees for Expressions

With expressions, we distinguish between *binary expressions*, *unary expressions*, and *leaf nodes* (Fig. 7.8).

Fig. 7.8 ASTs for binary expressions, unary expressions, and leaf nodes

As we have already seen, each node of the AST is represented by an object of a class derived from Node. Thus, we need classes for binary expressions, unary expressions, and leaf nodes, as well as an enumeration type for the various operators:

```
abstract class Expr extends Node {}
class BinExpr extends Expr {
   Operator op;
   Expr left, right;
   BinExpr (Expr e1, Operator op, Expr e2) { this.op = op; left = e1; right = e2; }
}
class UnaryExpr extends Expr {
   Operator op:
   Expr e;
   UnaryExpr (Operator op, Expr e) { this.op = op; this.e = e; }
}
class Ident extends Expr {
   Obj obj;
   Ident (Obj obj) { this.obj = obj; }
}
class IntCon extends Expr {
   int val;
   IntCon (int val) { this.val = val; }
}
class BoolCon extends Expr {
   boolean val;
   BoolCon (boolean val) { this.val = val; }
}
enum Operator {EQU, LSS, GTR, ADD, SUB, MUL, DIV}
```

7.5 Examples

Using an attributed grammar, we can now build ASTs for expressions. Nonterminal symbols provide sub-ASTs, which are assembled into new ASTs using the constructors of the classes described above.

```
Expr <out Expr e>            (. Operator op; Expr e2; .)
= SimExpr <out e>
  [ RelOp <out op>
    SimExpr <out e2>         (. e = new BinExpr(e, op, e2); .)
  ].
SimExpr <out Expr e>         (. Operator op; Expr e2; .)
= Term <out e>
  { AddOp <out op>
    Term <out e2>            (. e = new BinExpr(e, op, e2); .)
  }.
Term <out Expr e>            (. Operator op; Expr e2; .)
= Factor <out e>
  { MulOp <out op>
    Factor <out e2>          (. e = new BinExpr(e, op, e2); .)
  }.
Factor <out Expr e>          (. String name; .)
= Ident <out name>           (. e = new Ident(curProc.find(name)); .)
| number                     (. e = new IntCon(Integer.parseInt(t.val)); .)
| "-" Factor <out e>         (. e = new UnaryExpr(Operator.SUB, e); .)
| "true"                     (. e = new BoolCon(true); .)
| "false"                    (. e = new BoolCon(false); .).
Ident <out String name>
= ident                      (. name = t.val; .).
AddOp <out Operator op>
=   "+"                      (. op = Operator.ADD; .)
|   "-"                      (. op = Operator.SUB; .).
MulOp <out Operator op>
=   "*"                      (. op = Operator.MUL; .)
|   "/"                      (. op = Operator.DIV; .).
RelOp <out Operator op>
=   "=="                     (. op = Operator.EQU; .)
|   "<"                      (. op = Operator.LSS; .)
|   ">"                      (. op = Operator.GTR; .).
```

In principle, the grammar should be comprehensible to the reader without much explanation. Factor returns a leaf of a tree, while Expr, SimExpr and Term assemble subtrees into new trees. The call of curProc.find(name) in the production of Factor looks up a name in the scope of the current procedure and returns an object of type Obj, which will be explained in more detail later. Figure 7.9 shows the AST for the expression −3 * x + y.

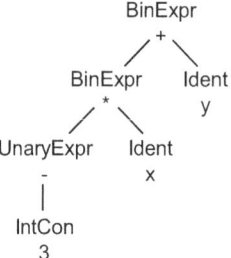

Fig. 7.9 AST for the expression -3 * x + y

Abstract Syntax Trees for Statements

For each kind of statement, there is an AST node that represents the root of a subtree for that statement. Figure 7.10 shows the different kinds of statements and their subtrees.

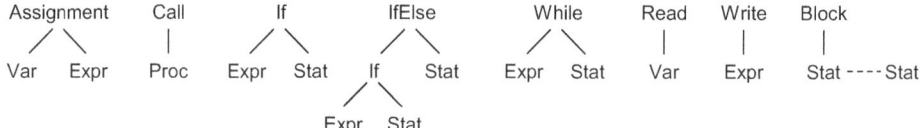

Fig. 7.10 ASTs for statements

We declare the necessary node classes as follows (the classes for Var and Proc will be described in the next section):

```
abstract class Stat extends Node {}
class Assignment extends Stat {
  Var left;
  Expr right;
  Assignment (Var v, Expr e) { left = v; right = e; }
}
class Call extends Stat {
  Proc proc;
  Call (Proc p) { proc = p; }
}
class If extends Stat {
  Expr cond;
  Stat stat;
  If (Expr e, Stat s) { cond = e; stat = s; }
}
class IfElse extends Stat {
  Stat ifPart;
  Stat elsePart;
  IfElse (Stat i, Stat e) { ifPart = i; elsePart = e; }
}
```

7.5 Examples

```
class While extends Stat {
    Expr cond;
    Stat stat;
    While (Expr e, Stat s) { cond = e; stat = s; }
}
class Read extends Stat {
    Var var;
    Read (var v) { var = v; }
}
class Write extends Stat {
    Expr e;
    Write (Expr e) { this.e = e; }
}
class Block extends Stat {
    List<Stat> stats = new ArrayList<Stat>();
    void add (Stat s) { stats.add(s); }
}
```

The following attributed grammar builds the ASTs for statements:

```
Block <out block b>                    (. Stat s; .)
= "{"                                  (. b = new Block(); .)
    { Stat <out s>                     (. b.add(s); .)
    | VarDecl
    }
    "}" .

Stat <out Stat s>                      (. String name; Expr e; Stat s2; Block b; .)
=                                      (. s = null; .)
    ( Ident <out name>                 (. Obj obj = curProc.find(name); .)
        ( "=" Expr <out e> ";"         (. s = new Assignment((Var)obj, e); .)
        | "(" ")" ";"                  (. s = new Call((Proc)obj); .)
        )
    | "if" "(" Expr <out e> ")"
        Stat <out s>                   (. s = new If(e, s); .)
        [ "else" Stat <out s2>         (. s = new IfElse(s, s2); .)
        ]
    | "while" "(" Expr <out e> ")"
        Stat <out s>                   (. s = new While(e, s); .)
    | "read" Ident <out name> ";"      (. s = new Read((Var)curProc.find(name)); .)
    | "write" Expr <out e> ";"         (. s = new Write(e); .)
    | Block <out b>                    (. s = b; .)
    ) .
```

For the following snippet of a *Taste* program

```
{ if (x > y) max = x; else max = y;
  while (max > 0) {
      z = max / 10;
      write max – 10 * z;
      max = z;
  }
}
```

the AST shown in Fig. 7.11 is generated.

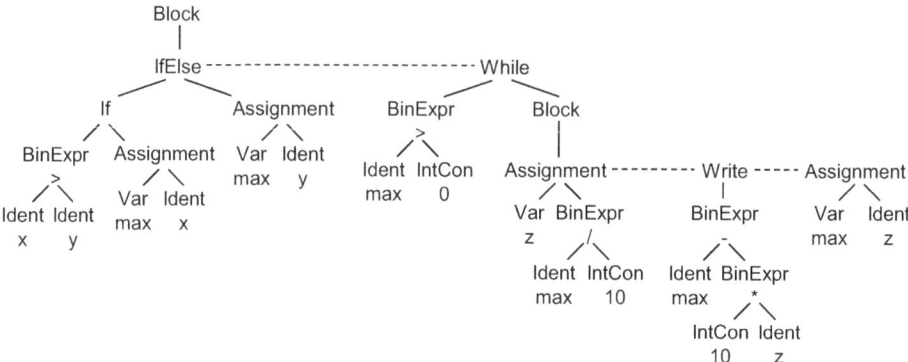

Fig. 7.11 AST for the Taste program snippet

Abstract Syntax Trees for Declarations and Procedures

Declared names are usually stored in the symbol table (see Chap. 5). In our example, however, we integrate the declarations into the AST as special nodes. There are two types of declarations in Taste: variables and procedures. So we declare the node classes Var and Proc, which are derived from a general class Obj. Nodes of type Proc maintain a list of local variables. They represent, so to speak, a scope of the symbol table, with the methods insert() for inserting and find() for looking up names. For objects, we store also their type (INT or BOOL). For procedures, we use the type VOID.

```
class Obj extends Node {     // any declared object that has a name
    String name;              // name of this object
    Type type;                // type of this object (VOID for procedures)
    Obj (String s, Type t) { name = s; type = t; }
}
class Var extends Obj {       // variable
    int adr;                  // address in memory
    Var (String name, Type type) { super(name, type); }
}
class Proc extends Obj {      // procedure (also used for the program)
    List<Obj> locals;         // objects declared in this procedure
    int nVars = 0;            // number of variables in this procedure == next free address
    Block block;              // block of this procedure (null for the program, which has no block)
    Proc program;             // link to the Proc node of the main program or null
    Proc (String name, Proc program) {
        super(name, Type.VOID);
        locals = new ArrayList<Obj>();
        this.program = program;
    }
    void insert (Obj obj) {
        for (Obj x: locals) {
            if (x.name.equals(obj.name)) SemErr(obj.name + " declared twice");
        }
```

7.5 Examples

```
    locals.add(obj);
    if (obj instanceof Var) ((Var)obj).adr = nVars++;
  }
  Obj find (String name) {
    for (Obj x: locals) { if (x.name.equals(name)) return x; }
    if (program != null) {
      for (Obj x: program.locals) { if (x.name.equals(name)) return x; }
    }
    SemErr(name + " undeclared"); // name not found
    return new Obj("_undef", Type.INT); // error object
  }
}
enum Type { VOID, INT, BOOL }
```

The following attributed grammar processes declarations and enters declared names into the symbol table:

Taste	(. String name; .)
= "program" Ident <out name>	(. curProc = new Proc(name, null); .)
"{"	
{ VarDecl | ProcDecl }	
"}" .	
VarDecl	(. String name; Type type; .)
= Type <out type>	
Ident <out name>	(. curProc.insert(new Var(name, type)); .)
{ "," Ident <out name>	(. curProc.insert(new Var(name, type)); .)
} ";" .	
Type <out Type type>	
= "int"	(. type = Type.INT; .)
| "bool"	(. type = Type.BOOL; .) .
ProcDecl	(. String name; .)
= "void" Ident <out name>	(. Proc program = curProc;
	curProc = new Proc(name, program);
	program.insert(curProc); .)
"(" ")"	
Block <out curProc.block>	(. curProc = program; .) .

curProc is a global variable that holds the current procedure. For the program fragment

```
program Sample {
  int x;
  bool y;
  void foo() { int a, b; ... }
  void bar() { int c, d; ... }
}
```

the AST shown in Fig. 7.12 is generated.

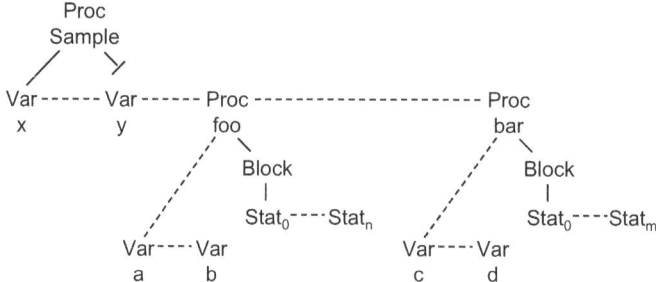

Fig. 7.12 AST for the program Sample

Figure 7.13 summarizes the hierarchy of the AST node classes.

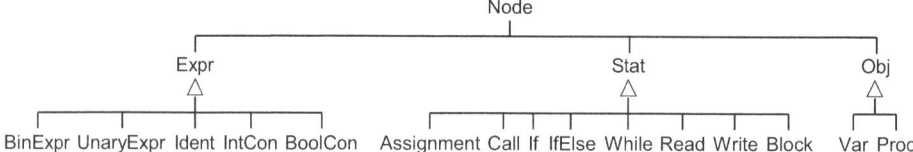

Fig. 7.13 Node classes of the AST

We have now covered all the language constructs of *Taste* and shown how to translate them into abstract syntax trees. The above productions can simply be inserted into a compiler specification for Coco/R. What is still missing, however, is the scanner description. The only two terminal symbols we need to declare are ident and number; all other terminal symbols are literals. The compiler specification therefore looks like this:

```
COMPILER Taste
   Proc curProc; // current program unit (procedure or main program)
CHARACTERS
   letter   = 'A' .. 'Z' + 'a' .. 'z'.
   digit    = '0' .. '9'.
TOKENS
   ident    = letter {letter | digit}.
   number   = digit {digit}.
COMMENTS FROM "//" to "\r\n"
IGNORE '\t' + '\r' + '\n'
PRODUCTIONS
   ... // productions as described above
END Taste.
```

The classes for the AST nodes can either be declared directly in the global semantic declarations or stored in separate files. We also need a main program, which is similar to the main program in the previous examples:

```
class Taste {
  public static void main (String[] arg) {
    Scanner scanner = new Scanner(arg[0]);
    Parser parser = new Parser(scanner);
    parser.Parse();
    System.out.println(parser.errors.count + " error(s) detected");
  }
}
```

Finally, the compiler specification must be processed with Coco/R, and the generated scanner and parser must be compiled together with the Java files for the classes of the AST nodes:

```
java -jar Coco.jar Taste.atg
javac Scanner.java Parser.java Taste.java ...
```

The *Taste* compiler can then be invoked as follows:

```
java Taste inputFile.tas
```

If you want to try out the Taste compiler and experiment with it further, you can download the necessary files from [Download].

Summary

The examples in this chapter have shown that Coco/R is a useful tool for generating compilers or compiler-like tools from a compact compiler specification. Coco/R and the techniques described in this book can be used whenever there is a syntactically structured input that can be described by a grammar. Examples of such applications are (in addition to compilers in the strict sense):

- Compilers for domain-specific languages
- Tools for static program analysis
- Tools for calculating metrics from source code
- Tools for instrumenting source code
- Tools for analyzing log files
- Tools for processing measurement data series

Coco/R is based on attributed grammars that satisfy the LL(*) property, i.e., where alternatives can be distinguished by an arbitrarily far lookahead or by semantic information. This makes Coco/R a powerful tool for many applications, even outside of compiler construction proper.

7.6 Exercises

For the tasks in this chapter, you will use Coco/R. So download the files Coco.jar, Scanner.frame and Parser.frame (for Java) from *https://ssw.jku.at/coco/* and store them in the same directory as the compiler specification for the respective task.

1. *Path calculation.* Given is a text file containing a sequence of points with coordinates in the format (n, m), where n and m are integer constants. Write an attributed grammar that processes this input by calculating and printing the length of the path from the first to the last point. Use Coco/R to generate a scanner and a parser and write a main program that starts the processing.

2. *Interpreter for Boolean expressions.* In Exercise 7 of Chap. 4, you specified a scripting language for Boolean expressions and described its processing by an attributed grammar. Use Coco/R now to implement an interpreter that processes and executes programs of this scripting language. No code should be generated, but the instructions should be executed immediately during parsing.

    As a parser specification, you can use the attributed grammar developed in Exercise 7 of Chap. 4 in Coco/R notation. In the scanner specification, you only need to declare the terminal symbol ident. The symbol table holding the names and values of the variables should be managed as a hash table that is declared in the global declarations of the compiler specification. Write a main program that creates a scanner and a parser (like in the previous sections), and then starts the parser (and thus the interpreter). The name of the file with the script program should be passed to the main program as a command line argument.

    Use Coco/R to generate a scanner and a parser, and compile them together with the main program to get the executable interpreter.

3. *Processing a phone book.* Assume that persons and their phone numbers are stored in a text file with the following format:

    Doe, John Maxwell
       home +44 (20) 24684567,
       work (020) 234567
    Miller, Ann
       23456789
       ...

    Each entry begins with a surname, a comma, and one or more first names. This is followed by a comma-separated list of phone numbers, which can take one of the following forms:

+44 (20) 24680	Country code, area code in brackets without leading 0, number
(020) 234567	Area code in brackets with leading 0, number
23456789	Number without country code and area code

    Each phone number can be preceded by the keyword "home" or "work". If it is missing, "home" is assumed. If the country code is missing, "+44" is used, if the area code is missing, "020" is assumed.

    (a) Describe the structure of this text file by a context-free grammar.

    (b) Turn this into an attributed grammar so that the names and phone numbers are read and stored in a suitable data structure with separate fields for the country code, the area code, the number and the identification home/work. Output this data structure for control. Use Coco/R to create a program that reads the input file, builds the data structure and outputs it.

4. *Complexity analysis.* To determine the complexity of a program, metrics can be calculated from its source code, which allow an estimate of how difficult a program is to understand and maintain. There are various complexity metrics, but let us define one here that calculates the complexity of MicroJava methods from the complexity of their statements. To do this, we define the basic complexity of each statement type as follows:

- assignment: 1
- method call: 2
- ++ or --:   1
- if statement: 1 + 2 * (complexity of nested statements)
- while statement: 1 + 2 * (complexity of nested statements)
- break statement: 5
- return statement: 1
- read statement: 1
- print statement: 1

The complexity of a method is the sum of the complexities of its statements. Since nesting increases complexity, the complexity of nested statements is multiplied by a factor of 2. For example, the statement

if (x > 0) val = 1; else val = 2;

has a total complexity of 5: each assignment has a basic complexity of 1, which is multiplied by a factor of 2, resulting in a total of 4. The if statement itself has a basic complexity of 1, which is added to the total, giving 5. If the if statement were also nested, its total complexity would again be multiplied by a factor of 2, and so on.

Use Coco/R to implement a tool that calculates and prints the complexity of all methods in a MicroJava program. Use the MicroJava grammar from Appendix A as the parser specification and turn it into an attributed grammar such that the complexity of methods is calculated from the basic complexities of their statements. You can ignore function calls in expressions.

5. *Extraction of documentation comments.* For Java, there is a tool *javadoc* [JavaDoc] that extracts documentation comments from a Java source program. We want to implement a similar tool for MicroJava. A documentation comment starts with /** and ends with */. Any text may be placed in between, but the comments must not be nested. In MicroJava, it should be possible to place documentation comments in front of the declaration of constants, variables, classes, and methods. Documentation comments can contain *tags*, of which we only implement two here, namely for comments that precede method declarations.

@param ident ... *text* ...
@returns ... *text* ...

The @param tag describes a parameter with the name ident, and the @returns tag describes the method's return value. The texts, which explain the parameter or return value, continue until the next tag or until the end of the comment.

Use Coco/R to implement a tool that extracts all documentation comments from a MicroJava program and outputs them. For each commented program element (constant, variable, class, or method), list its name as well as its documentation comment including any tags and their components.

In your grammar, you only need to specify the relevant parts of a MicroJava program. Irrelevant parts can be skipped by {ANY} (*fuzzy parsing*, see the description of the symbol ANY in Sect. 7.2).

Bottom-up Syntax Analysis

In Chap. 3, we discussed *top-down* syntax analysis using recursive descent. Recursive descent parsing is simple and sufficient for most languages (possibly after transforming their grammar or with multi-symbol lookahead). It is also the only parsing technique that can be implemented manually (i.e., without tools).

In this chapter, we take a look at an alternative syntax analysis technique that works *bottom-up* and has the advantage that a larger class of grammars can be processed without transformation. The disadvantages, however, are that tools (parser generators) are usually needed to generate the necessary parser tables and that semantic processing is more complicated and less powerful.

8.1 How a Bottom-up Parser Works

In contrast to a top-down parser, a bottom-up parser builds the syntax tree of a program from the bottom up. Note that grammars here must be in pure BNF and not in EBNF. Let's look at this with an example. The following grammar

```
S = X Y | S X Y.
X = a | a a b.
Y = b | b b a.
```

is not LL(1) because the first production is left-recursive and the other productions have alternatives that start with the same terminal symbols (see Sect. 3.3). To be able to process this grammar with recursive descent, it has to be transformed. A bottom-up parser, however, can process it without prior transformation. To analyze the input

```
a b b a a b
```

the syntax tree is built from the bottom up, using *reductions* instead of derivations, as shown in Fig. 8.1.

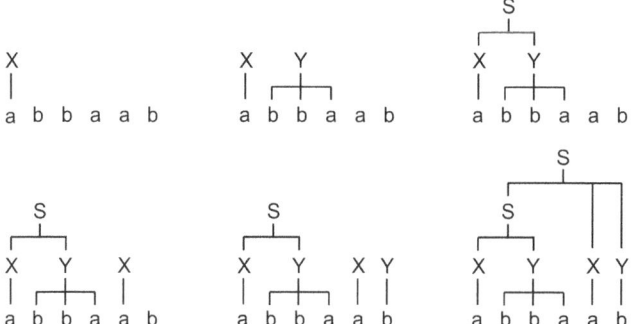

Fig. 8.1 Building a syntax tree bottom-up

First, a is reduced to X, then b b a to Y, and then X Y to S. Then the next a is reduced to X, then b to Y, and finally S X Y to S. The input has thus been recognized, and the syntax tree has been built bottom-up.

But how does the parser decide which parts of the input it should reduce? It follows the actions of a pushdown automaton (PDA), which we discussed in Sect. 3.1. For the input

a b b a a b #

(where # is the end-of-file symbol), the parser performs the following actions, using a stack to store the parts of the input that have already been processed:

stack	input	action
	a b b a a b #	shift
a	b b a a b #	reduce a to X
X	b b a a b #	shift
X b	b a a b #	shift (don't reduce b, otherwise the parser will run into a dead end)
X b b	a a b #	shift
X b b a	a b #	reduce b b a to Y
X Y	a b #	reduce X Y to S
S	a b #	shift
S a	b #	reduce a to X
S X	b #	shift
S X b	#	reduce b to Y
S X Y	#	reduce S X Y to S
S	#	input recognized (stack contains the start the symbol; input is empty)

The action shift reads the next input symbol and shifts it onto the stack, the action reduce reduces parts at the end of the stack (the so-called *handle*) to a nonterminal symbol. Which parts should be regarded as a handle is determined by the parser table (see Sect. 8.3). In the fourth line, it would be possible to reduce b to Y, but this would cause the parser to run into a dead end. Again, the parser table, which will be discussed later, tells the parser that it should shift and not reduce in this situation.

8.1 How a Bottom-up Parser Works

As you can see, a bottom-up parser processes the input by repeatedly executing shift and reduce actions. Such parsers are therefore also called *shift-reduce parsers*. There is a further action that is executed when the input has been fully recognized, as well as an action that is executed in the event of an error. In total, there are the following four actions:

- *shift*   read and shift the next input symbol onto the stack
- *reduce* reduce the end of the stack to a nonterminal symbol
- *accept* input successfully recognized (only for S . #)
- *error*   no other action possible (error handling begins)

But what does the parser table look like? Let's look at the example grammar used above:

1 S = X Y.
2 S = S X Y.
3 X = a.
4 X = a a b.
5 Y = b.
6 Y = b b a.

As shown in Sect. 3.1, a pushdown automaton (PDA) can be built from this grammar, and from the automaton a state transition table can be derived (Fig. 8.2). This table is then used by the parser for syntax analysis.

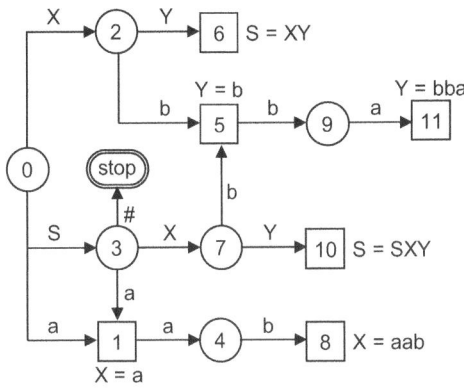

Fig. 8.2 PDA and the resulting parser table

The table contains the action to be executed for each state (line) and for each symbol (column). Actions can take one of the following forms:

sn	*shift n*	consume the next input symbol and go to state *n*
rp	*reduce p*	reduce according to production *p*
acc	*accept*	the input was successfully recognized
-	*error*	the current symbol cannot be recognized

Let's see how the parser uses this table to recognize the sentence a b b a a b #. To do this, it stores the *traversed states* on its stack (not the *processed symbols*, as indicated above in outline). The parser starts in state 0 with the as yet unprocessed input:

```
stack      input       action
    0      a b b a a b #    s1
```

It looks up the current state 0 and the next input symbol a in the table and finds the action s1 there *(shift 1)*. The symbol a is therefore consumed and the parser goes to state 1, which it shifted onto the stack:

```
    0 1    b b a a b #    r3 (X = a)
```

In state 1 with the symbol b, the action is r3; therefore, the parser must reduce according to production 3 (X = a). To do this, it pops as many states from the stack as the right-hand side of the production is long (i.e., 1 state) and then inserts the nonterminal symbol on the left-hand side of the production at the front of the input:

```
    0 X    b b a a b #    s2
```

In state 0 with the symbol X, the action is s2; therefore, X is consumed and the parser shifts to state 2 (after a reduction, there is always a shift with the recognized nonterminal symbol):

```
    0 2    b b a a b #    ...
```

In this way, the entire input is processed, with the parser being controlled by the parser table. The full analysis looks like this:

```
stack           input        action
      0         a b b a a b #    s1
    0 1         b b a a b #      r3 (X = a)
    0 X         b b a a b #      s2
    0 2         b b a a b #      s5
    0 2 5       b a a b #        s9
    0 2 5 9     a a b #          s11
  0 2 5 9 11    a b #            r6 (Y = bba)
    0 2 Y       a b #            s6
    0 2 6       a b #            r1 (S = XY)
    0 S         a b #            s3
    0 3         a b #            s1
    0 3 1       b #              r3 (X = a)
    0 3 X       b #              s7
    0 3 7       b #              s5
    0 3 7 5     #                r5 (Y = b)
    0 3 7 Y     #                s10
    0 3 7 10    #                r2 (S = SXY)
    0 S         #                s3
    0 3         #                acc
```

8.1 How a Bottom-up Parser Works

The last action is an *accept* (acc), which means that the input has been recognized. You can trace the actions using the PDA in Fig. 8.2 to understand how the parser moves as directed by the automaton. With each reduction, it builds a part of the syntax tree (see Fig. 8.1), although this is only an imaginary process (as with recursive descent)—it does not really build a syntax tree as a data structure. It is actually 'hidden' in the reductions of the parser.

Now let's turn to the parser as a program. It is controlled by three tables: the action table with the parser actions (see Fig. 8.2), the length table, in which the length of the right-hand side is encoded for each production, and the leftSide table, which contains the nonterminal symbol on the left-hand side of each production. The productions and the nonterminal symbols are numbered consecutively. For space reasons, the parser actions are stored here in entries of type short, where the first byte contains the kind of action (shift, reduce, accept, error) and the second byte contains the operand of the action.

```
void parse() {
  short[][] action = { {...}, {...}, ...};  // state transition table
  byte[]    length = { ... };                // production lengths
  byte[]    leftSide = { ... };              // left side nonterminal symbol of every production
  int       state;                           // current state
  int       sym;                             // next input symbol
  int       op, n, a;
  clearStack();
  state = 0; sym = next();   // get next symbol from the scanner
  for (;;) {
    push(state);
    a = action[state][sym];
    op = a / 256; n = a % 256;
    switch (op) {
      case shift:          // shift n
        state = n; sym = next();
        break;
      case reduce:         // reduce n
        for (int i = 0; i < length[n]; i++) pop();
        a = action[top()][leftSide[n]]; n = a % 256; // shift n
        state = n;
        break;
      case accept:
        return;
      case error:
        System.exit(1);   // error handling see later
    }
  }
}
```

The core of the parser is a loop in which the next parser action is determined from the current state (state) and the next input symbol (sym) using the action table. This action is split into the action kind op (first byte) and the operand n (second byte). A switch statement then handles the four kinds of actions, and the loop starts all over again. It is exited by either an accept or an error action.

The parser remembers the traversed states on the stack (push(state)). When a reduce action occurs, it goes back part of its way and continues from there with the reduced nonterminal symbol. To do this, it pops as many states as the reduced production is long (length[n]), and then uses the topmost state on the stack (top()) and the nonterminal symbol to which the production was reduced (leftSide[n]) to determine the state to which it should go.

A bottom-up parser is therefore a table-driven program that is identical for all grammars. The specific grammar is contained in the tables with which the parser is parameterized.

8.2 LR Grammars

Bottom-up parsers are also called *LR parsers*. The name is derived from "recognition from **l**eft to right with **r**ight-canonical derivations." Although such parsers do not work with derivations, but with reductions, a right-canonical derivation in which the rightmost nonterminal symbol is derived first

$$S \Rightarrow S\,X\,Y \Rightarrow S\,X\,b \Rightarrow S\,a\,b \Rightarrow X\,Y\,a\,b \Rightarrow X\,b\,b\,a\,a\,b \Rightarrow a\,b\,b\,a\,a\,b$$

corresponds in the opposite direction to a left-canonical reduction, in which the leftmost handle is reduced first. So the name is not particularly well chosen, but not wrong.

Depending on how far the parser looks ahead during parsing, we distinguish between LR(0) and LR(1) grammars.

8.2.1 LR(0) Grammars

Here, the parser does not use a lookahead symbol for reductions—it reduces regardless of the next input symbol. A grammar is called LR(0) if

- there is no reduce state in which also a shift is possible;
- in each reduce state it is only possible to reduce according to a single production.

Our example grammar is not LR(0), because the PDA in Fig. 8.2 has two states (1 and 5) in which both a reduction and shift are possible. It is therefore not possible to distinguish between reduce and shift without a lookahead symbol. LR(0) grammars have little significance in practice.

8.2.2 LR(1) Grammars

Here, the parser uses a lookahead symbol to decide between reduce and shift actions. A grammar is called LR(1) if in each state it is possible to decide with 1 lookahead symbol

8.2 LR Grammars

- whether a shift or a reduce action should be executed;
- to which nonterminal symbol it should be reduced.

Our example grammar is LR(1) because the PDA in Fig. 8.2 can use the lookahead symbol in states 1 and 5 to decide whether a shift or a reduce action should be executed. If the lookahead symbol in state 1 is a, a shift to state 4 is performed, otherwise a reduction. If the lookahead symbol in state 5 is b, a shift is done to state 9, otherwise a reduction is performed.

8.2.3 LALR(1) Grammars

LR(1) grammars are powerful, but lead to large parser tables. Thus, a variant of this is used in practice, which is called LALR(1) grammars (*lookahead LR(1) grammars*). The name is somewhat unfortunate because LR(1) grammars also look ahead, but that is the term that is used.

LALR(1) grammars are a subset of LR(1) grammars. They are only slightly less powerful, but have much smaller parser tables, because states with the same actions but possibly different successors are merged. Let's take a look at the following small example grammar:

E = v | E "+" v | "(" E ")".

Figure 8.3 shows on the left the PDA based on the LR(1) approach, and on the right the PDA based on the LALR(1) approach, in which certain states have been merged.

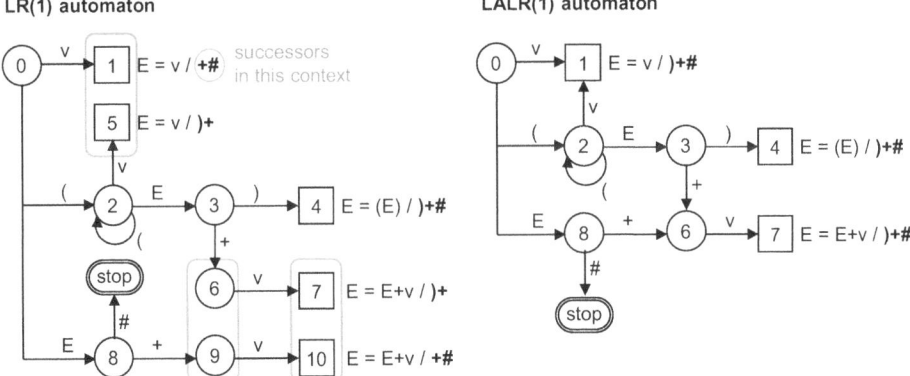

Fig. 8.3 PDA based on the LR(1) and the LALR(1) approach

First, you can see in state 1 of the left automaton that a reduction is performed according to the production E = v. However, you can also see that this reduction can only take place if one of the symbols "+" or "#" follows in the input stream (denoted by / +#). In state 5, there is also a reduction according to E = v, but only if ")" or "+" follows. The two states can therefore be merged to form state 1 of the right automaton, where the successors are the union of the previous successor sets, namely ")", "+" and "#". Similarly, states 6 and 9 as well as states 7 and 10 of the left automaton can be merged. If this results in an automaton in which it is still possible to decide in each state using 1 lookahead symbol whether a shift or a reduce action should be executed, the grammar is LALR(1), which is the case here. Three states have been eliminated by the merge. The parser table therefore became smaller.

But is it permissible to simply merge the successor sets when reduce states are merged? What if the automaton on the right goes from state 0 with v to state 1 and then the symbol ")" follows? By reducing according to E = v, the automaton goes back to state 0 and from there with E to state 8, where only "+" and "#" are allowed. If the symbol ")" follows there, an error is reported. The error is therefore not lost; it is simply reported later when the next shift with a terminal symbol is performed instead of being reported immediately during the reduction.

8.2.4 Strengths of Bottom-up Syntax Analysis

- LALR(1) grammars are more powerful than LL(1) grammars, which are used for recursive descent parsing. They allow left-recursive productions as well as alternatives with the same terminal start symbols. Such grammars can therefore be used for bottom-up syntax analysis without having to be transformed first.
- LALR(1) parsers are more compact in terms of code than recursive descent parsers. However, the tables require a significant amount of memory.
- The bottom-up parser shown above is a universal algorithm that is parameterized with tables.
- Table-driven bottom-up parsers allow for better error handling, as we will see in Sect. 8.6.

8.2.5 Weaknesses of Bottom-up Syntax Analysis

- LALR(1) tables are difficult to construct manually. We will see in Sect. 8.3 how to do this for small grammars, but for larger grammars, tools (i.e., parser generators) are needed.
- LALR(1) parsers are slightly slower than recursive descent parsers due to the table accesses.
- Semantic processing is more complicated and less powerful in bottom-up parsers than in recursive descent parsers (see Sect. 8.5).
- The actions of bottom-up parsers are hard to trace and check. The parser goes through a series of states, but these are difficult to map to the original grammar.
- LALR(1) parsers require BNF grammars, which are more awkward to read than EBNF grammars used in recursive descent parsing.

For these reasons, bottom-up syntax analysis is only worthwhile for really complex languages whose grammar is difficult to convert into LL(*) form. For smaller languages such as Java or MicroJava (and also for self-defined command languages), recursive descent parsing is much simpler and has the advantage that it can be implemented manually.

8.3 LR Table Generation

In Sect. 8.2 we saw how the parser uses the state transition table from Fig. 8.2 to analyze an input sentence. But how is this table created? That's what we are going to look at in this section. The parser table is derived from the grammar, but this is quite time-consuming to do by hand, i.e., only practical for small grammars. For larger grammars, parser generators are needed.

Assume that the parser is to parse a program according to the following grammar:

```
S = a X b
X = c
```

Let's simulate the analysis, in which the parser moves through the grammar. A dot indicates the current position of the parser:

```
S = . a X b
S = a . X b
X = . c      / b
X = c .      / b
S = a X . b
S = a X b .
```

The parser starts with the first production; the dot is at its beginning. After it has recognized a, the dot is moved across a and the parser is now in front of X. When it is in front of a nonterminal symbol, it is also at the beginning of its production, in this case in front of c. The successor of the X production in this context is b (represented as / b). Now the parser recognizes c and is then at the end of the X production and thus also after X in the higher-level production. Finally, it recognizes b, which concludes the analysis.

Let's take such a snapshot of the analysis and call it an *LR item*. Figure 8.4 shows the general structure of an LR item (α and β are strings of terminal or nonterminal symbols; γ denotes a set of terminal symbols).

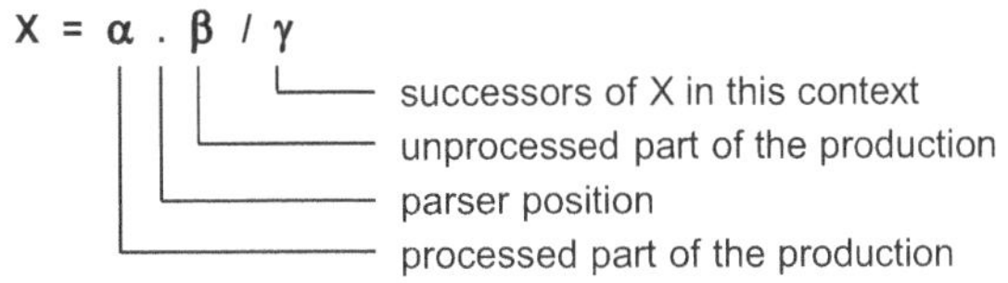

```
X = α . β / γ
        │   └──── successors of X in this context
        └──────── unprocessed part of the production
    ──────────── parser position
    ──────────── processed part of the production
```

Fig. 8.4 Structure of an LR item

There are two types of LR items: those where the dot is at the end of a production (*reduce items*) and those where it is not at the end (*shift items*). The symbol that immediately follows the dot is called the *control symbol*. In the shift item

X = a . a b / c

the control symbol is a, in the reduce item

X = a a b . / **c**

the control symbol is c (in principle, any symbol from the set of successors).

At all times, the parser is in a certain *state*, in which it is able to work on several items in parallel, i.e., on all the possible productions, for example:

S = X . Y c   / #
Y = . b   / c
Y = . b b a   / c

Therefore, we refer to the *parser state* as the *set of items* that the parser is currently working on. Since the parser is in front of the nonterminal symbol Y in the first item, it is at the same time also working on all productions of Y, where the dot is at the beginning and their successors are the successors of Y in this context (here c). So these items are also members of the state.

This example already shows the power of LR analysis. A top-down parser only works on a single production at a time, while a bottom-up parser can work on multiple productions in parallel. Figure 8.5 shows how a bottom-up parser can analyze two productions that start with the same terminal symbols in parallel until it finally has to choose one of the two.

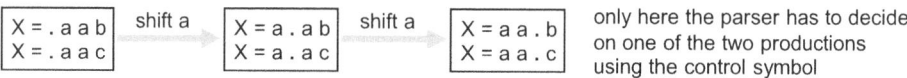

Fig. 8.5 Bottom-up parser working on two productions in parallel

8.3.1 Kernel, Closure, and Successor State

The set of all items of a state that do not begin with a dot is called the *kernel* of the state. In the example above, the item

S = X . Y c / #

comprises the kernel. From the kernel, the *closure* of the state can be computed: for all items, in which the dot is in front of a nonterminal symbol, the productions of this nonterminal symbol are added as new items to the state. If the grammar is:

S = X Y c
X = a
X = a a b
Y = b
Y = b b a

8.3 LR Table Generation

then the closure of the above kernel can be formed by adding the Y productions with the dot at the beginning and the respective successors (here c):

```
S = X . Y c    / #
Y = . b        / c
Y = . b b a    / c
```

The algorithm for forming the closure of a state is (in pseudocode; First($\beta\gamma$) denotes the terminal start symbols of β; if β is empty it is the successor set γ):

```
foreach (item in state) {
    if (item is of kind X = α . Y β / γ) {
        add all productions Y = . ω / First(βγ) as new items to state;
    }
}
```

The closure of a state describes all items that the parser is working on in this state. Once we have formed the closure, we can determine for each control symbol sym the successor state *Succ(state, sym)*, to which we get from state with sym (Fig. 8.6).

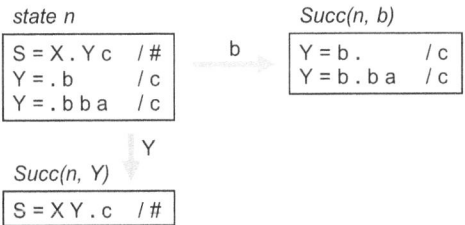

Fig. 8.6 Computing the successor states and their item sets

The control symbols in state n are Y and b (the symbols after the dot). The successor state Succ(n, b) contains all items of n with the control symbol b, where the point has been moved across b. The successor state Succ(n, Y) contains all items of n with the control symbol Y, where the point has been moved across Y.

The productions in the successor states are then analyzed in parallel again. Note that a successor state formed in this way just represents the kernel from which the closure may have to be computed, which is not necessary in this example, because none of the items has the dot in front of a nonterminal symbol.

8.3.2 Table Generation Algorithm

We will now look at the algorithm for LALR(1) table generation, which we will then apply to an example. The algorithm in pseudocode is:

```
extend the grammar with a pseudo-production S' = S #
create state 0 with the kernel S' = . S#  // exceptional kernel; see the comment below
while (not all states have been visited) {
    s = next unvisited state;
    build closure of s;
    for (all items of s) {
        switch (item kind) {
            case S' = S . # :       generate acc #;
                                    break;
            case X = α . y β / γ :  create auxiliary state s1 = Succ(s, y);
                                    if (∃ s2: kernel(s1) == kernel(s2)) {
                                        merge successors of s1 to s2;
                                        generate shift y, s2;
                                    } else {
                                        add s1 as a new state;
                                        generate shift y, s1;
                                    }
                                    break;
            case X = α . / γ :      generate reduce γ, (X = α);
                                    break;
        }
    }
    // all undefined transitions are error actions
}
```

The algorithm first extends the grammar by adding a pseudo production S' = S #, where S is the original start symbol and # the eof symbol. Then state 0 is created with the kernel S' = . S # (this is an exception; usually a kernel only contains items that do not start with a dot).

Now the table generation loop begins, in which all states are visited, new states are created, and the actions in the states are generated. For each visited state, the closure is first built from its kernel. Then all items of the state are inspected, of which there are three kinds:

- The item S' = S . # is the one where the original start symbol S has been recognized and the remaining input contains only the eof symbol #. An acc action is therefore generated in the current state.
- In shift items of type X = α . y β / γ, the dot is in front of a symbol y (which can be a terminal symbol or a nonterminal symbol). So there will be a shift action with y. The algorithm first creates an auxiliary state s1 using Succ(s, y). It then checks whether there is already another state s2 with the same kernel as s1 (differences in the successor symbols are ignored). If this is the case, the successors of the items in s1 are added to the successors of the same items in s2 and an action shift y, s2 is generated. If not, s1 is added as a new state and an action shift y, s1 is generated.
- In reduce items of type X = α . / γ, the dot is at the end of the production. Therefore, a reduce action is generated with the successor set γ.

Let's take a look at an example. The grammar (including the pseudo production for S') for which we want to generate a table is:

8.3 LR Table Generation

```
0  S' = S #
1  S = X Y
2  S = S X Y
3  X = a
4  X = a a b
5  Y = b
6  Y = b b a
```

We start with state 0, which initially contains just the following kernel:

S' = . S #

To build the closure of this state, we first need to add all S productions as items, with the dot at the beginning and the successor #:

S' = . S #
S = . X Y   / #
S = . S X Y   / #

In the added items, the dot is again in front of a nonterminal symbol, therefore we need to add the X and S productions as new items. The successors of X are the terminal start symbols of Y, i.e., b. The successors of S in the third item are the terminal start symbols of X, i.e., a. Thus, we add those new successors of S to the successors of the already existing S items (giving / #a):

```
S' = . S #
S = . X Y      / #a
S = . S X Y    / #a
X = . a        / b
X = . a a b    / b
```

The closure is now complete, as there are no further items with the dot in front of a nonterminal symbol. We now create the successor states to which we get with the control symbols a, X, and S. With the control symbol a we go to a new state 1 containing the items

```
X = a .        / b
X = a . a b    / b
```

With the control symbol X we go to a new state 2 containing the kernel item

S = X . Y   / #a

With the control symbol S we go to a new state 3 containing the kernel items

```
S' = S . #
S = S . X Y    / #a
```

The items of the new states are only the kernel, which must later be expanded to a closure when these states are visited (this is the case in states 2 and 3 that have the dot in front of a nonterminal symbol). The generated actions in state 0 are

```
shift a, 1    // shift with a to state 1
shift X, 2    // shift with X to state 2
shift S, 3    // shift with S to state 3
```

The states created by this algorithm with their items and the actions generated from them are as follows (kernel items are shown in bold):

```
0   S' = . S #                    shift  a   1
    S = . X Y      / #a           shift  X   2
    S = . S X Y    / #a           shift  S   3
    X = . a         / b
    X = . a a b     / b
1   X = a .         / b           red    b   3 (X = a)
    X = a . a b     / b           shift  a   4
2   S = X . Y      / #a           shift  b   5
    Y = . b        / #a           shift  Y   6
    Y = . b b a    / #a
3   S' = S . #                    acc    #
    S = S . X Y    / #a           shift  a   1 (!)
    X = . a         / b           shift  X   7
    X = . a a b     / b
4   X = a a . b     / b           shift  b   8
5   Y = b .        / #a           red    #,a  5 (Y = b)
    Y = b . b a    / #a           shift  b   9
6   S = X Y .      / #a           red    #,a  1 (S = X Y)
7   S = S X . Y    / #a           shift  b   5 (!)
    Y = . b        / #a           shift  Y   10
    Y = . b b a    / #a
8   X = a a b .     / b           red    b   4 (X = a a b)
9   Y = b b . a    / #a           shift  a   11
10  S = S X Y .    / #a           red    #,a  2 (S = S X Y)
11  Y = b b a .    / #a           red    #,a  6 (Y = b b a)
```

Note that in state 3, there is a shift with a to the already existing state 1 (no new state is created). Similarly, in state 7, there is a shift with b to the already existing state 5. The states and the generated actions result in the parser table shown in Fig. 8.7.

	a	b	#	S	X	Y
0	s1	-	-	s3	s2	-
1	s4	r3	-	-	-	-
2	-	s5	-	-	-	s6
3	s1	-	acc	-	s7	-
4	-	s8	-	-	-	-
5	r5	s9	r5	-	-	-
6	r1	-	r1	-	-	-
7	-	s5	-	-	-	s10
8	-	r4	-	-	-	-
9	s11	-	-	-	-	-
10	r2	-	r2	-	-	-
11	r6	-	r6	-	-	-

Fig. 8.7 Parser table for the example grammar

8.3 LR Table Generation

All table entries for which no action is defined are error entries. For example, the parser would report an error if it sees the symbol b in state 0. It would then start an error recovery, which we will look at in Sect. 8.6.

As you can see, this table is sparsely populated, which is even more the case for large grammars with many symbols. Therefore, the table is sometimes stored in list form, with the control symbol and the action specified for each state.

	T actions		NT actions	
0	a	s1	S	s3
	*	error	X	s2
1	a	s4		
	*	r3		
2	b	s5	Y	s6
	*	error		
3	a	s1	X	s7
	#	acc		
	*	error		
4	b	s8		
	*	error		
5	b	s9		
	*	r5		
6	*	r1		
7	b	s5	Y	s10
	*	error		
8	*	r4		
9	a	s11		
	*	error		
10	*	r2		
11	*	r6		

If the symbol a occurs in state 0, the action s1 (shift to state 1) is executed, otherwise (expressed by an asterisk) an error is reported. The actions of a state are checked sequentially for their control symbol. The last action of each state is always an "otherwise action" with an asterisk. As you can see, that action can also be used to reduce. If a reduction is made with an incorrect control symbol, the error will be noticed and reported with the next shift.

Since the table part for nonterminal symbols is even more sparsely populated than that for terminal symbols, separate lists are used for terminal and nonterminal symbols. There are no error actions in the nonterminal symbol part, because after a reduction there is always a shift with the reduced nonterminal symbol.

The list form is more memory-efficient than the table form, but it is also slower to access because the actions have to be checked sequentially. Therefore, we will use the table form in the following sections.

8.3.3 LR(1) Conflicts

In top-down syntax analysis, we have seen that LL(1) conflicts can occur, which usually must be eliminated (Sect. 3.3). Similarly, in bottom-up syntax analysis, LR(1) conflicts can occur that make a grammar unsuitable for bottom-up parsing. There are two types of such conflicts:

- A *shift-reduce conflict* occurs if the parser (using the lookahead symbol) cannot decide whether to shift or reduce:

    shift a, ...
    reduce a, ...

- A *reduce-reduce conflict* occurs if the parser (using the lookahead symbol) cannot decide according to which production it should reduce:

    reduce a, p1
    reduce a, p2

When such conflicts occur, they must be eliminated before the grammar can be used for bottom-up parsing. Unfortunately, eliminating LR(1) conflicts is much harder than eliminating LL(1) conflicts, and no general procedure can be given for this. You have to find out what causes the conflict and then transform the grammar so that the conflict disappears. This requires some intuition.

LALR(1) tables are more susceptible to conflicts than LR(1) tables because they merge states and successor sets, while LR(1) tables keep them separate. However, merging can only result in new reduce-reduce conflicts and not new shift-reduce conflicts, as shift-reduce conflicts would already have occurred in the LR(1) tables.

8.4 LR Table Compression

For realistic programming languages, the parser table can be very large. For example, if a grammar has 80 terminal symbols and 200 nonterminal symbols and the parser table has 2500 states, this table will have 280 × 2,500 = 700,000 elements. If each table element is stored in four bytes, the table takes 2.8 megabytes. While this is not a serious problem with today's memory sizes, there are techniques that can be used to compress such tables by up to 90%. We will review two of these techniques.

8.4.1 Combining Shift and Reduce Actions

Sometimes a shift action leads to a state in which only a reduction is possible. In state 4 of Fig. 8.8, for example, there is a shift with the symbol b to state 8, in which no further shift is possible, but only a reduction according to production 4 (error entries are ignored, because after a premature reduction, a possible error is noticed with the next shift).

8.4 LR Table Compression

	a	b	#
...	...	...	...
4	-	s8	-
...	...	...	...
8	-	r4	-
...	...	...	...

	a	b	#
...	...	...	...
4	-	sr4	-
...	...	...	...
...	...	...	...

Fig. 8.8 Combining shift and reduce actions

The action s8 can therefore be combined with the action r4 to form the action sr4 (shift and then reduce according to production 4). After that, state 8 is no longer reachable so the entire table line of state 8 can be eliminated. Combining shift and reduce actions does not slow down the parser, but on the contrary makes it faster, because instead of two actions, only one has to be interpreted. However, the parser (see Sect. 8.1) must be modified because there is now a new shiftred action:

```
switch (op) {
   ...
   case shiftred: // shiftred n
      sym = next();
      do {
         for (int i = 0; i < length[n] – 1; i++) pop(); // reduce, but pop one state less
         a = action[top()][leftSide[n]];
         op = a / 256; n = a % 256;
      } while (op == shiftred);
      // op == shift
      state = n; break;
   case reduce: // reduce n
      for (int i = 0; i < length[n]; i++) pop(); // reduce
      a = action[top()][leftSide[n]];
      op = a / 256; n = a % 256;
      while (op == shiftred) {
         for (int i = 0; i < length[n] – 1; i++) pop(); // reduce, but pop one state less
         a = action[top()][leftSide[n]];
         op = a / 256; n = a % 256;
      }
      // op == shift
      state = n; break;
}
```

The action shiftred n reads the next symbol, but does not execute a shift; instead, it reduces immediately according to production n, but pops one state less from the stack than the production n is long, because the last shift was not executed. A shiftred could now occur again with the reduced nonterminal symbol (leftside[n]), which is why a loop is executed, until there is a reduction to a nonterminal symbol with which a shift can take place.

The same applies to the reduce action. Here too, a shiftred with the reduced nonterminal symbol could occur, which is why a loop is executed until a shift follows.

8.4.2 Merging Lines

As we have seen, the parser table is sparsely populated. It therefore makes sense to merge lines whose actions do not conflict with each other. In doing so, the table is compressed. In Fig. 8.9, for example, lines 0, 3 and 4 are not in conflict (they contain the same actions or error entries) and can therefore be merged.

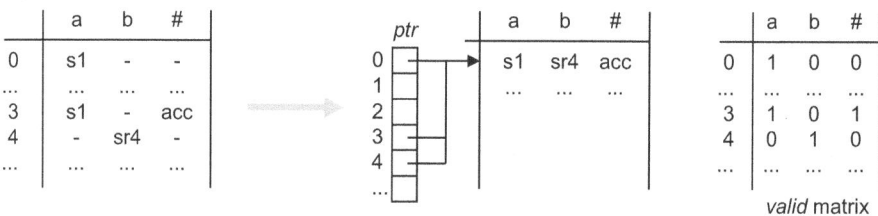

Fig. 8.9 Merging of lines

Merging eliminates some lines from the table. However, we need a pointer array ptr to map lines 0, 3, and 4 to line 0. In addition, we need a bit matrix valid that tells us which actions are valid in each original state. If the parser (see Sect. 8.1) is to work with such a merged table, some changes are necessary (printed in bold):

```
BitSet[] valid;
short[] ptr;
...
a = action[ptr[state]][sym];
op = a / 256; n = a % 256;
if (!valid[state].get(sym)) op = error;
switch (op) {
...
```

When looking up the table, the indirection via ptr must be taken into account. It is also necessary to check whether sym is valid in state at all. This slows down parsing slightly.

It is advisable to merge the table parts for terminal and nonterminal symbols separately, as the table part for nonterminal symbols is much sparser, which allows a greater compression.

In principle, the same technique could also be used to merge columns, but this would make parsing even slower. With today's large main memories, it is better to find a trade-off between the size of the table and the speed of the parser.

8.4.3 Example

As an example, let's look at the parser table from Sect. 8.3 and first combine shift and reduce actions into shiftred actions (Fig. 8.10).

8.5 Semantic Processing

	a	b	#	S	X	Y
0	s1	-	-	s3	s2	-
1	s4	r3	-	-	-	-
2	-	s5	-	-	-	(s6)
3	s1	-	acc	-	s7	-
4	-	(s8)	-	-	-	-
5	r5	s9	r5	-	-	-
6	r1	-	r1	-	-	-
7	-	s5	-	-	-	(s10)
8	-	r4	-	-	-	-
9	(s11)	-	-	-	-	-
10	r2	-	r2	-	-	-
11	r6	-	r6	-	-	-

	a	b	#	S	X	Y
0	s1	-	-	s3	s2	-
1	s4	r3	-	-	-	-
2	-	s5	-	-	-	sr1
3	s1	-	acc	-	s7	-
4	-	sr4	-	-	-	-
5	r5	s9	r5	-	-	-
7	-	s5	-	-	-	sr2
9	sr6	-	-	-	-	-

Fig. 8.10 Example: combining shift and reduce actions

The actions s6, s8, s10, and s11 can be combined into sr1, sr4, sr2, and sr6, thus eliminating lines 6, 8, 10, and 11. Whilst the original table had 12 lines of 6 columns of 2 bytes, i.e., 144 bytes, the new table has only 8 lines of 6 columns of 2 bytes, i.e., 96 bytes—a reduction by 33% without sacrificing speed in the parser.

Now let's do a line merge. In the terminal symbol part, lines 0, 3 and 4 as well as lines 2, 7 and 9 can be merged, in the nonterminal symbol part lines 0 and 2 as well as lines 3 and 7 (Fig. 8.11).

T actions

	a	b	#
0,3,4	s1	sr4	acc
1	s4	r3	-
2,7,9	sr6	s5	-
5	r5	s9	r5

NT actions

	S	X	Y
0,2	s3	s2	sr1
3,7	-	s7	sr2

valid

	a	b	#
0	1	0	0
1	1	1	0
2	0	1	0
3	1	0	1
4	0	1	0
5	1	1	1
7	0	1	0
9	1	0	0

Fig. 8.11 Example: Merging lines

We now need 6 lines of 3 columns of 2 bytes (36 bytes) for the actions, 2 × 8 lines of 2 bytes (32 bytes) for the ptr tables, and 8 bit arrays of 1 byte (8 bytes) for the valid matrix (assuming that each line can be stored as a bit array in one byte), a total of 76 bytes. This is a reduction by 47% compared to the original table, which required 144 bytes. For larger grammars, which usually have much sparser tables, the savings can be up to 90%.

8.5 Semantic Processing

So far, we have only talked about syntax analysis. However, a compiler must not only analyze a program, but also translate it, which requires semantic actions and attributes. How can these be integrated into a bottom-up parser?

8.5.1 Semantic Actions

As we have seen, a bottom-up parser can analyze several productions in parallel. In extreme cases, it only knows what production is the right one when there is a reduction. Therefore, semantic actions can only be performed during reductions. If a semantic action were allowed in the middle of a production

    X = a (. *semantic action* .) b.

we would have to insert an empty nonterminal symbol there and execute the semantic action during the reduction of this nonterminal symbol:

    X = a Y b.
    Y = (. *semantic action* .).

However, this could invalidate the LR(1) property. In the following example

    X = a b c.
    X = a (. *semantic action* .) b d.

the context-free grammar is LR(1). But if we transform it into

    X = a b c.
    X = a Y b d.
    Y = (. *semantic action* .).

a shift-reduce conflict arises:

```
i  X = a . b c     / #      shift  b  i+1
   X = a . Y b d   / #      red    b  p (Y = )
   Y = .           / b      shift  Y  i+2
```

With the lookahead symbol b, the parser cannot decide whether to shift or reduce (and execute the semantic action in the process). It can therefore no longer follow the two productions of X in parallel, because a semantic action is to be executed in the second X production. The semantic action in the middle of the production thus invalidated the LR(1) property of the grammar. For this reason, semantic actions may generally only be executed at the end of a production, once it is clear which of several productions being analyzed in parallel is the right one.

8.5.2 Attributes

Input attributes lead to a similar problem as semantic actions. In the attributed grammar

    X = a Y<↓v> b.
    Y<↓w> = ...

passing the attribute v to w can be regarded as an assignment in a semantic action:

    X = a (. w = v; .) Y b.
    Y = ...

8.5 Semantic Processing

which could again invalidate the LR(1) property. For this reason, bottom-up syntax analysis typically does not use input attributes.

Output attributes, on the other hand, are not a problem. However, it is usually assumed that a nonterminal symbol has just a single output attribute and leaves this on a special *attribute stack* from where it can be retrieved and processed. For example:

```
X<↑x> = A<↑a> B<↑b> C<↑c>   (. c = popAttr(); b = popAttr(); a = popAttr();
                                x = f(a, b, c);
                                pushAttr(x); .) .
```

The nonterminal symbols A, B, and C each leave their attribute on the attribute stack. In the production of X, these attributes are retrieved from this stack using popAttr() and processed into a value x, which is then pushed back on the attribute stack as the output attribute of X using pushAttr(x). This can all be done in a semantic action at the end of the production, which is executed when A B C is reduced to X.

Let's look at a concrete example of this kind of attribute evaluation, namely the calculation of simple constant expressions, which is described by the following attributed grammar:

```
Expr<↑x>   = Term<↑x>                  (. pushAttr(popAttr()); .) .
Expr<↑x>   = Expr<↑x> "+" Term<↑y>     (. pushAttr(popAttr() + popAttr()); .) .
Term<↑x>   = Factor<↑x>                (. pushAttr(popAttr()); .) .
Term<↑x>   = Term<↑x> "*" Factor<↑x>   (. pushAttr(popAttr() * popAttr()); .) .
Factor<↑x> = number                    (. pushAttr(t.numVal); .) .
Factor<↑x> = "(" Expr<↑x> ")"          (. pushAttr(popAttr()); .) .
```

All semantic actions take place at the end of the productions. In the first production, the attribute provided by Term can simply be reused as the output attribute of Expr and can therefore remain on the attribute stack. The situation is similar for the third and last production.

The remaining semantic actions are numbered consecutively, resulting in the following grammar:

```
Expr   = Term .
Expr   = Expr "+" Term    (. 1 .) .
Term   = Factor .
Term   = Term "*" Factor  (. 2 .) .
Factor = number           (. 3 .) .
Factor = "(" Expr ")" .
```

All semantic actions are collected in a method semAction(), which is parameterized with the number of the semantic action to be executed. The actions are then called via their number in a switch statement:

```
void semAction (int n) {
  switch (n) {
    case 1: pushAttr(popAttr() + popAttr()); break;
    case 2: pushAttr(popAttr() * popAttr()); break;
    case 3: pushAttr(t.numVal); break;
  }
}
```

Finally, we need to make sure that the semantic actions are executed in the right place. To do this, we create a table sem in which for each production the semantic action is listed that must be executed when the production is reduced. If no action is to be executed, the corresponding entry is 0. Figure 8.12 shows the tables leftSide, length, and sem for the above grammar.

	leftSide	length	sem
0	Expr	1	0
1	Expr	3	1
2	Term	1	0
3	Term	3	2
4	Factor	1	3
5	Factor	3	0

Fig. 8.12 Parser tables leftSide, length and sem

We have to extend the parser (see Sect. 8.1) so that a semantic action is executed on each reduction if sem provides one:

```
switch (op) {
  ...
  case reduce: // reduce n
    if (sem[n] != 0) semAction(sem[n]);
    for (int i = 0; i < length[n]; i++) pop();
    a = action[top()][leftSide[n]]; n = a % 256; // shift n
    state = n; break;
}
```

A similar adjustment is necessary if the parser also supports shiftred actions.

8.5.3 Assessment

As you can see, semantic processing is more awkward and less powerful in bottom-up parsers than in recursive descent parsers. One can only use output attributes, and semantic actions are only possible at the end of productions. In addition, all semantic actions are combined in a global method semAction() and can therefore only work with global variables, which have to be saved and restored across recursive nonterminals.

Therefore, semantic processing in bottom-up parsers is often done in such a way that a (real) syntax tree is built, which can then be traversed to check context conditions and perform translation actions. Building a syntax tree can be done easily with semantic actions at the end of productions. Each nonterminal symbol provides a subtree as its output attribute. The semantic actions then build a new tree from the provided subtrees, for example:

```
A<↑tree3> = B<↑tree1> C<↑tree2> (. tree2 = popAttr(); tree1 = popAttr();
                                    tree3 = new NodeA(tree1, tree2);
                                    pushAttr(tree3); .) .
```

8.6 LR Error Handling

A syntax error occurs when the next input symbol is not valid in the current state. The parser must then report the error and attempt a recovery, i.e., it must synchronize its state with the remaining input so that parsing can continue. This is easier to do with bottom-up syntax analysis than with recursive descent, because the grammar is implicitly encoded in the parser tables, which can be analyzed in the event of an error in order to find a synchronization point.

If a syntax error occurs, the stack contains a sequence of states $s_0...s_n$ and the remaining input is $t_0...t_m$ #:

$$s_0...s_n \, . \, t_0... \, t_m \, \#$$

The goal now is to synchronize the stack and the input so that there is a state s_i at the end of the stack and the next input symbol is t_j, so that t_j is valid in s_i and the analysis can continue:

$$s_0...s_i \, . \, t_j... \, t_m \, \#$$

To do this, states are pushed and/or popped, and tokens are inserted and/or deleted until the desired configuration is achieved (Fig. 8.13). The details will be explained in the next section.

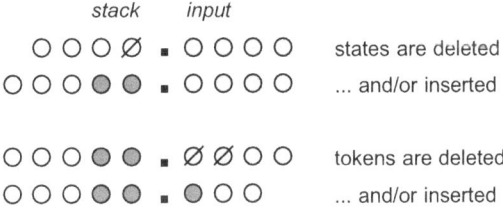

Fig. 8.13 Inserting/deleting states, inserting/deleting tokens

8.6.1 Algorithm for Error Recovery

The algorithm for recovery after syntax errors [Röhr80] consists of the following three steps:

1. **Search an escape route**
   The input $t_0...t_m$ is replaced with a virtual (fictitious) input $v_0...v_k$, which steers the parser from the error state s_n to the final state as quickly as possible (i.e., along an "escape route").

   $$s_0 ... s_n \, . \, t_0 \!\cdots\! t_m \, \#$$
   $$v_0 ... v_k \, \#$$

   On the escape route, all tokens that are valid in the traversed states are collected as *anchors*.

2. **Delete faulty tokens**

   Tokens are deleted from the original input $t_0...t_m$ until a token t_j occurs that is in the set of anchors.

   $s_0 ... s_n . \cancel{t_0 ... t_{j-1}} \; t_j ... t_m \; \#$

3. **Insert missing tokens**

   The parser is now again steered along the escape route, i.e., from the error state s_n with the virtual input $v_0...v_k$, until it gets to a state s_i where the anchor t_j is valid. Such a state must exist, because the anchors were collected along the escape route. This results in the following configuration with which syntax analysis can continue:

   $s_0 ... s_i . t_j ... t_m \; \#$

   In this step, all consumed tokens of the virtual input $v_0...v_k$ are inserted into the remaining input before t_j. This corresponds to a "correction" of the faulty input. If the inserted tokens had been there from the beginning, the error would not have occurred.

8.6.2 Example

Before we go to the implementation of the recovery algorithm, let's take a look at how it works using an example. Assume that the parser is represented by the PDA in Fig. 8.14 and is supposed to parse the input a b b #.

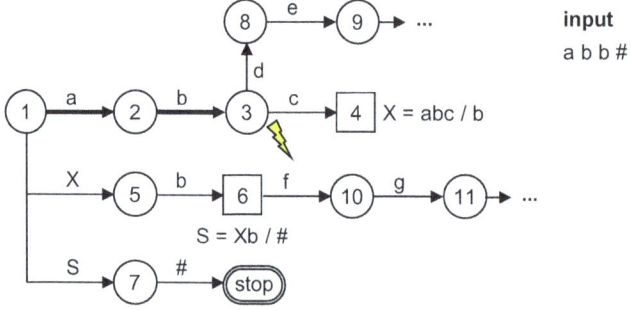

Fig. 8.14 Error handling using a PDA

The PDA starts in state 1 and goes with a to state 2 and then with b to state 3. The next input symbol b, however, does not fit in state 3, which is a syntax error. Now the recovery begins.

The PDA needs to find the shortest escape route from state 3 to the final state stop, but it must not run edges backward. However, it can go to state 4 with a fictitious input symbol c, where it can reduce a b c to X, thus going back three edges to state 1, and from there with X to state 5.

8.6 LR Error Handling

From state 5 it can go to state 6 with the fictitious input symbol b, where it can reduce X b to S, thus going back two edges to state 1 and from there with S to state 7. From state 7, it can reach the final state with the fictitious input symbol #. So the virtual input that steers the parser from the error state 3 to the final state is c b #. Along the escape route, the parser traverses the states shown in Fig. 8.15 and collects all the symbols valid there as anchors.

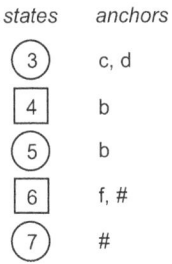

Fig. 8.15 Collecting anchors along the escape route

The set of anchors, i.e., the symbols with which the parser can continue in some state along the escape route, is therefore b, c, d, f, #.

The next step is to delete symbols from the remaining input b # until an anchor occurs. In our example, nothing needs to be deleted because b is already an anchor.

In the third step, the parser traverses the escape route again from the error state 3 with the virtual input c b # from above until it reaches a state in which the anchor b is valid. In state 3, b is not yet valid, so the parser goes to state 4 with the fictitious input symbol c and inserts c into the input as a "correction". In state 4, however, the anchor b is valid, and the recovery is thus completed. The corrected input is

    a b c b #

With this input, the syntax error would not have occurred. It is remarkable that this algorithm not only leads to a good error recovery, but even corrects the faulty input. Whether this is the correction intended by the programmer is arguable, but at least it is a valid input.

But what should be printed as an error message? The easiest way is to describe the correction made. For example, if the symbols a, b, and c have been deleted from the remaining input, the error message is:

    line ... col ...: "a b c" deleted

If the symbols x and y have been inserted before the remaining input, the error message is:

    line ... col ...: "x y" inserted

Finally, if the symbols a, b, and c have been deleted and the symbols x and y have been inserted, the error message is:

    line ... col ...: "a b c" replaced by "x y"

8.6.3 Guide Symbols for Finding the Escape Route

How does the parser actually find the escape route? In other words, how does it know that it should go from state 3 to state 4 and reduce there? To do this, the parser uses *guide symbols* that direct it along the escape route in each state. Figure 8.16 shows the parser table for our example grammar from Sect. 8.3. The *guide* column contains the guide symbol for each state.

grammar		a	b	#	S	X	Y	guide
0 S' = S #	0	s1	-	-	s3	s2	-	a
1 S = X Y	1	s4	r3	-	-	-	-	b
2 S = S X Y	2	-	s5	-	-	-	s6	b
3 X = a	3	s1	-	acc	-	s7	-	#
4 X = a a b	4	-	s8	-	-	-	-	b
5 Y = b	5	r5	s9	r5	-	-	-	#
6 Y = b b a	6	r1	-	r1	-	-	-	#
	7	-	s5	-	-	-	s10	b
	8	-	r4	-	-	-	-	b
	9	s11	-	-	-	-	-	a
	10	r2	-	r2	-	-	-	#
	11	r6	-	r6	-	-	-	#

Fig. 8.16 Parser table with guide symbols

We will later show how to compute these guide symbols, but first, let's see how the parser uses this table, this time to analyze the faulty input

a a a b #

The analysis begins with the part of the input that is still correct:

stack	input	action
0	a a a b #	s1
0 1	a a b #	s4
0 1 4	a b #	-- error!

In state 4, a syntax error occurs because the symbol a is not permitted there. Now the recovery begins. Using the guide symbols, the parser is steered from the error state 4 along the escape route to the final state. In all the traversed states, the symbols valid there are collected as anchors.

stack	guide	action	anchors
0 1 4	b	s8	b
0 1 4 8	b	r4, s2	b
0 2	b	s5	b
0 2 5	#	r5, s6	a, b, #
0 2 6	#	r1, s3	a, #
0 3	#	acc	a, #

In state 4, the guide symbol is b and the action in the table for b is s8. Also, the only valid terminal symbol in state 4 is b, so b is added to the set of anchors. The parser goes to state

8.6 LR Error Handling

8, where the guide symbol is b again. The corresponding action is r4, i.e., the parser reduces according to production 4 (X = a a b). This will pop 3 states and bring the parser back to state 0, from where it will go with X to state 2 (s2). In state 8, the only valid terminal symbol is b, so b is added as an anchor. In this way, the escape route is continued until finally the symbol # is accepted in state 3 and the final state has been reached. The set of collected anchors is a, b, and #.

Now, symbols are deleted from the remaining input a b #, until an anchor occurs, but since a is already an anchor, nothing is deleted.

In the last step, the parser follows the escape route again from the error state 4 using the guide symbols until it reaches a state in which the anchor a is valid. At each shift action with a guide symbol, this symbol is inserted into the input as a correction.

stack	guide	action	inserted
0 1 4	b	s8	b // only shifts with a guide symbol lead to an insertion
0 1 4 8	b	r4, s2	
0 2	b	s5	b
0 2 5			

In state 5, the anchor a is valid, and the analysis can be continued:

stack	input	action
0 2 5	a b #	r5, s6
0 2 6	a b #	r1, s3
0 3	a b #	s1
0 3 1	b #	r3, s7
0 3 7	b #	s5
0 3 7 5	#	r5, s10
0 3 7 10	#	r2, s3
0 3	#	acc

The analysis has been successfully completed. The corrected input is

a a **b** b a b #

and the error message is

line ... col ...: "b b" inserted

8.6.4 Finding the Guide Symbols

How are the guide symbols for each state computed? This is quite simple and is a by-product of creating the parser table. But first, we have to rearrange the productions of the grammar so that the first production of each nonterminal symbol is the shortest. Also, it must not be (left) recursive. Here is our sample grammar with the correct order of its productions:

```
0  S' = S #
1  S = X Y
```

2   S = S X Y
3   **X = a**
4   X = a a b
5   **Y = b**
6   Y = b b a

From this grammar we can now create the LALR(1) table. However, care has to be taken when building the closure of a state: new items must be inserted immediately after the item that triggered their insertion. For example, if we look at the state

S' = . S #
S = . X Y   / #
S = . S X Y   / #

when we add the productions of X as new items, we must insert them immediately after the item where the dot is in front of X, for example:

S' = . S #
S = . X Y   / #
X = . a   **/ b**
X = . a a b   **/ b**
S = . S X Y   / #

If we now apply the table generation algorithm, the first terminal symbol action of each state specifies the guide symbol (rightmost column).

0	S' = . S #		shift	a	1		a
	S = . X Y	/ #a	shift	X	2		
	X = . a	/ b	shift	S	3		
	X = . a a b	/ b					
	S = . S X Y	/ #a					
1	X = a .	/ b	red	b	3 (X = a)		b
	X = a . a b	/ b	shift	a	4		
2	S = X . Y	/ #a	shift	b	5		b
	Y = . b	/ #a	shift	Y	6		
	Y = . b b a	/ #a					
3	S' = S . #		acc	#			#
	S = S . X Y	/ #a	shift	a	1 (!)		
	X = . a	/ b	shift	X	7		
	X = . a a b	/ b					
4	X = a a . b	/ b	shift	b	8		b
5	Y = b .	/ #a	red	#,a	5 (Y = b)		#
	Y = b . b a	/ #a	shift	b	9		
6	X = X Y .	/ #a	red	#,a	1 (S = X Y)		#
7	S = S X . Y	/ #a	shift	b	5 (!)		b
	Y = . b	/ #a	shift	Y	10		
	Y = . b b a	/ #a					
8	X = a a b .	/ b	red	b	4 (X = a a b)		b
9	Y = b b . a	/ #a	shift	a	11		a
10	S = S X Y .	/ #a	red	#,a	2 (S = S X Y)		#
11	Y = b b a .	/ #a	red	#,a	6 (Y = b b a)		#

If the first terminal symbol action of a state is a reduce action with several control symbols (as in state 5), any of them can be selected as a guide symbol.

8.6.5 Assessment

The error handling technique described above is not trivial, but it is impressively powerful. It does not slow down error-free parsing, but only starts when a syntax error occurs. Some effort is then required for the recovery, but this is quite justified in the event of an error.

The recovery is guaranteed to terminate. Since the last transition on the escape route occurs with the eof symbol #, this symbol is always an anchor. In the worst case, the entire remaining input up to # must be skipped, but synchronization succeeds with # as a backstop.

The technique described here not only leads to a recovery after syntax errors, but even "corrects" such errors, although this correction may not always be what the programmer intended. At least the corrected input allows for consistent semantic processing, which is not always the case with recursive descent.

Last but not least, this error handling technique enables good error messages that simply describe the correction of the faulty input, which in most cases explains the errors well.

Overall, error handling is more powerful in bottom-up syntax analysis than in recursive descent, which is due to the fact that the grammar of the input is available in tabular form and can be analyzed in the event of an error to collect anchors and enable a good recovery.

8.7 Exercises

1. *Table generation (1)*. Given the following grammar, create the parser table for bottom-up syntax analysis.

    A = A B c.
    A = a.
    B = b.

    Is this grammar LR(0), LR(1) or LALR(1)? Give reasons for your answer.

2. *Table generation (2)*. Given the following grammar, create the parser table for bottom-up syntax analysis and compute the guide symbols for error recovery.

    S = a.
    S = S X.
    X = c.
    X = b X b.

    Is this grammar LR(0), LR(1) or LALR(1)? Give reasons for your answer.

3. *Table generation (3)*. The following grammar is LR(1), but not LALR(1):

   S = d X b.
   S = d Y a.
   S = X a.
   S = Y b.
   X = c.
   Y = c.

   Create the parser tables for both LR(1) and LALR(1) analysis and show where the conflict occurs. Also draw the PDA for the LR(1) and LALR(1) analysis and explain why the conflict occurs in the LALR(1) table but not in the LR(1) table.

4. *LR Error Handling (1)*. Given the grammar of Fig. 8.16 with the corresponding parser table and the guide symbols. Show the analysis of the faulty input

   a b b b a #

   including error recovery, as shown by the example in Sect. 8.6.

5. *LR Error Handling (2)*. Show that error recovery also works when shift and reduce actions are combined into shiftred actions. As in the previous exercise, use the grammar from Fig. 8.16 and its compressed form from Fig. 8.10, in which shift and reduce actions have been combined into shiftred actions. Use this to show the analysis of the faulty input

   b a b #

   including recovery.

A. The MicroJava Language

This appendix specifies the lexical structure, the syntax and the semantics of the MicroJava language, for which a compiler is built in this book. In particular, it specifies the context conditions for MicroJava, which are the requirements that the compiler needs to check in order to guarantee the semantic correctness of a program.

Lexical Structure

Character classes:	letter	= 'a' .. 'z' | 'A' .. 'Z'.
	digit	= '0' .. '9'.
	char	= ANY − '\''.
Terminal classes:	ident	= letter {letter | digit | '_'}.
	number	= digit {digit}.
	charCon	= "'" char "'". // can also contain '\r', '\n', and '\t'

Keywords:	program	class					
	if	else	while	read	print	return	break
	void	final	new				
Operators:	+	−	*	/	%	++	−−
	==	!=	>	>=	<	<=	
	&&	||					
	(	)	[	]	{	}	
	=	;	,	.			
Comments:	// ... until the end of the line						
Whitespace:	blanks, '\r', '\n', '\t'						

Syntax

```
Program    =  "program" ident {ConstDecl | VarDecl | ClassDecl} "{" {MethodDecl} "}".
ConstDecl  =  "final" Type ident "=" (number | charCon) ";".
VarDecl    =  Type ident {"," ident } ";".
ClassDecl  =  "class" ident "{" {VarDecl} "}".
MethodDecl =  (Type | "void") ident "(" [FormPars] ")" {VarDecl} Block.
FormPars   =  Type ident {"," Type ident}.
Type       =  ident ["[" "]"].
Block      =  "{" {Statement} "}".
Statement  =  Designator ("=" Expr | ActPars | "++" | "--") ";"
           |  "if" "(" Condition ")" Statement ["else" Statement]
           |  "while" "(" Condition ")" Statement
           |  "break" ";"
           |  "return" [Expr] ";"
           |  "read" "(" Designator ")" ";"
           |  "print" "(" Expr ["," number] ")" ";"
           |  Block
           |  ";".
ActPars    =  "(" [ Expr {"," Expr} ] ")".
Condition  =  CondTerm {"||" CondTerm}.
CondTerm   =  CondFactor {"&&" CondFactor}.
CondFactor =  Expr RelOp Expr.
RelOp      =  "==" | "!=" | ">" | ">=" | "<" | "<=".
Expr       =  ["–"] Term {AddOp Term}.
Term       =  Factor {MulOp Factor}.
Factor     =  Designator [ActPars]
           |  number
           |  charCon
           |  "new" ident [ "[" Expr "]" ]
           |  "(" Expr ")".
Designator =  ident {"." ident | "[" Expr "]"}.
AddOp      =  "+" | "–".
MulOp      =  "*" | "/" | "%".
```

Semantics

All subsequent terms for which there is a definition or which are regarded as a definition are underlined to emphasize their special meaning.

Reference Types
Arrays and classes are reference types.

Types of Constants
- The type of a number constant is int.
- The type of a character constant is char.

A. The MicroJava Language

Type Equality
Two types are the same,
- if they are denoted by the same type name, or
- if both types are arrays and their element types are the same.

Type Compatibility
Two types are compatible,
- if they are the same, or
- if one of them is a reference type and the other is the type of null.

Assignment Compatibility
A type *src* is assignment compatible with a type *dst*:
- If *src* and *dst* are the same, or
- if *dst* is a reference type and *src* is the type of null.

Predeclared Names

int	standard type
char	standard type
null	null value of a class or array variable
chr	standard method; chr(i) converts the int expression i into a char value
ord	standard method; ord(ch) converts the char value ch into an int value
len	standard method; len(a) returns the number of elements of the array a

Scope
A scope is the textual area of a program, method or class. It extends from the position after the program, method or class name to the closing curly brace (}). A scope excludes any nested scopes. There is an (artificial) outermost scope (the "universe") which contains the main program as well as all predeclared names. The declaration of a name in an inner scope hides any declaration of this name in an outer scope.

Note
- Indirect recursion is not allowed, because each name must be declared before it is used, which is not possible with indirect recursion.
- A predeclared name (e.g., int or char) can be overridden by a new declaration of the same name in an inner scope (although this is not recommended).

Context Conditions

General Context Conditions

- Each name must be declared before it is used.
- No name may be declared more than once in the same scope.
- The program must contain a method main(), which must be declared as void and must not have any parameters.

Context Conditions for Standard Methods

chr(e)	e must be an expression of type int
ord(c)	c must be of type char
len(a)	a must be an array

Context Conditions for Productions

In the following, we describe the context conditions that must be checked for each production of the MicroJava grammar. Note that there are some productions for which there are no context conditions.

Program = "program" ident {ConstDecl | VarDecl | ClassDecl} "{" {MethodDecl} "}".

ConstDecl = "final" Type ident "=" (number | charCon) ";".

- The type of number or charCon must be <u>the same</u> as the type described by Type.

VarDecl = Type ident {"," ident} ";". ClassDecl = "class" ident "{" {VarDecl} "}".

MethodDecl = (Type | "void") ident "(" [FormPars] ")" {VarDecl} Block.

- Type must be int or char.
- The main() method must be parameterless and void.
- Function methods must be exited via a return statement (checked at run time).

FormPars = Type ident {"," Type ident}.

Type = ident ["[" "]"].

- ident must denote a type.

Block = "{" {Statement} "}".

Statement = Designator "=" Expr ";".

- Designator must denote a variable, an array element, or an object field.
- The type of Expr must be <u>assignment compatible</u> with the type of Designator.

Statement = Designator ("++" | "--") ";".

- Designator must denote a variable, an array element, or an object field.
- Designator must be of type int.

Statement = Designator ActPars ";".

- Designator must denote a method.

A. The MicroJava Language

Statement = "return" [Expr] ";".
- The type of Expr must be <u>assignment compatible</u> with the function type of the current method.
- If the current method is a function method, Expr must not be missing.
- If Expr is missing, the current method must be declared as void.

Statement = "break" ";".
- The break statement must not occur outside a loop.

Statement = "read" "(" Designator ")" ";".
- Designator must denote a variable, an array element, or an object field.
- Designator must be of type int or char.

Statement = "print" "(" Expr ["," number] ")" ";".
- Expr must be of type int or char.

Statement = "if" "(" Condition ")" Statement ["else" Statement]
  | "while" "(" Condition ")" Statement
  | Block
  | ";".

ActPars = "(" [Expr {"," Expr}] ")".
- The number of actual and formal parameters must match.
- The type of each actual parameter must be <u>assignment compatible</u> with the type of its corresponding formal parameter.

Condition = CondTerm {"||" CondTerm}.

CondTerm = CondFactor {"&&" CondFactor}.

CondFactor = Expr RelOp Expr.
- The types of both expressions must be <u>compatible</u>.
- Classes and arrays may only be checked for equality or inequality.

Expr = Term.

Expr = "–" Term.
- Term must be of type int.

$Expr_0$ = $Expr_1$ AddOp Term.
- $Expr_1$ and Term must both be of type int.

Term = Factor.

$Term_0$ = $Term_1$ MulOp Factor.
- $Term_1$ and Factor must both be of type int.

Factor = Designator | number | charCon | "(" Expr ")".

Factor = Designator ActPars.
- Designator must denote a method.
- The type of the method denoted by Designator must not be void.

Factor = "new" ident.
- ident must denote a class.

Factor = "new" ident "[" Expr "]".
- ident must denote a type.
- The type of Expr must be int.

Designator = ident.

Designator$_0$ = Designator$_1$ "." ident.
- The type of Designator$_1$ must be a class.
- ident must denote a field of Designator$_1$.

Designator$_0$ = Designator$_1$ "[" Expr "]".
- The type of Designator$_1$ must be an array.
- The type of Expr must be int.

RelOp = "==" | "!=" | ">" | ">=" | "<" | "<=".

AddOp = "+" | "−".

MulOp = "*" | "/" | "%".

Implementation Restrictions

- There must be no more than 128 local variables.
- There must be no more than 32768 global variables.
- A class cannot have more than 32768 fields.

B. The MicroJava Compiler

This appendix describes the architecture of the MicroJava compiler and summarizes the interfaces of its classes

Overview

This book describes the necessary techniques for the implementation of a compiler for the programming language MicroJava. Readers can download and study this compiler in full source code [Download]. This appendix serves as an overview of its architecture and the interfaces of its classes.

The MicroJava compiler consists of 12 Java classes grouped into three packages (Fig. B.1).

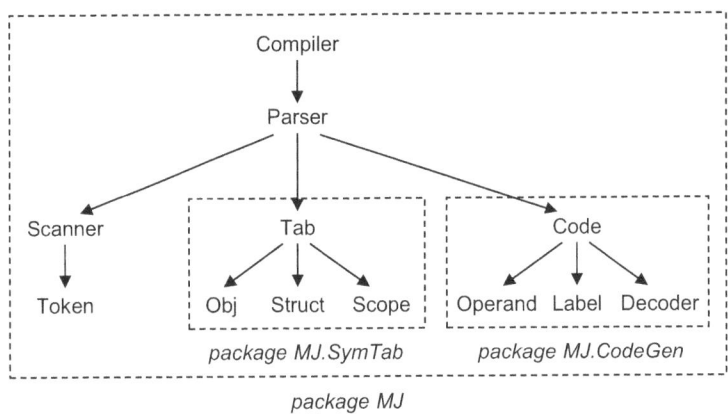

Fig. B.1 Architecture of the MicroJava compiler

Tab is the symbol table with classes for object nodes (Obj), structure nodes (Struct), and scope nodes (Scope). Code is the code generator with classes for the operands of code generation (Operand), for jump labels (Label) and for decoding the generated bytecode

(Decoder). The parser controls the compilation and calls the scanner, which supplies terminal symbols as Token objects. It also calls methods of the symbol table, which enter and look up names in scopes, as well as methods from the code generator, which generate the target code.

Interfaces of the Compiler Classes

For quick reference, we describe here the interfaces of the individual compiler classes. Their implementation can be found in the source code.

Compiler

The class Compiler is the main class of the MicroJava compiler. Its main() method reads the name of the MicroJava source file to be compiled from the command line, initializes the scanner with it, and calls the parser. The compiler is started as:

    java MJ.Compiler *sourceFileName*.mj

If no error was detected, the compiler generates a file *sourceFileName*.obj, which can be executed by the MicroJava VM (available at [Download]):

    java MJ.Run *sourceFileName*.obj [-debug]

By specifying the -debug option, the interpretation of the bytecode and the contents of the expression stack can be tracked.

Parser

The parser controls the compilation and calls methods of the scanner, the symbol table, and the code generator. Its interface is:

```
public class Parser {
    public static int errors;                          // error counter
    public static void error (String msg) {...}        // prints an error message with line and col number
    public static void parse() {...}                   // starts parsing
}
```

Scanner

The scanner reads the source program and delivers the terminal symbols in it as tokens to the parser. Comments and whitespace are filtered out. The scanner's interface is:

```
public class Scanner {
    public static void init (Reader r) {...}   // initializes the scanner with the input stream
    public static Token next() {...}           // returns the next token from the input stream
}
```

B. The MicroJava Compiler

Token

Tokens are supplied by the scanner and describe the kind, value, and position of terminal symbols in the source program.

```
public class Token {
    public int      kind;      // token kind
    public int      line;      // token line
    public int      col;       // token column
    public String   val;       // token value
    public int      numVal;    // numeric token value (for number and charCon)
}
```

The MicroJava compiler uses the following token kinds:

```
static final int
    //--- error token
    none = 0,
    //--- token classes
    ident = 1,       number = 2,        charCon = 3,
    //--- operators and special characters
    plus = 4,        minus = 5,         times = 6,       slash = 7,       rem = 8,
    eql = 9,         neq = 10,          lss = 11,        leq = 12,        gtr = 13,
    geq = 14,        and = 15,          or = 16,         assign = 17,     pplus = 18,
    mminus = 19,     semicolon = 20,    comma = 21,      period = 22,     lpar = 23,
    rpar = 24,       lbrack = 25,       rbrack = 26,     lbrace = 27,     rbrace = 28,
    //--- keywords
    break_ = 29,     class_ = 30,       else_ = 31,      final_ = 32,     if_ = 33,
    new_ = 34,       print_ = 35,       program_ = 36,   read_ = 37,      return_ = 38,
    void_ = 39,      while_ = 40,
    //--- end of file token
    eof = 41;
```

Tab

The class Tab implements the symbol table of the MicroJava compiler. The method insert() enters a declared name into the current scope, find() searches for a name in all open scopes, and findField() searches for a field name in a class.

```
public class Tab {
    public static Scope   curScope;                                    // current scope
    public static int     curLevel;                                    // nesting level of current scope
    public static Struct  intType, charType, nullType, noType;         // predeclared types
    public static Obj     chrObj, ordObj, lenObj, noObj;               // predeclared objects
    public static void openScope() {...}                               // opens a new scope
    public static void closeScope() {...}                              // closes the current scope
    public static Obj insert (int kind, String name, Struct type) {...}
    public static Obj find (String name) {...}
    public static Obj findField (String name, Struct type) {...}
}
```

Obj

The class Obj stores information about a declared name.

```
public class Obj {
    public static final int Con = 0, Var = 1, Type = 2, Meth = 3, Prog = 4;  // object kinds
    public int      kind;    // Con, Var, Type, Meth, Prog
    public String   name;    // object name
    public Struct   type;    // object type
    public Obj      next;    // next object in this scope
    public int      val;     // for Con: constant value
    public int      adr;     // for Var, Meth: address
    public int      level;   // for Var: declaration level
    public int      nPars;   // for Meth: number of parameters
    public Obj      locals;  // for Meth: parameters and local objects
    public Obj (int kind, String name, Struct type) {...}
}
```

Struct

The class Struct stores information about the kind and structure of a type. For each type, there is only a single Struct node in the whole symbol table.

```
public class Struct {
    public static final int None = 0, Int = 1, Char = 2, Arr = 3, Class = 4;  // structure kinds
    public int      kind;       // None, Int, Char, Arr, Class
    public Struct   elemType;   // for Arr: element type
    public int      nFields;    // for Class: number of fields
    public Obj      fields;     // for Class: field list
    public Struct (int kind) {...}
    public Struct (int kind, Struct elemType) {...}
    public boolean isRefType() {...}                        // true for arrays and classes
    public boolean equals (Struct other) {...}              // true if "this" and other are the same
    public boolean compatibleWith (Struct other) {...}      // true if "this" is comparable with other
    public boolean assignableTo (Struct dest) {...}         // true if "this" is assignable to dest
}
```

Scope

The class Scope defines the head node of a scope to which the object nodes of that scope are attached.

```
public class Scope {
    public Scope  outer;    // to next outer scope
    public Obj    locals;   // to local objects of this scope
    public int    nVars;    // number of variables in this scope
}
```

B. The MicroJava Compiler

Code

The class Code implements the code generator of the MicroJava compiler. It has methods for emitting instructions and generating jumps.

```
public class Code {
    public static final int   // instruction codes
        load = 1,         load0 = 2,        load1 = 3,        load2 = 4,        load3 = 5,
        store = 6,        store0 = 7,       store1 = 8,       store2 = 9,       store3 = 10,
        getstatic = 11,   putstatic = 12,   getfield = 13,    putfield = 14,    const0 = 15,
        const1 = 16,      const2 = 17,      const3 = 18,      const4 = 19,      const5 = 20,
        const_m1 = 21,    const_ = 22,      add = 23,         sub = 24,         mul = 25,
        div = 26,         rem = 27,         neg = 28,         shl = 29,         shr = 30,
        new_ = 31,        newarray = 32,    aload = 33,       astore = 34,      baload = 35,
        bastore = 36,     arraylength = 37, pop = 38,         jmp = 39,         jeq = 40,
        jne = 41,         jlt = 42,  jle = 43,  jgt = 44,     jge = 45,
        call = 46,        return_ = 47,     enter = 48,       exit = 49,        read = 50,
        print = 51,       bread = 52,       bprint = 53,      trap = 54;
    public static final int eq = 0, ne = 1, lt = 2, le = 3, gt = 4, ge = 5;  // compare operators
    public static int[] inverse = {ne, eq, ge, gt, le, lt};
    public static int pc;                    // next free address in the code buffer
    public static int mainPc;                // address of the main() method (set by the parser)
    public static int dataSize;              // length of the global data area in words (set by the parser)
    public static void put (int x) {...}     // appends 1 byte to the code buffer
    public static void put2 (int x) {...}    // appends 2 bytes to the code buffer
    public static void put2 (int pos, int x) {...}  // patches 2 bytes at pos in the code buffer
    public static void put4 (int x) {...}    // appends 4 bytes to the code buffer
    public static void load (Operand x) {...}        // loads x to the EStack
    public static void assignTo (Operand x) {...}    // assigns the top element of the EStack to x
    public static void callMethod (Operand m) {...}  // calls method m
    public static void inc (Operand x, int val) {...}  // increments x by val (which is +/- 1)
    public static void jump (Label lab) {...}        // unconditional jump
    public static void tJump (int op, Label lab) {...}  // true-jump depending on op
    public static void fJump (int op, Label lab) {...}  // false-jump depending on op
    public static void write (OutputStream s) {...}  // writes the code buffer to the object file
}
```

Operand

The code generator uses operand descriptors of the following type to hold the kind and location of operands during code generation.

```
public class Operand {
    public static final int  // operand kinds
        Con = 0, Local = 1, Static = 2, Stack = 3, Fld = 4, Elem = 5, Meth = 6, Cond = 7;
    public int     kind;   // Con, Local, Static, Stack, Fld, Elem, Meth, Cond
    public Struct  type;   // operand type
    public int     val;    // for Con: value
    public int     adr;    // for Local, Static, Fld, Meth: address
    public Obj     obj;    // for Meth: method object
```

```
    public int      op;        // for Cond: most recent compare operator
    public Label    tLabel;    // for Cond: target for true-jumps in condition
    publicLabel     fLabel;    // for Cond: target for false-jumps in condition
    public Operand (Obj obj) {...}
    public Operand (int val) {...}
    public Operand (int kind, int val, Struct type) {...}
}
```

Label

The Label class manages jump labels. Addresses in jump instructions to a yet undefined label are automatically patched when the label is defined.

```
public class Label {
    public Label() {...}       // creates a yet undefined label
    public void here() {...}   // defines the label at the current pc position
    public void putAdr() {...} // writes the jump distance to this label into the code
}
```

Decoder

To check the correctness of the generated bytecode, you can use a decoder that outputs the instructions in readable form.

```
public class Decoder {
    public static void decode (byte[] code, int beg, int end) {...}
}
```

The decode() method decodes the contents of the code buffer in the range [beg .. end] and writes it to the console. It is called by the code generator at the end of code generation to display the generated code.

There is also a stand-alone program Decode that can be used to decode a MicroJava object file. It is invoked as follows:

```
java MJ.Decode fileName.obj
```

The output will be written to the console.

References

[AGH00]	Arnold, K.; Gosling, J.; Holmes, D.: *The Java Programming Language*. Addison-Wesley, 2000.
[ALSU06]	Aho, A. V.; Lam, M.; Sethi, R.; Ullman, J. D.: *Compilers: Principles, Techniques, and Tools*. Pearson, 2nd ed., 2006.
[Appe02]	Appel, A. W.: *Modern Compiler Implementation in Java*. 2nd ed., Cambridge University Press, 2002.
[Back56]	Backus, J. et al.: *Programmer's Reference Manual Fortran*. IBM, 1956. http://bitsavers.informatik.uni-stuttgart.de/pdf/ibm/704/704_FortranProgRefMan_Oct56.pdf.
[Coco]	*The Compiler Generator Coco/R – User Manual*. https://ssw.jku.at/Coco/.
[Coop22]	Cooper, K. D.: *Engineering a Compiler*. 3rd ed., Morgan Kaufmann, 2022.
[Cope20]	Copeland, T.: *Generating Parsers with JavaCC*, 2020. https://javacc.github.io/javacc/.
[Download]	Complementary material for this book (slides, source code, sample solutions). https://ssw.jku.at/CompilerBook/.
[FCL09]	Fisher, C. N.; Cytron, R. K.; LeBlanc, R. J.: *Crafting a Compiler*. Pearson Education, 2009.
[GTWW77]	Goguen, J. A.; Thatcher, J. W.; Wagner, E. W.; Wright, J. B.: *Initial Algebra Semantics and Continuous Algebras*. Journal of the ACM, 24 (1): 68–95, 1977.
[HOPL-I]	Wexelblat, R. L.: *History of Programming Languages*. Academic Press, 2014, First ACM SIGPLAN conference on History of Programming Languages, 1978.
[HOPL-II]	Second ACM SIGPLAN conference on History of Programming Languages, 1993. https://dl.acm.org/doi/proceedings/10.1145/154766.
[HOPL-III]	Third ACM SIGPLAN conference on History of Programming Languages, 2007. https://dl.acm.org/doi/proceedings/10.1145/1238844.
[JavaDoc]	*Java documentation tool*. https://www.oracle.com/technical-resources/articles/java/javadoc-tool.html.
[JW77]	Jensen, K.; Wirth, N.: Pascal User Manual and Report. Springer, 1975.
[Knut68]	Knuth, D. E.: Semantics of Context-free Languages. Mathematical Systems Theory, vol. 2, no. 2, 1968, 127-145.
[LMB92]	Levine, J. R.; Mason, T.; Brown, D.: lex & yacc. O'Reilly, 1992.
[Much97]	Muchnick, S.: Advanced Compiler Design and Implementation. Morgan Kaufmann, 1997.
[Naur64]	Naur, P.: Revised Report on the Algorithmic Language Algol60. http://algol60.org/reports/algol60_rr.pdf.

[Oder08]	Odersky, M.: Programming in Scala. artima, 2008.
[Röhr80]	Röhrich, J.: Methods for the Automatic Construction of Error-correcting Parsers. Acta Informatica 13, 115-139, 1980.
[Schm86]	Schmidt, D. A.: Denotational Semantics: A Methodology for Language Development. William C. Brown Publishers, 1986.
[Stro85]	Stroustrup, B.: The C++ Programming Language. Addison-Wesley, 1985.
[Parr13]	Parr, T.: The Definitive ANTLR 4 Reference. Pragmatic Book shelf, 2013. see also: https://github.com/antlr/antlr4/blob/master/doc/index.md.
[Wirt77]	Wirth, N.: What can we do about the unnecessary diversity of notation for syntactic definitions?, Communications of the ACM, vol. 20, no. 11, November 1977, 822–823.

Index

A
Abstract syntax tree, 19, 111, 188
Accept action, 203, 205, 212
Accessing array elements, 134
Accessing fields, 133
Action table, 205
Actual attribute, 172
Actual parameter, 157
add instruction, 121, 136, 141
Address
   of global variables, 92
   of local variables, 93
Address assignment, 93, 98, 101
Addressing mode, 118, 128, 131
Algol60, 3
aload instruction, 123, 131, 134
Alphabet, 11, 14
Alternative, EBNF, 48, 52, 55, 66
Ambiguity, 20–21, 58
Anchor, 61, 69, 176, 223, 225, 226
ANY
   in character sets, 167
   in productions, 173
Arithmetic expression, 136
Arithmetic instruction, 121
Array, 99, 100, 103
Array access, 123, 134
Array allocation, 122, 138
Array element, 118, 128, 134, 139
Array length, 101, 116, 122, 123, 138, 154
arraylength instruction, 123, 154
Arr structure, 99, 101, 103, 104, 134, 240
ASCII, 21
assignableTo(), 104, 140, 157, 158, 240
Assignment, 139

Assignment compatibility, 104, 140, 157, 158, 233
assignTo(), 140, 241
astore instruction, 123, 139, 140
ATG, *see* Attributed grammar
Attribute, 77, 78, 171, 220
Attribute stack, 221
Attributed grammar, 75, 164, 170

B
Backend, 7
Backus, J., 3, 11
Backus-Naur form, 3, 18, 201, 208
Backward jump, 124, 142, 148
baload instruction, 123, 131, 134
bastore instruction, 123, 140
Blank character, 25, 169
BNF, *see* Backus-Naur form
Boolean expression, 143, 145, 150
Bottom-up parser, 15, 201, 206, 210
bprint instruction, 126
bread instruction, 126
break statement, 143, 149
Byte array, 116, 122, 123, 138
Bytecode, 2, 9, 117

C
C++, 4
call instruction, 125, 153, 155
callMethod(), 153, 154, 241
Case sensitivity, 169
Central recursion, 16, 27, 39, 42, 43
CFG, *see* Context-free grammar

char, 94, 100, 119
CHARACTERS, 167
Character set, 167
Char array, 116, 122, 123, 138
Char structure, 99, 240
charType, 107, 239
check(), 46, 51, 63
Chomsky, N., 17
chr(), 94, 154, 234
chrObj, 107, 239
Circularity of a grammar, 60, 178
Class, 99, 101, 122
Class object allocation, 122
Class scope, 95
Class structure, 99, 101, 133, 240
closeScope(), 96, 107, 156, 239
Closure, 210, 212, 228
Coco/R, 163
   invocation, 184
Code buffer, 127, 159
Code class, 127, 241
Code generation, 6, 75, 111
   for assignments, 139
   for Boolean expressions, 152
   for break statements, 149
   for expressions, 136
   for if statements, 148
   for methods, 153
   for while statements, 147
Code generator, 10, 127, 164, 241
Column number, 34, 170, 175, 177
Comment, 22, 25, 35, 168, 231
Comparable types, 233
Comparison operator, 142
compatibleWith(), 105, 152, 240
Compilation phases, 4
Compiler class, 238
Compiler generator, 163
Compiler optimization, 2
Compiler specification, 166
Complementary set, 167
Completeness of a grammar, 60, 178
Concrete syntax tree, 19
Condition, 145
Conditional jump, 124, 141, 145, 148
Cond operand, 145, 148, 149, 241
Conflict resolver, 179
Con object, 90, 240
Con operand, 128, 131, 132, 241

Constant, 120, 232
const instruction, 120, 131
const_m1 instruction, 120, 131
Context condition, 42, 75, 133, 134, 136, 137,
       139, 140, 152, 156, 234
Context-free grammar, 18, 28, 39, 43, 170
Context-sensitive grammar, 18, 42
Control flow structure, 147
Control symbol, 210
curLevel, 96, 99, 107, 239
curMethod, 97, 156, 158
Current scope, 96, 98
curScope, 96, 98, 99, 107, 156, 239

D
Dangling else, 20, 58, 178
data, 114
dataSize, 241
Declaration
   of a method, 96, 156
   of a name, 90
   of a variable, 93
Declaration level, 92, 93, 96, 98, 101
decode(), 242
Decoder class, 242
Decoding MicroJava bytecode, 242
Decrement statement, 140
Deletability, 16, 53
Derivation, 15, 202, 206
Designator, 133, 134, 139
Deterministic finite automaton, 28, 29, 43,
       164, 167
DFA, *see* Deterministic finite automaton
div instruction, 121, 137
dl, 126
Domain-specific language, 184
dup instruction, 124, 141
dup2 instruction, 124, 141
Dynamic compiler structure, 4
Dynamic link, 126, 155

E
EBNF, *see* Extended Backus-Naur form
Element type, 99
Elem operand, 128, 131, 134, 140, 241
Empty string of symbols, 15
End-of-file token, 14, 25, 47, 202, 212, 229

Index

enter instruction, 125, 127, 155, 156
eof, *see* End-of-file token
eof token, 47, 62, 69, 71
equals(), 104, 240
errDist, 65
error(), 46, 64, 70, 238
Error action, 203
Error correction, 224, 227, 229
Error distance, 65
Error handling
    in bottom-up parsing, 223
    in Coco/R, 175
    in recursive descent, 60
    panic mode, 61
    with general anchors, 61
    with specific anchors, 68, 176
Error message, 32, 46, 48, 64, 175, 225
Error recovery, 61, 68
    in bottom-up parsing, 223, 224, 226
    in Coco/R, 176
Errors class, 175, 177
Error state, 223–225
Error token, 33, 35
Escape route, 223, 224, 226
EStack, *see* Expression stack
exit instruction, 125, 127, 155, 156, 158
Expression stack, 113, 119, 131, 153, 154, 157, 158
Extended Backus-Naur form, 11, 27, 46, 167, 170

F
Factorization, 55, 179, 182
False jump, 145, 147–150, 152
Field, 99, 101, 116, 118, 120, 128, 133, 139
Final state, 28, 30, 223, 224
find(), 89, 95, 99, 107, 132, 239
findField(), 107, 133, 239
Finite automaton, 18
Fixup, 147, 148, 151, 152
Fixup list, 143, 144, 151
fJump(), 146, 147, 149, 151, 152, 241
Fld operand, 128, 131, 133, 140, 241
Follow-up error, 65, 70, 176
Formal attribute, 172
Formal language, 16
Formal parameter, 90, 92, 157
Fortran, 3

Forward jump, 124, 142, 145, 148
fp, 93, 115, 125
Frame, *see* Stack frame
Frame file, 174
Frame pointer, 93, 115, 125
Frontend, 7
Function method, 153, 155, 158
Fuzzy parsing, 173

G
Garbage collector, 115
getfield instruction, 120, 131, 133
getstatic instruction, 119, 131
Global data area, 92, 114, 159
Global scope, 95
Global semantic declaration, 166, 171, 179
Global variable, 92, 114, 119, 128, 139, 159
Grammar, 10, 59
Grammar classes, 17–18
Guide symbol, 226, 227

H
Handle, 202
Heap, 115
here(), 143, 147, 149, 151, 152, 242
Hidden alternative, EBNF, 57
Hidden LL(1) conflict, 57
History of compiler construction, 2
Hoare, C.A.R., 3

I
if statement, 148, 151
IGNORE, 169
IGNORECASE, 169
Immediate mode, 118
inc(), 241
inc instruction, 121, 141
Increment statement, 140
Index check, 122, 123
Indexed mode, 118
init(), 32, 33, 238
Input attribute, 77, 79, 172, 220
insert(), 89, 93, 98, 107, 156, 157, 239
Instruction set, 117
int, 94, 100

int array, 116, 122, 123, 138
Intermediate representation, 8, 188
Interpreter, 4, 9, 113
Int structure, 99, 240
intType, 107, 239
isRefType(), 104, 152, 156, 240
Item, *see* LR item
Iteration, EBNF, 17, 19, 49, 52, 57, 67

J
Java, 4
jeq instruction, 124, 141
jge instruction, 124, 142
jgt instruction, 124, 142
JIT, *see* Just-in-time compilation
jle instruction, 124, 127, 142
jlt instruction, 124, 142
jmp instruction, 124, 127, 141, 146
jne instruction, 124, 142
Jump, 124, 141
jump(), 146, 147, 149, 151, 241
Jump distance, 124, 125, 142, 143, 148
Just-in-time compilation, 4

K
Kernel, 210, 212
Keyword, 11, 35, 68, 94, 231
Knuth, D.E., 75

L
la, 45, 171, 175
Label, 141, 143, 147, 149
Label class, 144, 242
LALR parser, 208, 217, 218, 222
LALR(1), 208
LALR(1) grammar, 207
LALR(1) table generation, 211
Language, 16, 29
Layout of array objects, 116
Layout of class objects, 116
Left-canonical derivation, 15
Left-canonical reduction, 206
Left recursion, 16, 19, 201, 208
    elimination, 17, 56
leftSide table, 205
len(), 94, 104, 154, 234
length table, 205

lenObj, 107, 239
Lexical analysis, 5, 25
Linear-bounded automaton, 18
Line number, 34, 170, 175, 177
Literal, 167
LL(*), 164, 181
LL(1), 55, 57, 59, 105, 170, 178, 201
    conflict removal, 55, 57, 105, 179, 180
load(), 131, 241
Loading
    array elements, 134
    constants, 132
    fields, 133
    operands, 131
    variables, 132
load instruction, 119, 131
Local mode, 118
Local operand, 128, 131, 132, 140, 241
Local scope, 95
Local variable, 93, 115, 119, 125, 128, 139, 155, 156
    in production, 171
Lookahead symbol, 45, 55, 175
Lookup of names, 96, 99, 132
loop, 147
LR(1) conflict, 216, 220, 221
LR grammar, 206
LR(0) grammar, 206
LR(1) grammar, 206
LR item, 209
    successors, 209
LR parser, 206
LR table generation, 209

M
main(), 116, 156, 159, 238
mainPc, 116, 156, 159, 241
Merging
    of lines, 218, 219
    of states, 207, 212, 216
Meth object, 90, 240
Method, 22
Method call, 125, 153
Method call stack, 93, 113, 115, 125, 153, 155, 156, 159
Method declaration, 96, 156
Meth operand, 128, 131, 241
MicroJava, 21–22, 231
    compiler, 237

context conditions, 234
grammar, 231
implementation restrictions, 236
invocation, 238
VM, 92, 93, 112
μJVM, *see* MicroJava VM
MStack, *see* Method call stack
mul instruction, 121, 137
Multi-pass compiler, 7
Multi-symbol lookahead, 179

N

Name equivalence, 102–104
Naur, P., 3, 11
neg instruction, 121, 136
Nested comment, 28
Nesting, 16, 28, 43
newarray instruction, 122, 138
new instruction, 122, 138
next(), 32, 34, 238
nextCh(), 33
Non-deterministic finite automaton, 167
None structure, 99, 240
None token, 33, 35
Nonterminal symbol, 11, 47, 64, 172
noObj, 99, 107, 239
noType, 104, 107, 239
null, 94
nullType, 107, 239

O

Obj class, 91, 240
Object allocation, 122, 138
Object file, 159
Object kind, 90
Object node, 89, 90, 98, 101
openScope(), 96, 107, 156, 239
Operand class, 129, 145, 241
Operand descriptor, 128, 130, 131, 145, 241
Operator precedence, 13
Optimization, 2, 6, 8
Option, EBNF, 19, 49, 57, 67
ord(), 94, 154, 234
ordObj, 107, 239
out, 172
Output attribute, 77, 79, 172, 221
multiple, 81

P

Parameter passing, 126, 153–155, 157
parse(), 238
Parse tree, 19
Parser, 6, 10, 39, 44, 163
Parser class, 45, 238
Parser.frame, 174
Parser generator, 164, 201, 208
Parser method, 47, 172
integration of semantic actions, 78, 80, 81
resulting operand, 130, 138
Parser specification, 170
Parser table, 203, 205, 207, 214, 218, 226
compression, 216
generation, 209
in list form, 215
Pascal, 3
pc, 116, 124, 241
P-code, 3
PDA, *see* Pushdown automaton
Peek(), 169, 179
Phases of a compilation, 4
Phrase, 15
pop instruction, 124, 153
Portability, 8, 9, 113
Pragma, 168
Predeclared name, 94, 96, 233
Predeclared object, 107
Predeclared type, 107
Print instruction, 126
Production, 11, 47, 170, 203
Prog object, 90, 240
Program counter, 116, 124
Pseudo production, 212
Pushdown automaton, 18, 40, 43, 55, 202, 203, 207, 224
put(), 127, 241
put2(), 127, 241
put4(), 127, 241
putAdr(), 143, 242
putfield instruction, 120, 139, 140
putstatic instruction, 119, 139, 140

R

ra, 125
read instruction, 126
Read state, 40
Recursion, 16

Recursive descent, 44, 164, 170, 178
    optimization, 51
Reduce action, 203, 204, 206, 212, 216, 217
Reduce item, 210, 212
Reduce-reduce conflict, 216
Reduce state, 40
Reduction, 15, 202, 204, 206, 215, 216, 220, 221
Reference type, 21, 104, 232
Regular grammar, 18, 26, 43, 164
Relative mode, 118
rem instruction, 121, 137
Requirements for recursive descent, 59
Resolver, 179
Return address, 125, 153
return instruction, 125, 155, 156, 158
return statement, 158
Return value, 124, 126, 153–155, 158
Right-canonical derivation, 15, 206
Right recursion, 16
Run-time error, 126

S

Same type, 104
Sample solutions, 22
Scala, 4
scan(), 45, 51, 169
Scanner, 6, 10, 25, 29, 45, 163, 169
Scanner class, 32, 238
Scanner.frame, 174
Scanner generator, 164
Scanner specification, 166
Scope, 89, 95, 156, 194, 233
Scope class, 96, 240
Scope node, 89
semAction(), 221
Semantic action, 76, 78, 168, 171, 220, 221
Semantic analysis, 6, 10, 42, 75, 208, 219
Semantic error, 75, 177
Semantic lookahead, 180
SemErr(), 175, 177
Sentence, 15, 29, 203
Sentential form, 15
Shift action, 203, 204, 206, 212, 216, 227
Shift item, 210, 212
Shiftred action, 217, 218
Shift-reduce conflict, 216, 220
Shift-reduce parser, 203
shl instruction, 121

Short-circuit evaluation, 146, 150
shr instruction, 121
Simple terminal symbol, 12
Single-pass compiler, 7, 75
sp, 93, 115, 125
Spurious error, 65
Stack frame, 93, 113, 115, 125, 126, 155, 156
Stack machine, 113
Stack mode, 118
Stack of a PDA, 42, 55, 202, 223
Stack operand, 128, 131, 132, 154, 241
Stack pointer, 93, 115, 125
Start symbol, 11, 15, 44, 47, 63, 64, 166, 170, 212
State, 28
State of an LR parser, 203, 210
State transition function, 29, 30
State transition table, 203, 205, 207, 209, 214, 218, 226
Static compiler structure, 10
Static mode, 118
Static operand, 128, 131, 140, 241
store instruction, 119, 139, 140
String of symbols, 15
Struct class, 100, 240
Structural equivalence, 102, 104
Structure kind, 99
Structure node, 89, 99
sub instruction, 121, 136, 141
Successor in LR item, 209
Successors of a parser method, 62
Successor state, 211
sym, 45
Symbol table, 6, 10, 75, 78, 89, 150, 156, 164, 194, 239
    initialization, 106
    insertion of names, 93, 98
    lookup of names, 96, 99, 132
SYNC, 176
Synchronization after an error, 61
Syntax analysis, 6, 39, 201
Syntax diagram, 12
Syntax-directed translation, 76
Syntax error, 6
Syntax tree, 6, 18–21, 44, 54, 75, 201, 205, 222

T

t, 45, 79, 171, 175
Tab character, 25, 169
Tab class, 89, 106, 239

Table-driven parser, 206
Table-driven scanner, 30
Taste, 188
Terminal class, 12, 167, 231
Terminal start symbol, 13–14, 45, 48, 50, 53, 57, 71, 201, 208
Terminal successor, 14, 50, 53, 57, 71
Terminal symbol, 11, 46, 63, 167, 171, 175
Terminalizability of a grammar, 60
tJump(), 146, 152, 241
Tokens, 5, 10, 11, 25, 30, 32, 45, 79, 167, 170
Token class, 32, 239
Token code, 6, 25, 32, 239
Token stream, 25
Token value, 6, 25, 32
Top-down parser, 15, 44, 210
Transition, 28
Transpiler, 1
trap instruction, 126, 156
True jump, 145, 150, 152
Turing machine, 18
Two-pass compiler, 7
Type, 99
Type check, 102
    name equivalence, 102
    structural equivalence, 102
Type compatibility, 104, 233
Type object, 90, 240
Type equality, 233

U
Unconditional jump, 124, 141, 148, 149
Unicode, 167
Universe, 95, 97, 106

Unrestricted grammar, 17

V
Value type, 21
Variable
    global, 92, 114, 119, 128, 139, 159
    local, 93, 115, 119, 125, 128, 139, 155, 156
Variable declaration, 93
Var object, 90, 132
Virtual machine, 9, 112
VM, *see* Virtual machine

W
while statement, 147, 151
Whitespace, 25, 29, 34, 169, 231
Wirth, N., 3
Word array, 116, 122, 123, 138

Symbols
--, 121, 140
#, 202, 212, 229
(. .), 76
[ ], 12, 19
{ }, 12, 19
|, 12
++, 121, 140
< >, 77
↑, 77
⇒, 15
↓, 77
δ, 29
ε, 15

The manufacturer's authorised representative in the EU is Springer Nature Customer Service Centre GmbH, Europaplatz 3, 69115 Heidelberg, Germany. If you have any concerns regarding our products, please contact ProductSafety@springernature.com

Printed and bound by CPI Group (UK) Ltd, Croydon, CR0 4YY

26/03/2026

02078988-0005